Information Technology Management

A Business Plan Enabler
Book 1: Principles

Dennis McBreen

cover photo: iStock.com/FredFroese

Printed in the United States of America

First printing, 2018

ISBN: 978-1-970063-02-8

Library of Congress Control Number: 2018958244

Ordering information: Special discounts are available on quantity purchases by bookstores, corporations, associations, and others. For details, contact the publisher at:

sales@braughlerbooks.com
or at 937-58-BOOKS

For questions or comments about this book, please write to:

info@braughlerbooks.com

Braughler™
Books
braughlerbooks.com

Acknowledgements and Dedication

This book is dedicated to my entire family, and especially to my wife, Sharon. She possesses an energy and spirit that never surrenders, never quits exuding positive energy. I wanted to give up so many times in writing this book, but she inspired me to keep going. I used her energy and spirit to complete the book. Thank you so much Sharon.

Table of Contents

Figures

Preface

The overall objective of the S&D Information Technology Management series is to present an information technology management process that maximizes the utilization of information technology resources in the achievement of a company's business plan objectives, and increases the overall effectiveness of the service and technology products delivered to its business clients. These objectives are all achieved within the resource limitations (budget) established for the information technology complex (hereafter referred to as IT). What is described in the book won't cost millions of dollars to install and implement, but it can save your company millions of dollars.

These are noble objectives, but how does IT achieve these technology management objectives? A successful technology management process includes five major components:

- Imagination
- IT Management Model
- Company business plan and the enabling IT technology plans
- Work performed by IT
- Work management processes and system to manage the work

The book series discusses these components and presents the basic principles and concepts which underlie their use in enabling a company's business plan. In this book the principles and concepts are presented in terms of a "best company" scenario in which principles and concepts are presented in the context of a business environment that is conducive to the "best" enablement of the principles presented. The presentation of objectives, strategies, strengths, weaknesses, opportunities, threats, cost divers, architecture, organization, management philosophy, and deliverables lend themselves to a best company scenario, but detail projects and work initiatives cannot be easily demonstrated.

Book 2 should be considered a complementary extension of this book's ideas. It takes the approach one step further by building a model company and supporting prototype system in which the principles are applied in a practical manner to a model company. The model company is used as a means of injecting personal and industry-related management experience and expertise into the discussions of technology management. It discusses the principles from a practical perspective, and can enrich the discussions of the principles stated in this book.

The model company is more than just a fictional company. It provides the opportunity to discuss a management structure, best practices, and organization required by the information technology management process to be effective. The supporting processes and best practices are based upon actual experience, and therefore provide another learning opportunity. Book 2 recognizes that the IT management process cannot be implemented in a management vacuum, or in a management environment inconsistent with the process's assumptions. Anyone who is going to develop an IT technology management process in their company must address many of the same issues that were resolved in developing the model company.

A model company *prototype system* is included in Book 2. It demonstrates the minimal system requirements to support the technology management functions presented. The system demonstrates that the investment in a system doesn't have to be complicated or expensive.

About the Book

Why read the book?:

The main reason to read the book is to evaluate new and imaginative ways of viewing and managing technology to enable your company to reduce its expenses while increasing its service to the clients. It contains a wealth of IT information concepts and technology management experiences. This information goes beyond just information technology management. It presents a global view of IT management.

Important concepts included:

IT Management Model:

The IT management model is at the core of the ideas and management practices presented in the book. It is an information model that combines and delivers all information processing technologies over a common computer network to provide multi-technology based systems and services to its business clients. The model's primary objective is to reduce IT and company expenses by increasing IT and business client efficiency while increasing business client service. It uses resource leveraging and plan alignment concepts to achieve these objectives. It presents a layered view and method of managing IT that permeates all IT management functions. The model views IT in terms of 24 management functions. Functions are likened to IT areas of responsibility. Each function is equally applicable to all types of computer platforms and information processing technologies (i.e. data, voice, text, and image).

Information Processing:

IT manages information, not just data. Information is conveyed by the spoken word, the written word, images, and in the traditional digital (data) format. This universal view of information results in the concept of information processing. Based upon this assumption the IT management model includes traditional computer processing (data), voice processing, text/word processing, and image/document processing. IT should plan and manage these technologies in a coordinated manner.

Computer Architecture:

The computer architecture upon which the IT management model is based is a *computer platform, technology, and organization independent architecture (CPTOIA)*. In this architecture the development of systems and services is not directly linked to a particular computer platform, technology, or organizational support structure. The architecture enables resource leveraging by identifying common areas of support across computers, technologies, and support organizations. It also enables the concept of information processing.

Systems and Services Organization:

Part of the supporting management and organizational structure the model requires for successful implementation is delivered by a *systems and services organization*. In the systems and services organization IT products and services are not tied to individual computers, their processing technologies, or their support structures. The systems and services support organization is an organization independent structure designed to develop, maintain, and service information products.

Financial view of IT:

In a book about technology management, it probably seems inconsistent that the IT management model places a significant emphasis on the financial aspects of technology management. Reasons to take a financial view of IT are to assist IT in obtaining funding for the technologies the company wishes to implement, and to track the cost and utilization of the technologies within the company to ensure they are being properly implemented and utilized to maximize company profits. A financial view can also assist the company in promoting more effective use of limited IT resources. It promotes better technical decision making by adding financial considerations to the decision making process.

Managing IT as any other business unit:

The mystique of IT is long gone. The introduction of an information management process provides IT the opportunity to implement work management functions which clearly demonstrate IT as both a technology and business partner. The book emphasizes planning, costing, resource management, and service chargeback as being key building blocks in building these partnerships.

Book style and structure:

Chapter Structure:

The chapters in Book 1 are based upon a discussion of the major components and processes of the overall information technology management process. For each chapter, and where applicable, the major components are discussed in terms of:

- Description of the component
- Relationship of the component to the other components
- Ownership and organizational placement of the component
- Skills, disciplines, and character traits for successful component management
- Component processes
- Objectives
- Strategies
- Strengths, weaknesses, opportunities, and threats (SWOT)
- Critical success factors
- Deliverables
- Cost drivers
- Alignment of process objectives and strategies with management functions and planned work
- Impact Analysis of one process upon another

Theme Statement:

A *theme statement* is included at the beginning of each chapter, or in some cases, for a major section of a chapter. This statement will be in italics, and represents the central message that is intended to be conveyed in the chapter or major section.

Book nuances:

References to groups in the singular context:

References are made throughout the book to a technology manager, a plan administrator, a visionary, a strategist, and a chief architect, etc. These reference are primarily made in a singular context. This is done for simplicity and consistency's sake, but its use should not be interpreted to mean that a technology manager, planner, architect etc. are always, or even most of the time, an individual person. It would be naive to think that there is only one person involved with these IT functions in a company. How these positions are staffed within a particular company will vary depending upon culture, availability, and skills of the individuals. These "individuals" could refer to a team of associates responsible for a technology management function, or they could refer to a separate management function within the IT department led by a division manager. It doesn't really matter. What is important is that there is specific ownership designated for each of the IT management functions. The owner consolidates all the various ideas about the function into a single statement of IT policy. The owner makes final decisions regarding the owned function. Think in terms of the function, not necessarily the individual(s) staffing the function.

Graphical illustrations of the model:

A 24 layered management model is at the core of the book. Graphical illustrations of this model are used throughout the book. Illustrating 24 of anything can be quite detailed and utilize much book space. There are times when the full 24 layered model must be illustrated. At other times the exact detail of the model need not be illustrated. When a full 24 layer illustration is not needed to convey the message, a modified 14 layer model structure is used. Many graphics do not require the illustration of any of the layers, and for those only a "shell" of the model is illustrated. These modifications in presentation of the model in no way compromise the integrity of the material presented. Any detail not included was done for printing purposes only.

Team References and Structure:

A description of the basic teams involved with many of the management functions discussed in the book is provided here because these teams are referenced many times throughout the book. It was thought best to describe the teams once, and just reference "the team" throughout the text, instead of listing the individuals involved each time a team is referenced. In most cases the team description is sufficient to inform the reader of the type of individuals participating on the team. It is understood that each company is organized in different ways, and mangers of similar functions can be assigned different titles and teams. Relate the teams and titles referenced herein to your particular company.

The senior business management team is the primary business decision-making team. It is typically led by the Chief Executive Officer with possible input from the Board of Directors. It is composed of the Chief Financial Officer (CFO), the Chief Operations Officer (COO), Chief Legal Counsel, Security Officer, senior vice presidents of the strategic business units (SBUs), and a company planner, if one exists in the company. A second level business management team is typically composed of business department and division managers.

The IT senior management teams are classified into three major types: the IT senior management team that exercises overall responsibility for IT; the IT senior technical team that has overall responsibility for IT technical matters and issues; and the IT senior administrative team that has responsibility for all internal administrative support matters.

- The IT senior management team is headed by the Chief Information Officer (CIO) and includes the VP of Systems; the VP of Services; the Director of the Project Management Office (PMO); the Director of Application Systems; the Director of Production; the Director of Technical Services; the Chief Architect; and the IT Security Officer.

- The IT senior technical support team is headed by the VP of Services and includes the VP of Systems; the Director of Technical Services; the Systems Software Manager; the Database Manager; the Application Systems Tech Support Manager; the Network Communications Manager; the Imaging / Workflow / Document Tech Support Manager; the Computer Operations Manager; the Para-Techs Manager; the Help Desk Manager; the Records Center Manager; and the Print Shop/ Copy Manager.

- The IT senior administrative support team is headed by the IT Financial Manager and includes the IT Plan Administrator and the Education and Training Manager.

A second level of IT team support are the non-senior teams typically composed of IT division managers, group managers, team leaders, and project leaders who are the individuals closest to the technology management process.

Use of Italics:

Italics are used strictly for emphasis. They are used to highlight key terminology, or key system concepts, but they are typically used only on the first occurrence of the terminology in the book.

Introduction

Defining Information Technology Management

Information technology management can be a difficult term to define. It's a rather abstract term that can be defined in many ways. It is very important to first determine the definition as used in this book. It's easily observed that there are three major components that must be addressed in determining its definition.

- Information concept
- Technology products
- Management practices

Information concept:

A fundamental assumption made in the book is that information is conveyed digitally by *data* technologies and delivered by traditional data processing systems; by the spoken word as delivered by *voice* technologies such as the telephone system; by the written word as delivered by *text* and word processing technologies; and by *images* or pictures as delivered by document management and imaging technologies. These four individual processing technologies should be organized, managed, and delivered by a common information network, and supported by an information-oriented organizational structure.

Management practices:

The *management* environment into which technology is introduced is a major topic of the book. This environment is multi-faceted. It must be business plan and vision driven. It must be an environment in which IT is managed as any other business unit, and contributes to the "bottom line" of the company. In this environment the financial management of IT is important, as are the management functions of planning, resource management, costing, and service chargeback. Client relations become client partnerships. The IT management and organizational structures support the merger of the data, voice, text, and image technologies around the information processing concept. The computer architecture is such that it enables the leveraging of IT resources which expands career opportunities and increases staff morale.

Work is focused because projects and other work are closely aligned with business objectives. Architecture, discipline, ownership, and responsibility become common attributes in IT's approach to managing work. Training, education, and skills management are functions critical to the overall success of IT because they are linked to specific objectives and work initiatives.

Technology products:

Technologies are considered equal components to management methods and practices in the definition of information technology management. This is not to diminish the importance of the technologies, but it implies that technologies alone cannot satisfy the objectives of information technology management, and conversely stated, excellent management methods and practices can't "cover for" the use of ineffective technologies and systems. Technology management requires both parts. The book doesn't describe technology products in technical detail, nor does it involve itself in their technical analysis. Technology products today are introduced at such a rapid rate that any book whose topic is about the detail technology products can become rather obsolete before a book can be written. Concentrating only on the introduction of technology products without regard to the business objectives they are intended to achieve, or the best practices to manage them, is an example of the use of technology for technology's sake.

Information Technology Management Major Components

Some, or even all, of the technology management components discussed next may already exist in a company's environment. The architectural task is to identify what components exist, and which must be developed, and how will the components be organized and inter-related to create an architecture which fits the components together into a cohesive architecture. The components that already exist in a company are referred to as *legacy* components or systems. If any of the legacy system components exist in your company, by all means attempt to utilize them. One of the worst things to do when implementing something as large as information technology management is to arbitrarily "throw away" all legacy components to make room for a new management process. Utilization of legacy components can win over champions to a new management process as long as continued use of a legacy component does not represent a significant compromise of the assumptions upon which a new management process is built.

A typical company usually has: a business plan, although it may not be readily accessible to associates; a planning and resource management system; possibly a formal costing system, but probably not a formal service chargeback system. A management model, if it exists at all, probably exists in "someone's head". The ability to imagine IT in new and different ways is a major component of information technology management. Hopefully a company abounds in imagination.

Imagination:

Is the reader surprised to see that *imagination* is listed as a major component of IT technology management? There's a common saying - "It's all in the way you look at things", and this statement certainly applies to information technology management. The entire IT technology management process begins with the technology manager's ability to imagine IT in ways other than just its physical attributes.

Company business plan and the enabling IT technology plans:

Information technology management requires both the company and IT to cooperatively imagine where the company wants to be positioned in the future (the *company business plan*), and how technology can enable the achievement of that vision (the *IT technology plan*). The company business plan is ground zero from which technology management is launched. The business plan and its supporting objectives provide meaning and purpose to the work IT performs. Technology management is a collaborative process between business planners and visionaries and their IT counterparts. IT is not a passive partner in the development of the company business plan.

Work performed by IT:

IT plans and manages work. In order to plan and mange work in a consistent and comprehensive manner a work classification scheme must be developed which identifies, classifies, and organize the work IT performs in support of business plan objectives. Once work is defined it must be aligned with the management functions it supports. Different work types can require different management approaches and skill levels.

The reader can liken a work classification scheme to a chart of accounts used in a company's accounting department. Just as a company would not like to base its financial reporting on a chart of accounts indiscriminately built from a host of accountants, or worse yet, produce financial reports with no chart of accounts, neither can IT plan, manage, and report its work without a chart of work.

Work management process and systems to manage the work:

How is work planned and managed to accomplish IT and company objectives? There are four key processes that are the concern of IT technology work management: planning, resource management, costing, and service chargeback. They are designated key processes because they *manage the work* required to achieve the business plan objectives. Information technology management provides coordination of these processes using a *work management system* which identifies, costs, plans, deploys, tracks, utilizes, and reports the status of the resources.

IT management model:

The *IT management model* (hereafter referred to as the model except as may be noted) is an imagined view of IT, and just like automobiles, there are many possible models from which to choose. The IT technology manager needs to select, or build, a model which not only fits their view of IT, but whose effectiveness can be measured objectively, and one that can be easily adapted to address changing situations. The model presented in this book is measured by its ability to best achieve company business plan objectives; provide excellent, cost effective client service; and remain within the bounds of its assigned resource limitations.

As will be described in greater detail in the chapter 2, *IT Management Model*, the model is at the core of the ideas and management practices presented in the book. It is an information model that combines and delivers all information processing technologies (i.e. data, voice, text, and image) over a common computer network architecture which provides multi-technology based systems and services to its business clients. The computer architecture upon which the model is based is a *computer platform, technology, and organization independent architecture (CPTOIA)*. In this architecture the development of systems and services is not directly linked to a particular computer, technology, or organizational support structure. The architecture enables resource leveraging by identifying common areas of support across computers, technologies, and support organizations. It enables the concept of information processing.

The supporting management and organizational structure the model requires for successful implementation is delivered by a *systems and services organization* (discussed in Chapter 2). In the systems and services organization IT products are not tied to individual computers and processing technologies and their support structures, but are developed and delivered by a common computer network which manages computers and processes across all technologies under a common banner of information processing.

At the core of the model are the *management function structures* which view IT in terms of 24 management functions that IT must successfully plan and manage. These are the basic building blocks of the model. Management functions can be likened to IT areas of responsibility required to manage IT. These functions are layered on top of each other in a hierarchical fashion, and are based upon the function's perceived priority. All functions are equally applicable to all computer platforms and information processing technologies. The model provides a method of cooperatively managing these functions.

From the management functions structure a process model is created for each of the 24 management functions. IT is managed by the development and management of these processes. These processes are identified as *basic IT management processes.* APPIAN.com defines a *business process* "as a set of activities and tasks that, once completed, will accomplish an organizational goal." A process can include associates, software, hardware, and technologies involved in the process, and even other processes. The rules by which the various process components interact with each other in order to successfully complete a process are defined as part of the process definition. The organizational goal to be accomplished by a basic IT management processes is to plan and manage the work aligned with each management function's objectives.

Other, non-basic, processes can be developed using various combinations of the basic IT management processes as their base building blocks. Each of these other processes has an owner who can include projects, tasks, activities, and other processes. The process owner defines the process and determines the component pieces required to complete the process. Information documenting the process is collected in a *strategic management plan worksheet.* These worksheets are made available to other process owners so that planning information can be shared and coordinated with other process owners and IT planners.

Defining information technology management:

Information technology management is a *process* identified as "Information Technology Management Process". It includes the components of the business plan; the model; the work classification scheme; the strategic management plan worksheets; a work management system; and the basic IT management processes of planning, resource management, costing, and service chargeback.

Important Roles Played in Technology Management

A role is defined by *www.merriam-webster.com* as a "function, or part, performed especially in a particular operation or process". In this book roles are contrasted with specific technical skills or management responsibilities. Six critical roles or functions have been identified as part of the IT technology management process:

- Visionary
- Strategist
- Chemist
- Architect
- Opportunist
- Facilitator

Who and how these roles are played in a company is dependent upon the company's culture, organization, and skills and talents of its employees. Typically these roles or functions are provided by a wide-range of IT and business associates and organizational units. The key to successful technology management is to ensure that these roles play an active and visible part in your technology management efforts.

Visionary:

A *visionary* is someone who uses their imaginations to envision the potential of future technology to shape the world and the company. These individuals see technology as something more than just the technical components of the IT products and services. The visionary asks the "what if" and "What can be" types of questions. "What if government regulations become too onerous?"; "What if e-commerce becomes the dominant form of commerce?"; "What will be Internet's impact upon company brick and mortar facilities?"; "What will be the impact of future technology on job growth?"; "What will be the dominant technology of the next decade?"; etc., etc.

Strategist:

A *strategist* assists in the development of an IT plan of action designed to achieve the IT and company vision and major business objectives. The strategist aligns strategies and work initiatives with the business objectives ensuring that company and IT visions and objectives are accomplished. Like the visionaries, there are multiple strategists in an IT department. The technology manager and the management model developer tend to play large strategist roles.

Chemist:

The *chemist* assists in identifying, decomposing, and classifying the IT elements and compounds that IT wants to plan, cost, bill, and manage. The managers need to dust-off their old Periodic Table of Elements document from their high school chemistry class days. It seems as though chemists are always trying to reduce matter to its lowest form called elements (i.e. IT cost components). All other matter is made of these base elements, and are called compounds (i.e. IT products and services). The goal of the chemist is to see how elements and compounds are arranged to create the various forms of matter (i.e. IT products and services) we see in everyday life. Everything has to fit perfectly into this nice table. There is an architecture to these elements and compounds. If something as complex as the "matter" of the world can be explained by the workings of these elemental structures, then surely IT can define its elemental and compound technical and management structures.

Instead of fitting these elements and compounds into a Periodic Table of Elements, the managers fit them into an overall IT technology architecture. This is not a simple task because IT's elements and compounds are not as clearly identified as the ones found in chemistry, but the analogy still holds true. IT elements and compounds are more subjective in nature, unscientific. For example, a computer processor can be viewed as a compound in an IT planning or costing scheme. The elements that comprise the compound (cost components) are the central processing unit, main memory, channels (bus), external storage, input, and output. The managers may only want to plan and manage the computer hardware at a computer processor level from a planning perspective, but from an IT costing perspective, the IT financial manager may want to further identify the computer hardware at lower elemental levels. The level of elemental technology at which an IT manager wants to plan and manage elements and compounds is a judgement call depending upon IT's management objectives.

Each technology element and compound must have an owner who is responsible for the element/compound's development and use within the overall IT architecture. The owner enforces the management functions required to manage the element/compound; the specific work required to develop and deliver the element/compound; the cost: and the method of recovering the cost for utilizing the element/compound. It's amazing how many IT departments have not officially identified their basic IT elements/compounds, much less their owners. A significant IT payback is realized just ensuring that all IT elements/compound have specific owners and assigned responsibility for their development and use.

Architect:

Architecture is the general framework or structure, within and around which, the various elements/compounds are defined, arranged and executed to achieve a specific objective. Architecture defines both the primary and secondary purposes of each of the elements or compounds. It strives for consistent and predictable relationships among elements/compounds. All elements/compounds of IT, regardless of computer platform, processing technology, or business application should "fit" within an overall architecture and be extensions of each other. Architectures must be supportive of the function they are intended to deliver. Architecture doesn't just happen. It must be specifically planned, designed, and managed. Discipline is a significant ingredient of architecture.

The IT chief architect plays the role of master IT architect, but needs to organize the IT managers of all the technical skills areas to work together as a team to plan out the technical architectures upon which the business applications operate. The master IT architect must assist in ensuring that all architectures defined within IT are planned and developed consistent with each other.

Resistance to architecture is often cloaked as the need for expediency. Technology managers acting in the role of an architect can easily be viewed as an obstructionist. Architecture can be a tiring job because of the requirement to fit all the pieces together just like a jig-saw puzzle. To make it even more difficult, all the puzzle pieces may not be currently known or clearly defined. The architect often has to suggest the missing puzzle pieces. It seems like it would be so much easier to just plunge into things and let things fall in place rather than examine every new system element to make sure it fits, or will fit, within the current and planned system architecture. Fitting elements and compounds may appear to be a bit slower in the beginning of the technology management process, but it is faster in the end. It's all about the old saying of "pay me now or pay me later". When you pay later the negative consequences are always greater. For just a few extra steps upfront, the downline processes are significantly streamlined.

Opportunist:

The *opportunist* knows where the company and IT wants to be in the future, mainly because of their knowledge of the vision and business plan objectives. The opportunist recognizes when an opportunity to achieve business plan objectives presents itself because they know the plan. They also know there are always alternative paths to achieving the objectives. As the opportunists these managers travel along the path of a technology development plan, and when an alternate path to achieve an objective presents itself, or a different objective appears, the opportunist knows which path of action to take because they know their objective and what course of action will achieve it. The opportunistic managers know when a door of opportunity opens, they must seize the opportunity quickly before it passes by them. Luck sometimes is not just a thing of chance, although it may appear that way. You hear someone say - "That person really got a lucky break". Did they? Maybe they knew their objective, and they knew what events or actions would advance them towards it. They recognized those events and activities and when they occurred they were there to snatch the prize. Were they lucky? Probably not. Maybe they were just opportunistic.

Facilitator:

The *facilitator* enables associates to work together in the achievement of planned goals and objectives. Many individuals may have the image of the "Thinker" when they envision technology managers. They see individuals working all alone in their cubicle thinking-up all these visions and grandiose technology plans for the company. Not so. The facilitator role can be played by a wide range of managers and even associates. Facilitators are what we refer to as team players who enjoy seeing individuals working to achieve team goals,

Factors Shaping the Model

In many books this section would be entitled "About the Author". Because we all have different experiences and different interpretations of what we observe, there can be multiple versions of a model. That's as it should be. The best model is the one that works best for you. The reader must judge for themselves whether the model presented in the book can work for their company.

As the reader has probably surmised, I'm a promoter of the concept how nothing, except maybe an incandescent light bulb, operates effectively in a "vacuum". The model will definitely be impacted, either negatively or positively, by the company culture, management structure and organization, and general infrastructure in which it is developed and implemented.

The technology manager who creates the model doesn't operate in a vacuum either. Their entire professional career has been influenced by their life values learnt at home; from trusted friends and mentors; experiences with coaches; lessons and tips from previous managers and career mentors; and the observations and professional experiences they've made as they progressed through their professional careers and employment experiences. All these things help shape how the technology manager perceives and develops an approach to IT technology management. One truly brings themselves to the technology management process. Development of our views and values is a continuing process, so be humble enough to consider the ideas of others when developing your approach to managing technology because you never know when the next person you meet, or the next observation you make, could have an impact on your views. Always seek the truth in what you do, no matter where you discover it.

The following sections discuss the experiences and factors that have influenced the model's design. I'm going to list a lot of experiences and factors, some times in a "shot gun fashion", hopefully to create a sense of excitement for the ideas and experiences discussed in the book.

Life's lessons influence :

From a life's lessons perspective, I've first learnt the value of *humility*, not in the sense of bowing or cowering to authority, but valuing others' opinions as you value your own. Humility causes technology managers to listen and include others' ideas in the model's design. It motivates a manager to praise the effort of others and their contribution to the technology management effort. Humility can create a drive within a person to continually educate themselves and improve their skills. We come to realize that maybe we don't know everything, and there are other people who have some really good ideas.

We've all experienced many types of *leadership styles* in our careers. The same style of leadership doesn't always work in all companies, and with all associates. Technical leadership is about the formation of teams representing both the business and the technical organizations of the company. It's based upon pride, teamwork, and effort beyond the call of duty. A leader should inspire their teams to achieve management objectives by their actions, results, and enthusiasm for ideas, not just with words or fancy slogans. Associates need to take responsibility for motivating themselves too. It takes *courage* to manage and lead. Being a leader can be lonely and stressful. The leader's job is to make 1 + 1 equal something greater than 2.

Technology managers need to make decisions concerning how associates want to be treated? The neat thing is everyone is a living laboratory. Look no further than inside yourself for answers concerning how people want to be treated. If all else fails, fall back upon the age-old principles - "Do unto others as you would have them do unto you", or "Walk in the shoes of others". Associates want respect and appreciation for what they do. Accept what is good in the current company environment. Everything doesn't have to have the technology manager's ownership tag on it. A technology manager may gain a lot of respect by using what others created as long as its use doesn't significantly compromise their fundamental beliefs and assumptions. Associates want to know what is expected of them. They want to feel a sense of importance, and perform meaningful work. They need to feel challenged and empowered. They want to see measurable results reflecting their work effort on significant projects. Most associates want a forum in which they can participate and present their ideas.

Choose battles carefully, and know when to *compromise*. Arguments aren't always going to be "won". Let the associate "win" once in a while. Making compromises is all about learning how to identify situations in which alternative courses of action are possible. The key is to know beforehand which alternatives can't be compromised, and which alternatives represent only an accidental change, nuisance, or insignificant modification of plans. Sensitivity to alternative courses of action must be considered, but in the end, the technology manager must do what they think is right, and accept the consequences.

It may surprise some technology managers, but there are some associates who fear accepting additional responsibility. Responsible people are the ones who tend to want more responsibility. The book, *Escape from Freedom*, by the psychologist and social theorist Erich Fromm has a message applicable to three of the values required for successful technology management – *ownership*, *responsibility* and *accountability*. The reason some people refuse to accept responsibility can be motivated by the idea that once responsibility is accepted for something, the individual is no longer free to blame others for their own failure. Blaming others for bad results can be a big part of many company cultures. It's called "CYA". A reason for avoiding responsibility can be a lack of personal confidence. *Confidence* originates from achievement. The model and process should assign ownership, and thus responsibility and accountability, for all IT objectives, work, projects and tasks.

We've all been in very difficult situations in our careers, and a thought that can motivate a technology manager to get through the toughest of these situations is - In all we do, the *truth* will ultimately win out. It's kind of like saying good will win out over evil. Some associates take courses of action in the work place environment which are obviously motivated by reasons other than the common good of the company. Egos, power struggles and politics are a few of the motivating factors witnessed. It's so easy to want to respond in kind to associates so motivated, but maybe the best response is no response, or at least a response which is objective and professional. Technology managers need to *believe* in their ideas. If their ideas are true, other responsible associates can see their merit. Responding in kind could cause an associate to be viewed in the same context as those they are criticizing.

Business managers' and mentors' influence:

We've all had previous business managers and mentors who have influenced the manner in which we view IT technology management. We can learn from the negative experiences as well as from the positive ones. The following comments relate more to general IT management best practices rather than "hard core" technology management advice. It's this kind of wisdom imparted to us that helps fill-up our management "vacuum". Each of us will have different experiences causing us to arrive at different approaches to technology management. I've italicized some of the advice I thought was particularly helpful. The next several sections present a collage of ideas gained from those with whom I worked. It may appear rambling in the presentation method, but I chose to do it this way versus some structured method because I hope this outpouring of ideas in this manner promotes a sense of energy for the ideas.

Management skills and traits:

Be *disciplined* and *focused* in your management approach. Don't let expediency continually determine your actions. *Compromise grudgingly*. Have the *courage* to stand-out from your peers. Don't rest on your laurels. Always look to improve, never be satisfied with the current situation because it will change. Ask lots of questions, and *be driven to learn*. The next challenge is just "waiting around the corner". Seek knowledge from all sources. Use peers and vendors as sources of technical knowledge. Don't get too carried away with yourself. "Perfect is often the enemy of the good". *Be able to make decisions with less than 100% of the information available.* Know when "to roll the dice." *Take calculated risks, but not fool-hardy chances.* Be decisive. Seek the truth in all you do. Avoid the political games if at all possible. Don't take anything for granted.

Management best practices:

Communicate with your associates and your superiors. Talking to each other is not necessarily communications. Always have a plan in mind.

Communicate that plan. Follow-up on the status of your plan. Know where you want to be so that when an opportunity presents itself you can seize it. Get others involved in the management process. Practice distributed management by pushing management responsibility to the lowest organizational level at which it can be executed. Emphasize architecture. Look for the connections in all that you manage. Fit every possible technology component piece to the technology puzzle. The time to plan is when things are "going well". Experience dictates that the good times won't last forever. It's easy to manage and plan when budgets are overflowing with dollars. If a technology manager begins to develop an action plan only when IT events take a turn for the worse, they're probably too late to effectively respond to the events. Well-run business organizations value the time of their managers. A specific meeting agenda is required when conducting meetings with managers at all levels of the organization. Presentations should be brief and to the point. Technology manager's decisions should be made on the basis of simple principles, concepts, and values whenever possible. Managing by simple principles and simple values "trumps" all the complicated processes and procedures a manager can devise. Excessive procedures and management structures can "suffocate" associate creativity, and create procedural "work arounds". Manage the delicate balance between creating a sense of enthusiasm for work while not losing control of the situation by having a fully communicated plan in place in which every associate knows the objectives and their role in achieving them. There's no one style of leadership that fits all situations. Know your associates and fit the leadership style to their psyche. The client is "always" right. Be client service and relationship oriented. Remember who pays IT's salaries, your business clients. Form synergistic partnerships within IT and with your business clients. Create service agreements with your business clients, and report against those standards. Create objective measures of your own performance.

Management perspectives:

No one is indispensable, including yourself. Management can be a *lonely and intimidating* experience. Always have a "skill in your back pocket." It's not always the most talented team that achieves its objectives, sometimes it's the most motivated team. Working in a company where managers think resources are unlimited and IT expense budgets will keep escalating can be a difficult environment within which to manage and plan work. *Without limitations, it is difficult to develop teamwork and remained focused.* Without limitations a manager may believe that they have many more options from which to choose, when in reality their options may be limited. Think of the time lost looking at technologies and projects that are not affordable. Resource limitations can be the source of innovative ideas and creative solutions to problems.

A final management perspective to be mentioned is closely connected with the quality of humility. If an individual builds a process, and if the successful operation of the process requires the individual's participation in the process, then maybe that individual has failed in their original objective of creating a successful process.

Influence of our professional observations of IT management:

The IT technology manager is not just passive to the ideas presented to them by others. Our own observations and management experiences in IT are very important. We need to keep our "eyes and ears open" and observe and note things within IT that you believe are important, and those things you think could be better managed if given the chance to change them. These new and better ways of viewing IT will become a part of your management model as your experiences increase. The following are some of the items that I observed and determined were either important or problematic to effective IT technology management. I attempt to address these items in the model presented in the book.

Observations on company practices:

I observed that a *company's business plan* was not always accessible or visible to IT. The business plan should be distributed to all managers in the company with the directive that they must read it and *internalize* it in their daily management activities. *How can anyone expect associates to support the company business plan if they've never seen it?* Some companies focus on the technical management of the computers and technologies to the exclusion of the management functions such as management best practices, organization, financials, business applications, client service strategies, and education/training. All management functions must be considered in the management of technology.

Observations on IT departments:

The mystique of working with computers is long gone. *IT can be managed just like any other business unit.* IT doesn't need special treatment. In some companies I sensed a feeling of arrogance on IT's part because of their work with computers and all the new technologies and gadgets. This arrogance can negatively impact business client relationships. IT needs to share their enthusiasm for their work with their clients. Many IT departments manage the four technologies of data, voice, text, and image as independent technologies, or they use traditional data processing management and organizational structures to manage these disparate technologies. Non-integrated management of these technologies requires a significant amount of redundant resource utilization. The IT products and services developed and delivered to the business client by these *"silo" managed* technology structures are often ineffective.

In many IT departments I observed that formal planning is a once a year event that produces a plan document which is not always *internalized into daily management practices.* Once a plan is completed, managers must manage to it every day. Managers can't go back to their old ways of managing work.

Some IT associates view the business clients as a nuisance. Others view the business clients as "their meal ticket". Client service management should represent a significant part of any model. Many IT departments continually face IT control issues with business units. Some business units would like to own and manage their own IT capability. They develop various ways of escaping IT control. Responsibility for some IT functions and facilities should be allocated to the business units, but the *indiscriminant allocation of IT responsibilities to the business units can result in chaos for IT management.* There are IT business clients who acquire application systems based upon the computer platform upon which it operates, rather the ability of the application system to satisfy business requirements. The business units believe that some computer platforms, the personal computer and possibly a limited client/server network, should be business unit owned and managed. In these situations the functionality of the business application system becomes secondary to the computer platform choice, and this can result in the installation of ineffective business application systems. The practice of distributing technology products and functionality to business units can also have the effect of distorting true technology costs of doing company business because these costs are directly recorded to the business unit ledgers and act to "scatter" the total cost of technology throughout the company. Care must be exercised in comparing total costs of IT operations when using professional organizations' surveys or cost comparison analyses reports because the cost components included in the surveys may not be the same as the cost components used in your company's cost analysis.

Some managers hoard work and are reluctant to delegate it because they fear that by giving up work they may not have other work to do. An individual grows in their career by passing on to others what they have mastered and accepting new challenges. *Lack of measurement awareness and performance against standards* is not always prominent in IT departments. Without having results reported against expectations it is difficult to improve service to the business client.

Observations on skills:
Programming is a core technology skill that provides a solid basis for understanding technology. It promotes logic, discipline, architecture, and responsibility for your actions. These are all traits required for effective technology management. A program does exactly as it is instructed. There are no mysterious "gremlins" in a computer messing with the program logic. *System Design is another key technology skill* which complements programming. I observed a reluctance of some programmers and designers to create

detail work specifications before work was initiated. There was a tendency to "jump right into the detail work task without much forethought on business requirements or system design. The result of such actions is usually the development of poorly designed and functionally-deficient systems. *If a system is designed well, it is easy to build, easy to install, easy to maintain, and easy to change.* The problem of poor upfront design can be exacerbated with the advancement of more sophisticated system development tools. Be disciplined, and don't let expediency continually determine your actions. *Architecture* is another significant trait of successful IT technology management. A lack of architecture promotes short-range thinking and solutions. Training is not always selected and aligned with work plans. Some associates are reluctant to take training because of production commitments.

Influence of personal technology management experiences:

The final influences upon the development of the model presented in the book are my own professional career experiences. These experience are based upon a 46 year career in the information technology industry working in both the manufacturing and financial services industries. The model was not developed all at once. It developed and refined over the years as I experienced and observed what was happening around me.

Beginnings of a career in information technology:

Like many young individuals graduating from college, I really had no idea what career I wanted to pursue. I was 26 years old when I finally decided to pursue a career in data processing. I started at the lowest position in the administrative data processing department at a local college, a Programmer I. I've never second-guessed this decision. I thought I was "big stuff" because I had a title of programmer and a business card that proved it. From that original position of a programmer, I advanced over my 46 year career to become a vice president of information technology. In-between, I developed my own technology consulting company which provided various project and system development services to both the manufacturing and financial services industries. Looking back at my information technology roots, I've personally witnessed this field advance from a single computer, data processing only facility to a multi-computer information processing complex fully integrating the technologies of data, voice, text, and image in the development and delivery of multi-tech information products and services.

When I look back over my career, I still carry the same sense of excitement about the information technology field as I did when I was handed my business cards indicating I was a Programmer I. In many ways my experience in programming was the key that unlocked the doors to success in this field. It is this sense of excitement and experience that I want to share with you in this book. I mention my programming experience because I believe programming is one of the major keys to managing information technology. Programming is the language we use to "talk" with the computers. It isn't about knowing a particular program language (e.g. COBOL, there's a dinosaur that hasn't gone extinct), but the pure logic and methodology that is so important. Programming taught me discipline and logic like no logic class in college could.

IT management - rescue artist:

My professional career had three distinct patterns, each reflecting my varying roles in information technology management. The first pattern reflects my consulting experiences in which I was brought into companies to assist in turning-around major projects that were in significant jeopardy of failing, both technically and financially. Some of these projects were described "as betting the company". One project involved a diversified holding corporation that wanted to use a third party's software product to reengineer the entire corporation's IT software and hardware infrastructure. Another project involved moving and assimilating the data processing capability of a newly acquired company into the company's headquarters computer center. Yet another project involved removing a facilities management group that had totally managed a company's computer operations for 25 years, and replacing the entire IT operation with an in-house staff and facilities. These projects required every management skill imaginable to provide a successful outcome.

IT management - on-going information management:

A second pattern of career development followed from this first pattern of career experiences. Typically I was asked to remain with the company and assume control of the on-going IT operation. I took the same basic technical and management approach in developing each IT operation for which I assumed responsibility. I introduced the company business plan as the driver of the technology plan for each company. The IT management model described in this book was used to develop and manage a complete technology "make-over" of the IT departments. I formed alliances with the Chief Financial Officers (CFO). The CFO is normally a trusted part of the senior business management team in most companies. They exercise a tremendous amount of influence in a company. The CFO tends to keep IT locked to reality. They talk the language of the other senior staff members - dollars. I took a financial view of IT management as well as a technical view. Emphasis was placed on expense and revenue management, budgeting, service chargeback, cost management, planning, resource management, and work management. A distributed management style was introduced in which management functions were deployed to the lowest organizational level at which they could be effectively executed. This management style "flattened" the IT organization structure.

Each company was transitioned from a data processing facility to an integrated information processing complex by integrating the formerly independent processing technologies of data, voice, text, and image. This was enabled by the introduction of an IT model and supporting architecture that provided IT the ability to develop and manage a computer platform, technology, and organization independent architecture (CPTOIA), and a systems and services organizational support structure to deliver it. The critical importance of client relationships and effective business system applications were given priority. Business client service and partnerships were always major objectives along with increasing profits for the company.

Consulting:

The third pattern of my career development involved my 15 years of experience as an independent contractor/consultant working out of my technology consulting company. I designed and implemented work management systems, as well as consulted on major corporate projects.

Adjunct Professor:

Concurrent with most of my professional IT career, I taught computer-related courses at both the undergraduate and MBA levels. At the undergraduate level I taught courses ranging from communications/networking, office automation, data processing management, and networked computing environments. My specialty at the MBA graduate level was IT strategic planning and management. I was lucky to be able to develop the synergy between my teaching and my professional careers. The impact of these teaching experiences provided me the opportunity to stay current with emerging technologies. I believed that if I was to be an effective planner, I needed to be able to discuss and challenge the technical managers with whom I dealt.

In the following chapters the reader will witness the influence of these experiences on the development of the model and its impact on technology management.

CHAPTER 1

Company Business Plan Ground Zero

Without a destination there really isn't much need for a map.

Ground Zero is defined as "the very beginning" on www.merriam-webster.com/dictionary's website. How appropriate that the business plan is considered Ground Zero in technology management. It's where everything starts. The business plan provides the answer to the basic technology management questions—Where does a company want to be positioned in the future, and what are the business and IT objectives, strategies, technologies, and major initiatives that will enable the company to achieve its business plan vision? The key to answering these questions is the company's business plan. The business plan is driven by a vision that looks out in time, and is heavily influenced by the assumptions it makes about what factors in the world economy, government, society, the market place, competition, and technology development can, and most probably will, shape the company's future. The business plan evaluates the potential impact of these factors on company management, organization, operational structure requirements; the technologies it must acquire; the physical plant capacity and capability the company must have; the employees it must recruit and retain; and the products it must deliver and service. The business plan vision allows a company to escape the requirement to analyze and evaluate all possible technologies that are "out there". It concentrates on those technologies which best advance the company towards the achievement of its business objectives.

Companies typically produce a very detailed business plan along with a summary business plan. Obviously such a detailed business plan cannot be illustrated in a book about principles. A summary business plan is usually created and presented at various company-wide presentations. A summary business plan is sufficient for illustration purposes in this book. The following represents a sample statement of the high level business objectives of a summary business plan used in this book. The business objectives illustrated are typical of those found in many summary business plans. The statement that they are classified as typical should not be interpreted to mean that they are irrelevant. It is these business objectives to which IT objectives, strategies, and work initiatives should align.

Organizational Effectiveness:

- Continuous improvement initiatives
- Effective organizational structures
- Cost awareness
- Plan driven
- Embrace Quality

Value Staff:

- Empower staff
- Career development opportunities
- Fair compensation
- Increase skills and training opportunities

Foster Customer Loyalty:

- Exceed expectations
- Customer-focused solutions
- Cost effective products

Financial Responsibility:

- Bottom-line oriented
- Financial awareness
- Cost management

Competitive and Imaginative Products:

- Introduce new technologies and systems in support of business plan

Maybe there's a complementary visioning strategy which concentrates on human behavior as a driving force in the technology visioning process. Technology should mimic and enable what we do today, and what we want to do tomorrow. Business and IT visions need to address trends in human behavior, not just technology trends. Technology visionaries need to look beyond the application of existing technologies to current human behavior that "can" be automated, and imagine what technologies will be required to facilitate the manner in which individuals would like to do things in the future.

A changing society

A significant example of how social practices can impact a company's technology plan is Facebook and other Internet based social media products. Just look at what is occurring in the retail world today with the movement away from "brick and mortar" retail outlets to online shopping based around smart phones and Internet. Think of the impact on technology required to support the new mobile Apps that must be created, the required support of extended warehouse operations, robotics, and ground transportation delivery capabilities. How many companies had the assumption of social media impact or online shopping in their business plans? Of the companies that didn't, how many of them are still in business? Planners must envision these social events because there is normally a long ramp-up time to get the technologies and systems in place to develop and support them. Even today it seems like some companies still "don't get it" because shopping malls and strip malls are continually being built, while stores seem to be closing at a rapid rate.

There is a big concern today about the impact of technology on jobs. That surely shouldn't come as a surprise to anyone. Going back to the early 1970s a common cost justification offered for new systems implementation was the elimination of jobs. History documents the fact that IT did its job well over the years, and jobs have been eliminated. It's been a lot of years, and a lot of jobs. Why should the general population be surprised at the job losses? This trend continues today as witnessed by the increasing use of self-checkout lines versus those serviced by a person, and the continued growth in the robotics industry. Companies need to plan for this type of job impact.

Social behavioral changes also migrate to a company's work environment and must be envisioned. Most of these changes revolve about the people management issues of hiring and management practices. The newer managers hired can have a completely different view of associates and management practices than older generation managers. These differences can cause some tension and conflict in the work place. Today's managers need to be more understanding and tolerant of a changing world. Electronic communication seems to override face-to-face communications today. Political correctness makes it more difficult to bring-up the real issues facing a company. Unfortunately society seems more focused on image and spin than on reality and truth. This attitude has migrated into many companies. These factors can be part of the reason why companies don't always find lasting solutions to work place problems and issues. Substantive change requires substantive effort. Managers can't work around the edges of problems and expect to solve them. The true test of finding a management truth is that it remains over time and people.

History's impact

A factor that can help in facilitating the effort to analyze the myriad of possible technologies is "history". You read that correctly, history. The connotation of the word "history" seems totally out of context with the concept of visioning, but it can have a forward look to it if it is put in a proper context. What's the old saying - "If you fail to recognize history, you are doomed to repeat it". In many instances of new technology introduction, what's happening today is not much different in substance from what has happened in the past. A good question to ask when new technologies are introduced in the industry is - "Does this new technology look or function like any existing technologies, or is it radically new?"

Many new technologies evolve from older ones, so if a technology manager knows to what existing technology phylum a new technology is likened, they already know something about the new technology and how it can be used. For example, if a technology manager understood the architecture of the telephone network, they could have seen the similarities between it and the introduction of Internet. The telephone system operates across a worldwide network of call switching centers (computers) to establish telephone call connections between users of the telephone system much like the Internet IP addresses and Uniform Resource Locators (URLs) operate across a worldwide network of computers to establish connections of computer users. The telephone number operates like an address and steps the call across the network of telephone switches (computers) much like is done in Internet. If a planner had knowledge of the telephone system, they could have much easier imagined and planned for information networks as contrasted with disparate telephone and data networks and their redundant support requirements. Minicomputers represent a forerunner technology of the desktop personal computers. If the trend towards smaller computers was properly recognized and addressed early in their development cycle, the introduction of the personal computer may not have been such an unanticipated revolution. Knowledge of history advances the ability to assimilate new knowledge.

History can also teach us humility. IT has the cumulative technical knowledge and experience gained from its ancestors. Technologies have advanced and progressively built upon the older technologies. There is a lot to be learnt from the past, especially as it relates to human behavior and management practices. Today there seems to be a big rush to automate everything by the use of the smartphone and a multitude of APSs. One particular type of current application involves the use of kiosk or smart phone to order meals at a restaurant. The order is placed, and the meal is served to the person at their table. It may be humbling to think that more than 50 years ago there was a small, carhop type, fast food restaurant in a little Indiana town that provided an in-house phone system that allowed diners to order directly from their tables, and have the food directly served to them at their tables. Today the delivery technology has changed, and maybe now there is equipment in the kitchen automatically preparing the food, but isn't the concept exactly the same. Someone had a vision back then, just like someone today is having a grander vision because now there are more enabling technologies available. Newer generations are moving from personal communication methods to more electronic method of communicating. Certainly online retailing is reflecting that trend. We have engineers today that still marvel how certain archeological structures were built thousands of years ago. Just because we have all these advanced technologies today doesn't mean we are wiser than those in our past. We may be technically smarter, but technology is only one part of the solution to achieving company objectives. What we gain in technology we may lose in something more important. The basics of good planning and management remain much the same today.

Ownership

The primary business owner of this management function is the Chief Executive Officer (CEO). The CEO develops the plan at the request of the Board of Directors. It can include direct input from the Board of Directors. Frequently the owner may be the champion and sponsor of the plan, but in developing it, the CEO will probably rely upon a member of the company's senior management team to effectively lead the project with oversight from the CEO. Leadership of plan development is most often delegated to the company business planner, assuming there is a company planner, else the next logical choices for delegation are the Chief Operations Officer (COO) or the Chief Financial Officer (CFO). In any scenario the lead individual must surround themselves with a comprehensive base of business and IT senior managers. Ultimately the business plan development process has "tentacles" that reach down into every level of the company's organizational structure. This far reaching scope indicates the importance of the process. More details of team composition and the process to integrate the business plan with the IT plan development process are contained later in this chapter under "Shared Responsibility", and in chapters 2 (IT Management Model) and chapter 7 (Planning and Resource Management). Clearly a balanced ownership team must be developed to ensure both the business and the technical plans are coordinated.

Obviously the developer of the business plan must be a visionary, or be surrounded by strong visionaries. The business plan owner must be a champion of the role the plan plays in the company and within IT. The business plan owner needs to lead the process which assembles and directs the teams that will develop the plan. The planner needs to assist in developing the strategies required to deliver the plan, or be able create a team of strategists who can perform the same function. Lastly the business plan owner must be an opportunist that takes advantage of new opportunities to enhance the plan that arise during the course of plan development.

Business Plan Development Process

Shared responsibility:

The business vision can narrow IT's search for vision-enabling technologies. Determining the actual enabling technologies required by the business plan is normally a shared responsibility with IT. Even though IT is business plan driven, IT is not anything close to being passive in the technology implementation process. IT has its own vision of technology that can help shape and broaden the business vision. IT must partner with the company in the sharing of these visions. IT needs to integrate the IT planning efforts of the company, the individual business units, and IT itself. Use of the business plan as a guide in evaluating the need to introduce new technology requires business management to share with IT in the responsibility for technology innovation.

The company's vision and supporting business plan are a major driver of IT cost. If IT cannot fund the technology required by the company's vision, it is the company's responsibility to either provide the needed funds or reduce the scope of their vision. Senior company management needs to ask itself the questions - "Does the company need all the technology that is available in the market place, and can the company afford the technology even if it thinks it needs it?" The CIO could be asked the question – "Can a company of our medium size compete technologically with larger companies?" Business management needs to work with IT in finding answers to these questions. The answers to these questions can be negative in which case the company may have to rewrite its business plan including a new mission statement and business objectives. The solution to developing a positive response to these questions is to have in place an IT plan tightly aligned with business plan objectives, and an IT operation which leverages and focuses its resources on the achievement of those objectives, and operates as any other business unit in order to contribute to the company's bottom line.

Gaining access to the company's business plan is a first step in discovering a glimpse of the business vision. Without a shared business plan, or some reasonable facsimile of one, what standard does a company's senior business management team have to judge IT's current performance and overall effectiveness in support of the company? The company business plan should be the barometer against which IT's performance is judged.

There is no way technology can be an enabling factor in the achievement of the company's vision if IT doesn't know the vision, yet the absence of a formal business plan document, including the vision, does not excuse IT from developing a technology plan. Clearly the technology plan would be more effective if IT had possession of a formal business plan.

The "plan" is out there in the company somewhere. IT needs to get aggressive and analyze any and all types of items that may convey company plan information. Business plan type information can be found in company presentations; company literature published to outside stakeholders; in memos; in minutes of meetings; in conversations with managers; in status reports; and in any fragmented planning reports they may discover.

Common business plan and IT plan development process – Why not?:

If a company has a common business plan that drives the utilization of business and IT resources on behalf of achieving common business plan objectives, why shouldn't there be a common plan, model, and development process shared by both the business and technical staffs of the company?

Think how nice it would be if the business community and IT not only worked together in a common planning process, but also used a common plan model. Too often the individual business units and the IT planners are out of synch with each other in both approach and scheduling of planned work. Coordinating all company planning initiatives and procedures is a real possibility if all groups agree upon a common process and plan model. Imagine the IT payback associated with the development of such a coordinated planning effort? As the saying goes, "priceless".

The business units can develop a management model and process similar to IT's model and management practices, but adapt it to their specific work components and management functions. There doesn't seem to be any substantive differences in work types and management functions between the business units and IT to preclude the two groups from using a common model. For example, the business units have the following management functions in common with IT.

- Business plan driven
- Align work to support the company's vision, and business objectives
- Perform comparable work types (general management, administration, production support, maintenance, regulatory/compliance work, and projects)
- Create a budget (plan) to manage business expenses
- Identify and address cost drivers, strengths, weaknesses, opportunities and threats
- Identify and address general management, organization, staff recruitment and retention, and compensation issues
- Support business applications (e.g. billing, accounts payable and receivables, etc.)
- Train and develop skills to support work requirements
- Create service strategies for internal and external clients
- Utilize technologies in support of their work efforts

The bulleted-list presented follows the IT management functions contained in the IT model. This fact further advances the idea that a common planning model and plan development process is feasible.

CHAPTER 2
IT Management Model

Some men see things as they are and say why.
I dream things that never were, and say why not.

Edward M. Kennedy
Address at the Public Memorial Service for Robert F. Kennedy
Delivered 8 June 1968 at St. Patrick's Cathedral, New York

Some IT managers may enter an IT department and see office space and equipment; staff sitting in front of personal computers working on the development of various business applications; staff meetings taking place discussing the status of various projects; etc. They enter the computer or equipment room and see many types of computers, big and small. They see lots of wiring and cabling, modems, flashing lights, etc. The staff is moving all over the place holding computer reports in their hands. What are they working on, and on whose behalf is the work being performed? Who are the clients and what type of applications are they utilizing? IT managers don't always look beyond the physical aspects of technology management.

The model enables the planner to imagine IT in terms of visions; financials; organization; client relationships; technologies; the commonality of computers; architecture; strategies; cost drivers; work structures; business applications; and the products and services IT delivers to its clients. The model is a comprehensive view in that it combines the technologies of data, voice, text, and image around the singular concept of information. The model creates a view of how IT resources are structured, arranged, deployed, and managed to enable the company's business plan. The model uses the management techniques of resource leveraging, plan alignment, and focusing to achieve its results. Each of us must imagine our own view of IT, and like Edward M. Kennedy said, "why not?

Figure 1 presents a graphical representation of how viewing IT through the structure of a model can impact the technology manager's perception of IT.

The model should provide impetus to IT actions, and not be just a nice graphic presented at various management meetings. It is a crucial component of the IT management process. It permeates every part of IT. Architecture, discipline, and a structured approach are key ingredients to the success of the model's impact, but imagination is the source of energy which makes the model something more than just a structured view of a process. Imagination provides the power to view information technology in new and challenging ways. Imagination allows a planner to get outside the bounds of their perceptual limitations. Imagination answers that "why not" question.

Figure 1 Imagining Information Technology through the Model

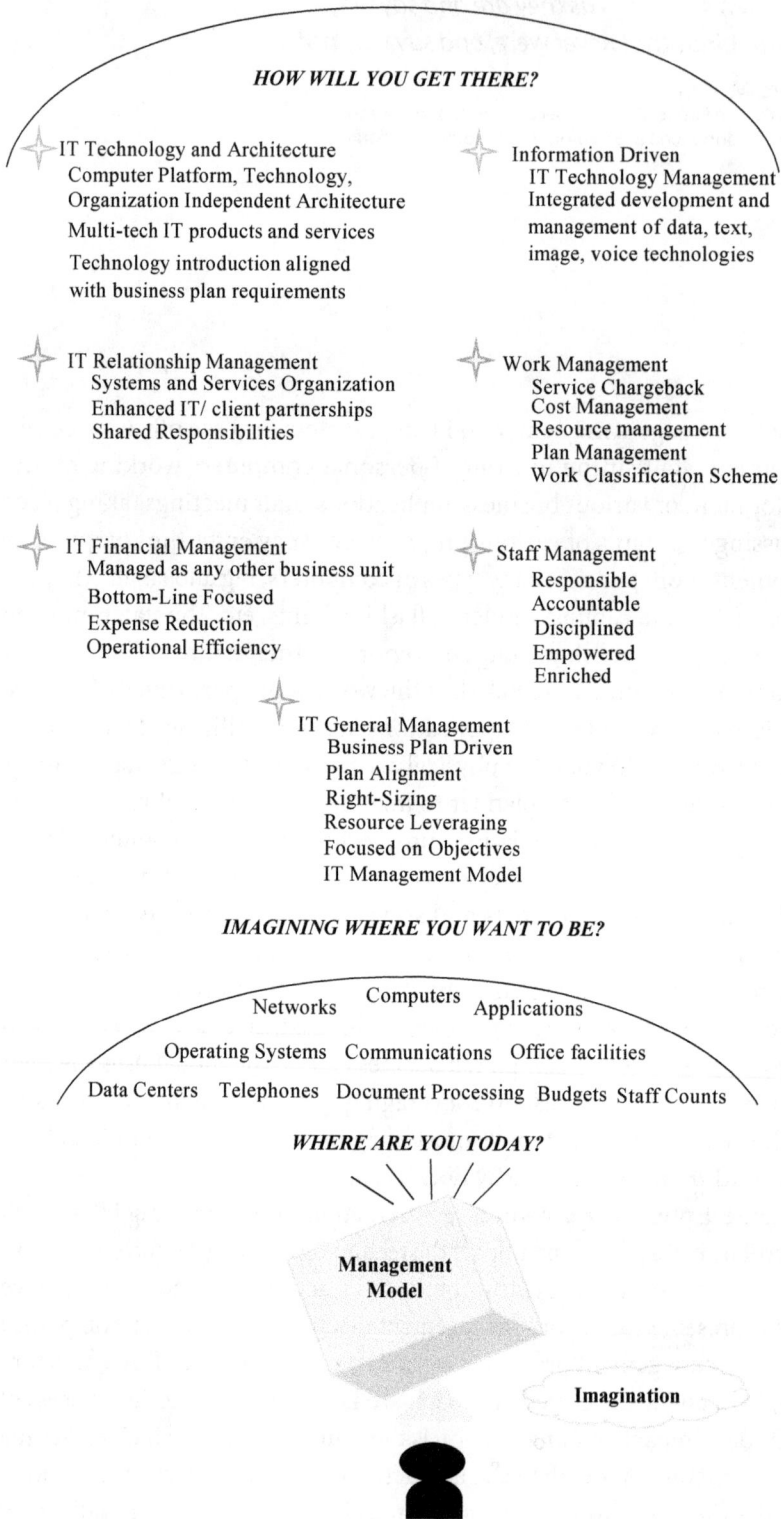

HOW WILL YOU GET THERE?

IT Technology and Architecture
Computer Platform, Technology,
Organization Independent Architecture
Multi-tech IT products and services
Technology introduction aligned
with business plan requirements

Information Driven
IT Technology Management
Integrated development and
management of data, text,
image, voice technologies

IT Relationship Management
Systems and Services Organization
Enhanced IT/ client partnerships
Shared Responsibilities

Work Management
Service Chargeback
Cost Management
Resource management
Plan Management
Work Classification Scheme

IT Financial Management
Managed as any other business unit
Bottom-Line Focused
Expense Reduction
Operational Efficiency

Staff Management
Responsible
Accountable
Disciplined
Empowered
Enriched

IT General Management
Business Plan Driven
Plan Alignment
Right-Sizing
Resource Leveraging
Focused on Objectives
IT Management Model

IMAGINING WHERE YOU WANT TO BE?

Networks   Computers   Applications

Operating Systems   Communications   Office facilities

Data Centers   Telephones   Document Processing   Budgets   Staff Counts

WHERE ARE YOU TODAY?

**Management
Model**

Imagination

*The model is fueled by our imagination concerning how we
view and want to manage IT*

The introduction of technologies in a company does not occur in a management vacuum, nor can it be introduced in a management or systems environment that is inconsistent with the model's basic assumptions and architecture. Choose whatever management model which satisfies the view of IT taken, but be aware that the model alone does not ensure success.

Ownership

If ownership of the model had to be placed with an individual, the best guess is this individual would be the Chief Information Officer (CIO). The model is at basis of the entire IT operation. Given the probable unavailability of the CIO, and considering the level of technical skills and experience required to develop the model, reality dictates that the CIO would be more of a champion of the model development effort, and would rely upon a team of other senior IT staff to develop and maintain the model. Not dealing with an actual company and real individuals, the only thing that can be done on the ownership issue is to present a list of candidates who can be considered, or even eliminated, as candidates for ownership.

- Consider – Vice president of IT Systems or Vice President of IT Services
- Consider – The IT plan administrator
- Consider – The chief IT architect
- Consider – A senior business manager, possibly the company planner
- Consider – Services of a consulting group, or independent consultant. Sometimes consultants receive more favorable acceptance on major initiatives like this one than do in-house staff associates.

Regardless who actually owns the model, a team of senior IT staff will be required to assist in its delivery because it touches every facet of IT. Putting in a model and its supporting infrastructure is on the scale of a major IT reengineering effort.

The management model builder will require a plethora of IT knowledge, skills, and energy. It would be difficult to create a job description for this position. The individual needs to be a visionary, strategist, architect, opportunist, and facilitator. Creation of a workable model is a very difficult task, one not to be taken lightly. The model developer must be tenacious in their beliefs, and relentless in their energy.

Major Model Components

There are four major components of the model presented in the book:

- The assumptions upon which the model is based.
- The management functions (responsibilities) required to identify and manage IT work.

- The management functions structure
- The extended management functions structure including non-traditional computer technologies (i.e. voice, text, and image)

In addition to these four model components, the infrastructural impact of company culture, management structure, and management best practices must be considered.

Model Assumptions

The assumptions upon which a model is based are critical to the development of an effective model.

Technology's role in support of the company's business plan:

The ultimate objective of technology management should be the achievement of business plan objectives within the IT resource limitations established by the company.

A management model cannot be developed in a management vacuum:

The IT components of architecture, hardware, software, communications, networking, and technologies cannot be managed independent of the management functions of visioning, financial control, general management and administration, client relationships, education and training, and other IT management functions such as resource management, change management, security, facilities management, etc.

Manage information, not just data:

A fundamental assumption of the model is the belief that information is conveyed by the:

- Spoken word (voice technologies, aka telephone systems)
- Text and the written word (aka text and word processing technologies)
- Pictures and images (aka image and document management technologies)
- Digital format (aka traditional data processing technologies)

The four information types and their supporting technologies were historically processed by independent hardware platforms. Today these technologies are processed by a common computer processing capability originating from traditional data processing technologies. The computers are connected by a sophisticated computer network which enables the development and delivery of multi-computer and multi-technology business applications to the business client under a variety of service options. The integration of these formerly independent processing technologies is referred to as information processing. The continued introduction of new technologies and support facilities makes information integration technically possible today, but if IT continues to use independent technology management support structures to manage these newer technologies, it cannot maximize its investments in new technology.

Commonality of computer functions:

The management model is based upon an assumption that all computers are functionally alike. Each has the same basic functional components of:

- Central processing unit (aka CPU)
- Main memory
- Input
- Output
- Channels or bus
- External storage

Computers differ mostly in size, power, performance, capacity, internal processing speed, and the manner in which they interface with the computer user. A good analogy that illustrates the idea that all computers are functionally alike is a transportation company which owns a fleet of transportation vehicles to haul freight. The fleet of vehicles could be composed of large tractor trailers, trucks of all sizes and shapes, vans, pick-up trucks, and even automobiles. These vehicles are all functionally alike in that they have: an engine, steering, braking, and fuel systems, cargo space, and wheels, but each vehicle differs in horsepower, speed, carrying capacity, performance, and cost to operate and maintain. The objective is to match the vehicle whose performance characteristics, capacity, and cost best aligns with the freight's physical characteristics and the shipper's budget.

The computer management functions required to operate and maintain each computer have not fundamentally changed either. Computers require a secure environment; an adequate and stable power supply; data back-up and recovery capabilities; constant system upgrades; hardware maintenance and upgrades; organized naming standards; education in the use of the computer; and most of all, excellent business applications that are secured and maintained.

Because any given computer can concurrently process all information technology types (i.e. data, voice, text, and image), and each computer is fundamentally alike in function and management support, IT can leverage management support and staff skills across a common network of computers and technologies, and realize significant cost savings.

Manage a computer network, not just a group of independent computers:

Computer support of information processing technologies is delivered by a common computer network architecture. The computer network is the "thing" to manage, not a singular computer platform or technology. The network brings added-value to each computer platform and technology in the network.

Computer Platform, Technology, Organization Independent Architecture (CPTOIA):

If it is assumed that all computers are fundamentally alike in function; process all forms of technology as information; and operate across a common network, then it can be further assumed that IT management support structures and organizations can be leveraged across the network. In this architecture the development of systems and services is not directly linked to a particular computer platform, technology, or organizational support structure. The architecture enables resource leveraging by identifying common areas of support across computers, technologies, and support organizations. It also enables the concept of information processing.

Business application systems are a primary concern:

Business application systems development and support are key products delivered by the IT department. Choose and implement the business application systems by their ability to first satisfy business requirements. The computer platform and system delivery choice follows the business application system decision. This is how platform independence in the application development process is achieved.

Distributed business application systems:

Business application systems development and delivery in the CPTOIA environment require a distributed application systems design methodology in which the basic business application system functions of input, output, processing, and data storage can be independently allocated and performed on any computer platform in the network based upon business requirements of the application.

Systems should mimic and facilitate business processes, not determine or constrain them:

The idea is to ensure the business requirements of functionality, accessibility, workflow, performance, cost and capacity are satisfied with the installation of any business application system. IT doesn't want to be in a position in which the business client must accept systems that require them to fundamentally compromise how they do business.

Systems design is a critical skill:

The IT systems designer is a key IT associate. If a system is designed well, it is easy to build, install, maintain, operate and enhance. Nothing beats good systems design. A critical part of any business application system design plan is its fit within a sound application systems architecture.

Tapping into the synergy between the system user and system developer:

A great source of creative energy in a company is the synergy which exists between the individual having the system need (the IT business client) and the individual providing the required service (IT service provider). Tapping into this synergy requires the development of specific business client servicing strategies. Synergistic relationships won't happen of their own accord.

Model Structure

The model's vision, assumptions, and structure will of necessity be influenced by the educational, professional and societal experiences the model developer(s) has experienced. Because each of these experiences will probably differ among management model developers, there will be variances in the design of management models. That's OK. Like the saying goes, "It's all in the way we view things".

The model can be referenced as the plan model when discussing planning and resource management; the cost model when discussing cost management; or the service chargeback model when discussing service chargeback management (i.e. billing). The model used in all these applications is simply an implementation of the IT management model.

This section of the book defines the how the model is structured around several basic components and concepts.

- Business plan
- Management functions
- Management functions structure
- Strategic management plan worksheet
- Basic IT management processes
- Other processes

Business plan:

The business plan resides in the highest layer of the model (reference Figure 2). It's at the top layer for a reason. It drives the entire modeling process. It provides the "why" for the work IT plans to do. Copies of this plan, or access to it, should be provided to all IT managers.

Figure 2 Illustrates the management functions structure upon which the IT management model is built.

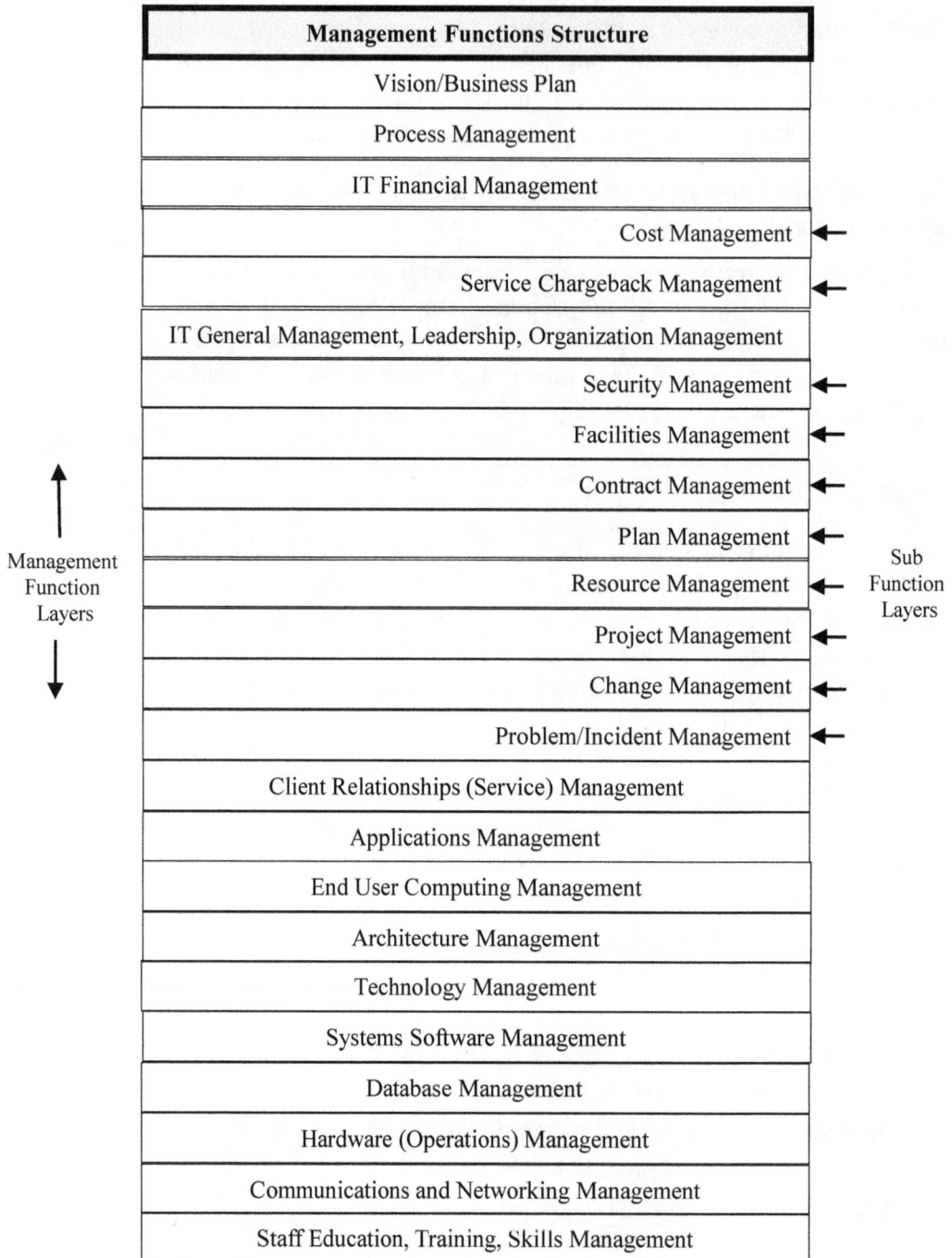

Management Function Layers	Management Functions Structure	Sub Function Layers
	Vision/Business Plan	
	Process Management	
	IT Financial Management	
	Cost Management ←	
	Service Chargeback Management ←	
	IT General Management, Leadership, Organization Management	
	Security Management ←	
	Facilities Management ←	
	Contract Management ←	
	Plan Management ←	
	Resource Management ←	
	Project Management ←	
	Change Management ←	
	Problem/Incident Management ←	
	Client Relationships (Service) Management	
	Applications Management	
	End User Computing Management	
	Architecture Management	
	Technology Management	
	Systems Software Management	
	Database Management	
	Hardware (Operations) Management	
	Communications and Networking Management	
	Staff Education, Training, Skills Management	

Includes all Model Layers

Management functions:

IT has multiple areas of management responsibility. These areas are alternately referred to in the model as management functions. The objective is to create a model which ensures that every management function performed by IT is identified and assigned an owner. IT management functions must be inclusive and comprehensive of all computer platforms and technologies, not just the traditional data services. The owner has the responsibility to the plan, manage, cost, and chargeback for utilization of their management functions. The owner must also establish the objectives, strategies, and work performed on behalf of the management function. If these items aren't completed for a management function, why would anyone expect to satisfy the responsibilities associated with a management function?

The management functions structure identifies 24 IT management functions and/or sub-functions. It views the management of IT from the perspective of these 24 management functions. Manage these basic functions and you manage IT. Figure 2 illustrates these management functions and the manner in which they are organized around what is referred to as the *management functions structure*. The management functions are presented in the model as IT management layers. Each management layer represents a management function that IT performs. The term management layer is sometimes used interchangeably with management function especially when illustrating the model because the layering concept is so integral to the model. The term management function is often used when discussing specific IT management work activities.

The decision concerning the number and types of management functions and sub-management functions to include in the model is strictly a technology manager's choice. Nothing prevents an IT technology manager from identifying 5, 10, 30, 50 management functions and sub-management functions. The IT technology manager, working with IT senior management teams, decide how granular IT wants to be in its work management approach. It may be a surprise to the reader that in a book about technology management that the model places a significant emphasis on the financial aspects of technology management. A major reason for the financial "flavor" of the model is its alignment with the business plan. Dollars are the common language of business. "Dollars do talk." A financial slant on IT technology management can assist IT in obtaining funding for the technologies the company wishes to implement. Tracking the cost and utilization of the technologies can ensure that the technologies are being properly implemented to maximize profits of the company.

Management layers are arranged in a hierarchical manner with the highest priority layers placed at the top of the model. It is important to note that sub-management functions were not prioritized along with the management functions. Neither were they prioritized within a management function. Sub-management functions assumed the priority of the layer within which they were included. Most sub-management functions are considered support functions; therefore, prioritizing them in this manner is not considered a compromise.

A rectangle represents any computer or technology platform. All 24 of the management functions and sub-functions are executed on all computer and technology platforms. The layers can exert a downward and upward level of influence on other layers, but the vision and business plan layers positioned at the top of the model exercises influence on all the other layers. In this manner the model can truly be labeled business plan driven. Note that the staff, training and skills layer is at the bottom of the model. This is done intentionally. Staff are the most critical part of the management process, but until all the requirements driven by the upper layers are known, the staff levels, training, education and new skills required by the upper layers cannot be determined.

There is flexibility in establishing the model's layers. The important thing is that the model reflects management's objectives. It is not unusual to go "round and round" with some of the layer choices. For example. IT Financial Management could be listed as a separate layer, or it could be made a sub-management function under General Management, Leadership and Organization. The reason for isolating it as a separate layer is purely for emphasis and priority. As a separate layer a management function stands-out so that senior management knows the importance of financial management to IT. Cost and service chargeback management could have been listed as a separate layers, but are included under IT Financial Management. A similar decision was made for Client Relationships (Service). It could have been made a sub-management function by creating it as a client service management sub-layer under IT General Management, Leadership, and Organization. Leaving it as a separate layer makes a statement about the importance of IT's business clients. The beauty of the model is it can be shaped to fit varying requirements, but the modifications to the layers won't change the model's fundamental structure and use.

The layers apply to all the technologies (data, voice, text, and image) with few exceptions. The layer most impacted by the inclusion of the non-data technologies in the model is the General Management, Leadership and Organization layer because of the requirement to create an organization which develops, manages, and services a multi-tech client product. The model addresses this requirement with its systems and services organizational structure.

A feature of the model is the placement of the technical management layers at the mid and lower layers of the model. One would think that these technical layers would be in the upper layers of the model since it is a technology management model. This arrangement of the layers represents a uniqueness of the model. It reinforces the idea that technology management is more than an exercise in managing technologies, hardware, software, database, and communications. Without the upper layers of vision, financial management, general management and administration, and client relationships, technology management would be an exercise in managing technology for technology's sake. It is these upper layers of the model that provide direction in the use of technologies. They add a business perspective to the management of technology, and make it comprehensive in scope. Note that the Applications management layer is positioned towards the middle of the model, book-ended between the management and the technical layers. This reinforces the idea that if we didn't have the business applications there wouldn't be any need for the computers or IT.

Processes:

Recall from the Introduction that a "*business process* is a set of activities and tasks that, once completed, will accomplish an organizational goal." A process can include associates, software, hardware, technologies, and even other processes. The rules by which the various process components interact with each other in order to successfully complete a process are defined as part of the process definition. Processes are important because they organize and focus the work for which IT is responsible. *The objective of this book is to simply create a process whose organizational goal is to manage information technology* in support of the company's business plan objectives. This process includes among other components: the business plan; the model; the type of work IT performs; a system to manage the work; other basic IT management processes; a statement of management best practices; a technical architecture; and supporting organizational structure. These process components are further discussed in this and subsequent chapters

All processes must be developed and documented by their owners in terms of identifying the:

- Process owner
- Process description
- Process objectives and strategies
- Work performed in the process
- The critical success factors
- Major initiatives to achieve process objectives
- Strengths, weaknesses, opportunities, and threats, (SWOT) analysis
- Process cost drivers
- Process deliverables
- Impact on process owner's management functions
- Impact on other process owners' management functions

Process plan information is entered into the *strategic management plan worksheet* (to be explained in the following sections).

Basic IT management processes:

A process must be created for each of the management functions included in the management functions structure. These processes are defined as the *basic IT management processes*. Processes must include all technologies and all management functions pertinent to the process. IT is managed by the development and management of these processes. The basic IT management process information is entered into the *strategic management plan worksheets* (hereafter referred to as worksheet, except as may be noted). Each worksheet now represents a process plan. Since the IT basic management processes encompass the core of IT's work, the collection of all the worksheets represents the base planning information used to initiate and support the plan development process for next year's plan. The only process information items not collected on the initial worksheet are the operational or production support requirements of the process. This information will be provided by the IT support units during the plan development process.

The cost management function is used as an example of how a basic IT management process is created. Cost management is one of the 24 management functions. This management function is the basis for developing the cost management process. Figure 3 illustrates an example of the 4 step process used in creating the basic IT management process for the cost management function. Each basic IT management process is created in the same manner.

Other Types of Processes:

The basic IT management processes are not the only types of IT processes. There are other processes which complement the work performed by the basic IT management processes. These other processes are developed and managed in the same manner as the basic IT management processes, but they have different organizational goals to accomplish, and they can contain different process components. As such, the process owner defines the process and determines the component pieces that are required to complete the process. The process owner documents the process in a strategic management plan worksheet which represents the process plan. The process plan is used to support the plan development process. Two examples of these other processes are: Information Technology Management Process, and Manage the Plan Development Process.

Strategic management plan worksheet:

Worksheet structure:

Figure 4 illustrates an example of a strategic management plan worksheet designed to collect information about the *Application Management* basic IT management process. It contains the questions the process owners must answer concerning the process. The design of the worksheet is a matter of choice for each company as long as each company is consistent in the format used across all processes.

The worksheet has two parts. Part 1 relates to the process owner's objectives, strategies, SWOT analysis, cost drivers, deliverables, and critical success factors established for the process. The process owner completes all information request items in this part of the worksheet. Part 2 of the worksheet involves two impact analyses. One is conducted individually by

Figure 3 Create a Basic IT Management Process from a Management Functions Structure

Step 1
Process owner creates a basic IT
management process from the
management functions structure, and
creates the strategic management plan
worksheet

Step 2
Process owner completes the
initial information requirements
of the strategic management plan
worksheet

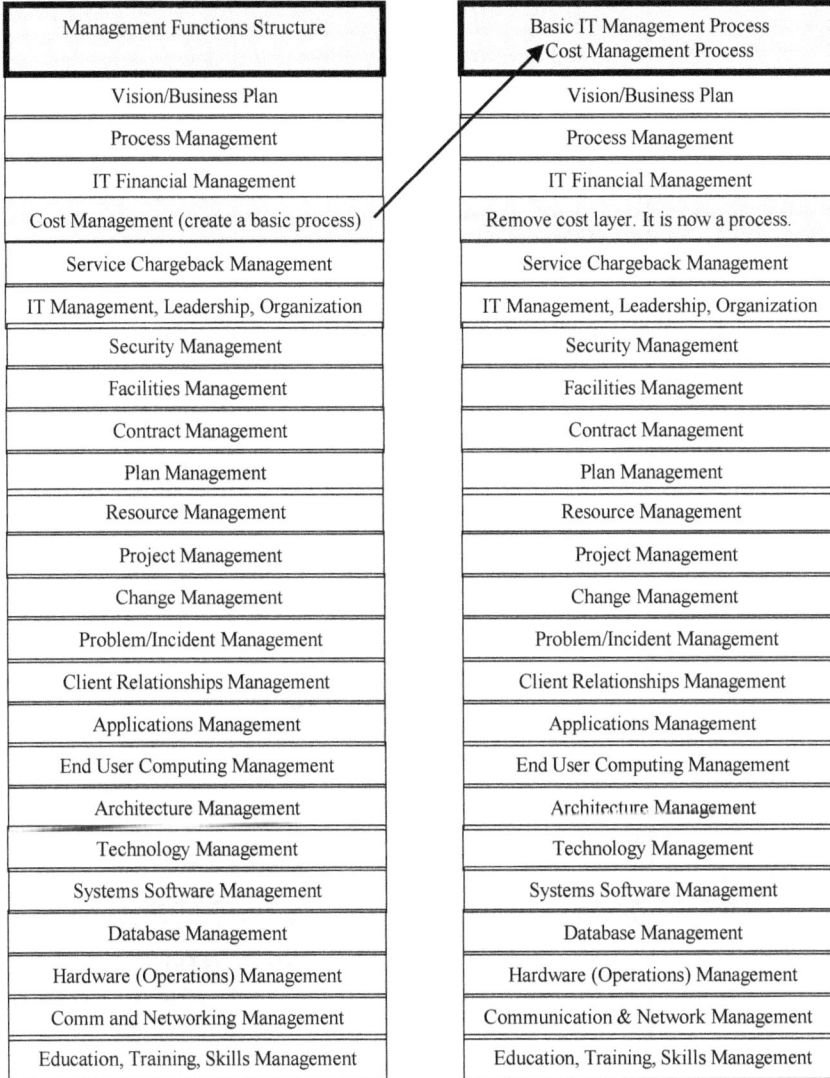

Management Functions Structure
Vision/Business Plan
Process Management
IT Financial Management
Cost Management (create a basic process)
Service Chargeback Management
IT Management, Leadership, Organization
Security Management
Facilities Management
Contract Management
Plan Management
Resource Management
Project Management
Change Management
Problem/Incident Management
Client Relationships Management
Applications Management
End User Computing Management
Architecture Management
Technology Management
Systems Software Management
Database Management
Hardware (Operations) Management
Comm and Networking Management
Education, Training, Skills Management

Basic IT Management Process / Cost Management Process
Vision/Business Plan
Process Management
IT Financial Management
Remove cost layer. It is now a process.
Service Chargeback Management
IT Management, Leadership, Organization
Security Management
Facilities Management
Contract Management
Plan Management
Resource Management
Project Management
Change Management
Problem/Incident Management
Client Relationships Management
Applications Management
End User Computing Management
Architecture Management
Technology Management
Systems Software Management
Database Management
Hardware (Operations) Management
Communication & Network Management
Education, Training, Skills Management

*Note: Model formatting has been slightly
modified to fit graphic to page.*

Step 3 Distribute and review the
worksheet with other process owners
to determine possible impact of the
new process on their areas of
responsibility.

Step 4 Update the worksheet with other process owner impact analysis
information, and export the completed worksheet to the repository.

Figure 4 Example of IT Strategic Management Plan Worksheet

IT STRATEGIC MANAGEMENT PLAN WORKSHEET	
Process Name: Applications *Process Owner:* Manager of Applications Systems	
Part 1: General Process Information	
Item	**Information Requested**
Process Owner	Individual assigned responsibility for coordination and completion of the process information. The owner establishes the process's policy and management best practices. The owner must include all managers involved, or potentially involved, in the development of the process.
Process Description	A concise description of the process.
Process Objectives and strategies	List business and IT objectives to which the process is aligned.
Work performed in the process	List the general types of work performed.
Critical Success Factors	What events or actions must occur to ensure successful execution of the process plan?
Major Initiatives to Achieve Objectives	Include all major planned work which enables IT to achieve its process objectives.
Strengths, Weaknesses, Opportunities and Threats, (SWOT) Analysis	List strengths and plan to exploit them. List weaknesses and plan to reduce them. List opportunities and plan to seize them. List threats and plan to mitigate them.
Process Cost Drivers	List cost drivers, both internal and external to IT, that impact the process.
Process deliverables	List the major deliverables resulting from the successful implementation of this process.
Part 2: Management Function Impact Analysis	
Impact on process owner's management functions	What is the impact of the process upon the owner's management functions. When this item is completed, workshheet will be distributed to other owners for review.
Impact on other process owners' management functions	What other process owners are impacted by the owner's plan for the process.

the process owner, the other is conducted by the process owner working in cooperation with the other process owners who may be impacted by the process owner's plan.

In the initial impact analysis the process owner reviews the impact of the process's objectives, strategies, SWOT analysis, cost drivers, deliverables, and critical success factors on each management function included in the process. The management functions structure is used as the framework around which to organize this impact analysis because it includes all areas of process owner's responsibilities. This ensures that all areas of process management will be assessed for impact. The process owner documents the impact in the strategic management plan worksheet. The worksheet is sent to a data repository.

The process owner is not always in the best position to assess the impact of their process plan on processes of which they are not the owners. There are 23 other process stakeholders who have a need to make their own assessment of impact of the process owner's plan upon their processes. A second impact analysis is initiated in response to this requirement. This analysis includes the process owner and the other 23 potentially impacted process owners. This analysis is triggered when the process owner's worksheet is sent to the data repository. When this occurs, notification is sent to the other process owners to review and comment upon the process owner's plan, and its potential impact upon the processes for which they are responsible. The circulation of the process owner's worksheets to all other process owners gives each owner a "heads up" concerning what may impact their area of responsibility in the coming plan year. There is a section at the end of the process owner's worksheet identified as *Potential Impact on other Management Functions* in which the other process owners can record their impact analysis information for the process owner.

Planning oversights in updating or creating a process plan should be discovered and addressed by sharing of the process worksheet information. This procedure not only assists the process owner in completing and validating their process plan, but also assists each of the contributing process owners in updating their own process plans.

The entire procedure can be completely automated or manually performed with some computer assistance. In some ways a manual based method of sharing information is preferred because it encourages more face-to-face conversations amongst the IT managers. The choice of repository, and the general information sharing procedure, depends upon each company's preferences.

Exercises in the application and use of the strategic management plan worksheet:

There are five basic IT management processes discussed in the book. Each of these processes are illustrated with a an example of a Strategic Management Plan Worksheet. The processes are:

- Develop and Manage the IT Management Model
- Information Technology Management Process
- Cost Management Process
- Planning and Resource Management Process
- Service Chargeback Management Process

Since the strategic management plan worksheet is used as the vehicle to capture the information relating to each of these major processes, it was decided to conclude each chapter with an exercise designed to complete a "best company" worksheet for each process presented. The procedures used to complete the worksheets are common to all processes discussed in the book; therefore, it was decided that additional explanations required to complete and use the strategic management plan worksheet would not be repeated in the discussions of each process.

The process worksheet information illustrated in the book is of benefit, but it's the *exercise* of completing the worksheet that is most informative and beneficial to the reader. The exercise is very comprehensive. It represents the essence of the planning concept. Key information items like objectives, strategies, work initiatives, and SWOT items must be identified. Strategies and work initiatives must be aligned with objectives. Impact of the process on existing processes must be determined and communicated to those potentially impacted. The reader is encouraged to think of the information and the exercise in terms of their own company. What values would your company assign to these information items? It's a good way of learning about your own company.

Concept of "Best Company":

This book is about principles. Because of this fact it cannot discuss the principles in terms of a "real company", but instead illustrates the principles and supporting information in terms of a "best company" approach. Under the "best company" concept, objectives, strategies, strengths, weaknesses, opportunities, threats (SWOT), critical success factors etc. are all presented in the context of a business environment that is conducive to the "best" enablement of the items and issues presented. "Best" connotes a business environment that has a positive culture; a clear-cut business vision; an effective business and IT management structure and organization; team-oriented and skilled staff; computer facilities; and a general working environment which welcomes and nurtures creative ideas and provides support for significant initiatives. In other words, it's the ideal working environment. The presentation of information items like objectives, strategies, strengths, weaknesses, opportunities, threats, etc. lend themselves to a "best company" approach, but any attempt to illustrate detail projects and work initiatives is not possible. Because the "best company" is the same for each process presented in the book, a detailed SWOT analysis will not be presented for each process. Instead, the detailed SWOT is presented once in chapter 2, *IT Management Model,* in the sections entitled *Strategic Management Plan Worksheet,* and *Strengths, Weaknesses, Opportunities, and Threats (SWOT),* and only referenced in each subsequent process.

Management Function Layer Descriptions

Descriptions of the management function layers included in the management functions structure are generally described in the context of planning, and include only traditional data technology. Brevity is the reason for presenting the layers in this fashion.

Vision/Business plan management layer:

This is the first management function layer in the model. The vision/business plan layer has been discussed in detail in chapter 1, *Company Business Plan, Ground Zero*, and in this chapter. It is sufficient here to emphasize that the business plan is located at the highest layer in the management functions structure. As such it impacts all other management function layers, and is a major driver of IT costs. Business management needs to be made aware of this fact.

This statement isn't intended to diminish costs driven by IT management and operational practices. Both types of cost drivers must be addressed. From a "best company" approach IT wants to partner with their business clients to address these costs. At an objectives and strategy level IT is promoting its financial mission to the rest of the company. The objective is to create for the business community a view of IT as not only technicians, but also as business partners who contribute to the "bottom line" of the company, just as any other business unit does. At a tactical level IT has a threefold strategy to reduce costs. First, tightly align IT work with business plan objectives so that IT is working on initiatives which provide the company the highest return on their investment in IT. Second, use planning, resource management, costing, and service chargeback to identify areas of excessive or inefficient use of IT resources, and take appropriate action to correct the issues. Third, introduce new architecture and organizational structures which will utilize the concept of resource leveraging to reduce costs.

A major threat to IT is that company business management won't accept IT's role as a business partner, but continue to view IT in its technical role only. Another threat is that the satisfaction of business plan objectives could require resources far beyond IT's budget, and the gap in resources could be perceived as a lack in IT effectiveness, not the aggressive nature of the plan objectives.

Process management layer:

This layer addresses the participants, processes, and procedures required to ensure the proper flow and interchange of information amongst the key managers involved in the development and maintenance of a process. It defines the context in which a process is developed and utilized. It ensures that all the required partners of the process are brought together in a coordinated fashion. The objective is to ensure the process is properly designed and implemented.

Figure 5 illustrates an example of a process management layer supporting the plan development process. Think of the process management layer as a bridge between the business and the technology planning processes. The process management layer does not only occur at the top level of the model, but appears all up and down the model layers. These bridges must be carefully planned, encouraged, and managed. It is a major tenet of the book that a common business/IT plan management model and plan development process should be created for both IT and the business units.

Financial management layer:

The financial management function layer refers to the manner in which IT is fiscally managed. Major questions to be answered at this layer are: "Will IT be managed as an overhead department whose expenses are allocated in total to the business units on the basis of some high level formula?" "Will it be a cost center whose expense for developing and delivering its services is allocated to the business units on some cost utilization basis?" "Will IT be a profit center in which IT revenue can exceed its expense?" The general type of IT work performed at this plan layer includes: expense and revenue management; budgeting; cost management; service chargeback management; financial analysis and general financial reporting; and the exchange of information with company payroll, accounting, and other financial departments.

Management function layers can be further decomposed into sub-management functions. The option to further decompose layers depends upon the level of specificity at which IT wishes to plan and manage its work. Two major sub-management functions are separately identified in the Financial Management Layer.

Figure 5 Example of a Process Management Layer

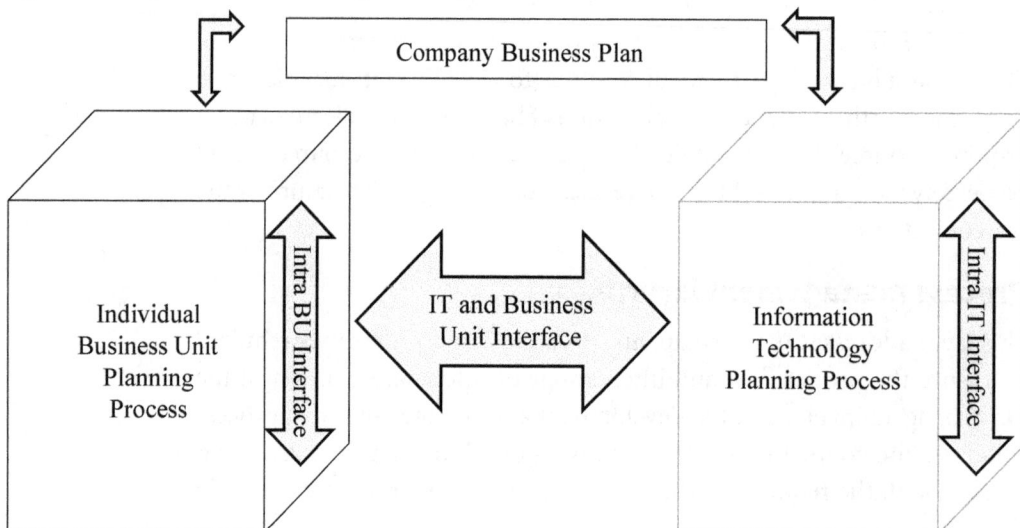

Sub-Management Functions of the IT Financial Management Function:

Cost Management	This sub-management layer is a part of IT's expense management program. Availability of costing information enables IT and business managers to make technology decisions based on sound business principles as well as a technical analysis. Cost management identifies and assigns expenses (costs) to IT elements and compounds which together comprise the products IT sells to its business clients.
Service Chargeback Management	This sub-management layer is a part of IT's revenue management program. It addresses the question, "Who is going to pay for the work IT performs?" Its ultimate deliverable is the billing of IT business clients for utilization of IT products and services. Don't think of this management function only in terms of a financial function. Service chargeback can have a significant impact on the manner in which work is requested and managed by both IT and the business client. A far greater impact of service chargeback is on IT and business client behavior. Implement service chargeback very cautiously.

The introduction of work management systems like planning, resource management, cost management, and service chargeback, can cause angst and possible negative behavior in both IT and the business unit associates. IT associates can get the impression they are being singled-out from other business units by the placement of more financial controls upon them. Another significant concern often experienced at this layer is the issue of whether business units are permitted to budget any computer or technology expense in their own budgets. IT's concern is they could lose control of managing total information technology costs for the company under such budgeting procedures.

General Management, Leadership and Organization Management Layer:

The general management, leadership and organization management function layer addresses the issues and manner in which IT recruits, manages, develops, compensates, deploys, and retains its staff. It includes the issues of management philosophy, staff objectives and strategies, management best practices, staff levels, and organization.

If the model were implemented in a "best company" environment, the objectives, strategies and projects required to support it would include such initiatives as: create an organizational and management structure that combines the disparate management technologies of data, voice, text, and image into a integrated information processing organization; make IT management policies, practices and procedures equally adaptable and applicable to all IT computer platforms, technologies, and organizations; reduce excessive management layers and eliminate ineffective management practices by delegating management functions to the lowest organizational level at which the functions can most effectively be executed and managed; develop competitive compensation strategies; provide excellent benefits and career growth opportunities to associates; and build the management practices and systems support capabilities to operate IT as any other business is operated.

A major cost driver at this management function layer can be IT's organizational structure. Ineffective organizational structures can create excess staff levels and work. The implementation of a systems and services organizational structure based upon the computer platform, technology, and organization independent architecture (CPTOIA) provides a major opportunity to increase organizational effectiveness. Frequent organizational changes can be a significant cost driver at this layer because of lost time in assimilating into the new organization structures, and changes to office configurations and equipment. Ineffective use of education and training resources can drive excessive costs if these programs are not aligned with specific business and IT objectives and strategies. Significant increases in operating efficiency, a reduction in staff expense, and improved customer support are all opportunities that can normally be seized at this layer.

Sub-Management Layers of the General Management, Leadership and Organization Management Function:

Eight sub-management layers are identified in the model within the General Management, Leadership and Organization management layer. Note that no attempt is made to prioritize the sub-management layers. The sub-management layers assume the priority of the management function within which they are included.

Security Management
This sub-management layer includes all facilities and practices designed to secure access to, and use of, IT's computing facilities. Tornados or other environmental factors are considered security issues. Security has become a huge issue throughout the world. The objective here is to protect the integrity of company information by denying access to unauthorized users. This is one of those "you bet the company" type of management functions. Obviously this sub-management layer affects all other IT management layers. A significant success factor at this sub-management layer is the creation of a sense of urgency in all associates of the critical importance of security. The type of work activities performed at this layer include disaster recovery preparedness; system security reviews; evaluation of new

security techniques; securing the data center; performing tests of the security systems and procedures; keeping abreast of new security techniques and facilities; and working with system developers to ensure adequate security is included in their business application systems. There is little IT can do to contain the cost of security. The risk has become too great.

Facilities Management
This sub-management layer involves the management of the physical facilities supporting all IT operations. Some might call this the IT physical plant layer. In the "best company" environment, the company's facilities management group has control and policy setting authority of this management function working in cooperation with IT management. IT provides their requirements to the facilities group for implementation of the required IT facilities. Implementation of the computer platform, technology, and organization independent architecture (CPTOIA) can provide a significant opportunity to reduce facilities costs. To better understand the potential impact of this architecture on facilities, visualize the situation in which telephone systems, imaging systems, computer systems all co-exist within the same physical facility, and are managed by a leveraged operations staff. Think of the leveraging and cost savings opportunities that can flow from such an arrangement. Shared security, backup systems, environmental controls, etc. are all possibilities. Significant cost drivers observed at this layer are the constant IT organizational changes that can occur within IT, and the desire to have the latest and greatest office facilities to accommodate these changes.

Contract Management
Contracts can be a source of significant expense reductions, if properly negotiated and managed, or if mismanaged, they can be the source of significant expense increases. Some IT departments have a centralized unit that evaluates, negotiates, modifies and approves all vendor contracts. A "best company" practice is to allocate a greater role to IT managers in contract negotiations consistent with a distributed management style. Regardless of the approach taken, many companies expect that each IT manager have some basic negotiating and contract knowledge so that they can discuss issues with the vendors and prepare proper documentation, but they must involve the company lawyer and IT senior management at critical points in the negotiation process. In a "best company" the lawyer and IT senior management

must approve and sign all major contracts on behalf of IT. Usually some dollar amount is used to designate a contract as major. Relationships between IT managers and vendors can be a significant source of technical knowledge, and present opportunities for IT management to leverage technologies within the company. Conversely, vendor relationships can be the source of significant negative issues if not properly managed. Vendors should not be left free to pander their wares to the company without IT's involvement.

Plan Management	This sub-management layer includes the management functions required to manage the plan development process; develop and publish the formal IT plans; and manage/administer the plan and resource management functions in the ongoing production environment. A critical success factor is the ability to instill in the IT staff the need to internalize the concept of planning in their daily management activities. Planning can't be an add-on responsibility performed once a year to satisfy senior managers.
Project Management	This sub-management layer includes all activities surrounding the management of IT enterprise projects. Unlike operational work, projects have a formal project leader, specific objectives and deliverables, start and end target dates, and a strict project development methodology. A Project Management Office (PMO) normally owns and manages all IT enterprise projects. The scope of project management should extend to all technologies and computer platforms. If a PMO does not exist in a company, or if a company does not have a formal project management system, a sub-management layer owner should be designated to develop the project management practices used in developing and managing projects. A PMO is a very important part of the information technology management process.
Resource Management	IT resource management is the "partner" to the planning sub-management function. It ensures that the necessary resources are available with the proper skills or capabilities to deliver the planned work when required. It enables IT to right-size its plan. The IT plan administrator is the owner of this sub-management layer by default, but every IT manager should possess some of level of basic resource management skills in order to be effective.
Change Management	This sub-management layer addresses practices, procedures and systems designed to allow IT managers to have significant control over any changes in the IT environment. The

first issue to be addressed is -"How does a manager know a change has been made to the IT environment? "Just as importantly - "To which IT component has the change been made, and what type of change was made?" Without some type of controls, how does IT know if changes are being made correctly, and with the proper authorization? In this age of serious computer hacking, managing changes to the computer environment is crucial to the company's survival. Change management is a form of security management. How many times have IT managers left their division thinking all was in good shape only to arrive at work the next day and be told that none of the production work has been completed because of system changes that were put in the system overnight? Many, many times, right?

Formal IT change management is most frequently associated with changes to business application systems, or to system software (i.e. operating systems and system utilities), but change management applies to all the management function layers. There are changes to management practices and procedures, organizational changes, changes to financial practices, changes in client relationship practices, changes to plans, hardware changes, database changes, facilities changes, the list goes on and on. Critical success factors for good change management are ownership, responsibility and communication.

All IT elements and compounds must be assigned owners. IT owners must be tenacious in protecting their areas of IT responsibility and the environments in which they exist. They must also be totally aware of who relies upon their activities so that when changes are contemplated, individuals who could be potentially affected by the change can be notified and solicited for their ideas on the impact of the proposed change, before it is implemented. There are not enough procedures that can cover for a lack of ownership and responsibility. How can anyone manage a facility, and be responsible for its operation, if they cannot exercise absolute control over it. Individuals make enough of their own mistakes.

All IT managers have a level of change management requirements for their area of responsibility. It would be nearly impossible to establish a central change management function for every possible event that could change the IT environment. Change management must have a broad base of responsibility, but only one owner of the sub-management function.

| Problem / | This sub-management layer is concerned with the manage- |

Problem /
Incident /
Service Request
Management

This sub-management layer is concerned with the management and resolution of production type problems, incident reporting, and service requests. A help desk, or some other type of service center, is usually the organizational unit that responds to problems, incidents, and service requests. Problems and incidents can include events like production system failures, hardware and software problems, errors in computer operations, equipment problems, etc. Service requests include such activities as adds, moves and changes to office based equipment such as PC's; questions about the status of a production system's processing status, etc. These incidents are bound to happen, even in the best of computer environments. The type and length of service interruptions need to be tracked so that problem areas can be identified, and a plan developed to fix the underlying causes of the problems. Systems with high support costs, and serious performance issues, should be reviewed as systems potentially needing replacement or significant overhaul.

The IT vision presented in this book places significant pressure on this sub-management layer to support more and more client service options required by IT clients. The scope of service needs to include an integrated support capability for all computers and technologies provided by IT. The increase in IT production complexity makes management very critical at this sub-management function. System disruption and the time and effort to fix problems and address incidents are significant drivers of IT costs.

Client relationship (service) management layer:

This management function layer is all about how IT wants to partner with its clients in the delivery of its systems and services across all computer platforms and technologies. Client relationships should not be allowed to happen by chance. Does IT view the client as a valued partner, one who pays the check for technology, or a nuisance? How will IT organize its staff to best support the client's utilization of IT's products and services.

One method of client support is to organize the support staff into a common pool of resources, and assign staff to clients as resources are required. The resource pool is rather generic in IT skills and management experience. Their knowledge of business applications is also rather generic. Normally this is not a very effective method of providing client service in a smaller IT environment. It tends to be more effective in larger environments.

Another approach to client relationships is an IT value-added client relationship strategy based upon the alignment of quasi-permanent IT team assignments whose team members have general knowledge of the business areas they support. Use of permanent or quasi-permanent support teams can be effective in creating partnerships, but they can be very ineffective in the utilization IT resources. The problem occurs when the business client doesn't require the use of all the resources assigned to them. What happens in many cases is the resources are not released to other teams which could use the extra resources for fear that the resources might not get reassigned to the original team. This results in ineffective use of resources because one team is under-staffed to do the work required of them, and the other team is using scarce resources to work on initiatives that don't satisfy priority objectives. Another service challenge faced by IT at the service layer is acquiring the skills and training required to support information products that are delivered across multiple platforms and technologies.

It is critical that IT delivers on its client strategies and supporting initiatives, but the business units also have responsibilities in this matter. Business units must work to improve communications by involving IT in the systems development initiatives early in the process: provide accurate definitions of their business requirements; and be available when needed by IT.

There is a very real issue of balancing central control of IT client relationship policies and best practices with the policies and best practices required to satisfy potentially unique products and services delivered by each IT unit. Different IT products sometimes can require different client relationships, but the basic relationship principles and best practices established by the management layer owner shouldn't be compromised at lower layer implementation without sufficient cause.

For example, business application systems development normally requires a longer-term client relationship based on a value-added partnership between the business client and the IT support associate because of the complexity of the product. IT computer operations relies heavily on a help desk/service center concept as its implementation of a client service capability. End user computing, because of its broad customer base resulting from everyone having a personal computer on their desk, implements a client relationship which has significant, direct one-on-one type interaction with their business clients. They also partner with the help desk and technical services support areas to resolve many of their client service issues.

Costs at this layer are heavily driven by the requirements for more client service options; a 24X7 extended service window; and the need to support multi-tech products. The ability to provide the new service options and improve the business community's participation in the planning process represent very significant opportunities. Threats are that IT won't be able to develop the necessary skills to support such a service environment, or they will encounter difficulties in establishing the systems and services organization required to support the IT client products and services.

Applications management layer:

This management function plan layer includes the "things we want computers to do for us", the business applications. Business applications are the end information products that IT delivers to its business clients. Business applications give meaning and purpose to computer technology. Without applications, or services, computers would be operating for the computer's sake, not the client's interest. Not a good idea.

This layer includes the system development functions of system requirements definition, system design specifications, program development, testing, systems installation, and the system maintenance functions of enhancements, required maintenance, and on-going production support.

The applications layer is positioned above the more technical management layers in the model, but beneath the vision/business plan, financial, general management /organizational/ leadership, and the client relationship layers. The positioning of the application plan layer in this middle area of the model reinforces the idea that if IT doesn't have a vision/business plan, the management structure and organization, adequate financial controls, a good working relationship with the business community, then no amount of computer technology can satisfy the business application requirements. Conversely, if IT properly manages the top layers of the model, but has a deficient technology base supporting the business applications, the business applications running on top of that technology base are similarly compromised. IT needs to manage all the layers of the model in a coordinated manner to develop effective business applications.

A significant "best company" opportunity at this plan layer is the expansion of the scope of business application systems development to include support for systems based in the non-traditional technologies of voice, text, and imaging. This expanded development not only allows IT to develop more effective products for the clients, but expands the staff's career opportunities to include support of the non-traditional technologies.

IT "best company" application cost drivers are typically: the sheer number and complexity of active projects; requirements for more client service options; system customization and the need to accommodate exceptions; client service coverage extension to 24 X 7; perceived need of a company's sales and marketing departments to have the "first" product or service to the market; inadequate, erroneous, late, or incomplete system/program definition; and failure to involve IT early in the project development cycle. A significant threat (risk) is that the staff won't be able to assimilate the new skills required to deliver the business and IT objectives in the timeframe required.

End user computing (EUC) management layer:

It's rather obvious that the IT business clients have gained significant computer skills over the years. Now they can do a lot of computer work for themselves. The desktop personal computer (PC) was truly a revolution in the IT industry because it placed a fully functional computer on a business client's desktop. Even though the PCs are fundamentally like all other computers, they required some new management strategies to effectively manage their acquisition and utilization. End user computing in the "best company" is like "self-service" computing for select IT systems and programming functions. The critical issue is how to define the "select IT systems and programming functions" that IT is willing to let the business clients manage without IT's intervention. The relationship between IT and the business clients can become quite contentious if not properly managed by a value-added support strategy.

Initially the typical work activities performed by a "best company" EUC division included such things as: evaluating and managing a standard portfolio of PC products, purchasing new PCs, making changes to PC's, installing and moving PCs, responding to user trouble calls and incidents, supporting PC business applications, installing new releases of software and hardware, and educating business clients in best practices. The typical software products supported were system utilities, commonly referred to as "shrink wrap" software, which included major system packages like word processing, spreadsheet, presentation software, database management systems, and a basic communications utility. These software packages were truly revolutionary in their impact on IT.

Managing desktop PCs was thought to be difficult, but it's nothing like the management challenge IT faces today. The number of hardware, software, and communications/networking options have geometrically increased. Today a typical desktop system includes something like Microsoft Office with its suite of business back-office support applications. It not only has the classic "shrink wrap" software installed, but also network-based office application systems such as calendar management, e-mail, meeting scheduling, bulletin boards, social media networking systems, and Internet access. These are business applications in every sense of the word, but they don't fit easily under the traditional systems support umbrella. "Best company" IT refers to these network-based systems and technologies as *administration support systems*. They are easy to overlook in creating a plan. Special attention must be paid to social media and Internet delivered network applications which can have significant impact on company-wide business applications. Definition of clear ownership and responsibility for the development and maintenance of these IT products is a very challenging task.

EUC is a management layer within which a singular client service strategy doesn't fit all the business clients. The term "personal" computer seems to fit well with the idea of individual service strategies. This situation places a premium on developing a flexible client service relationship plan in order to address the varying needs of the business clients. IT/client relationships at this plan layer certainly have the potential to bring-out the pettiness on both sides of issues. One of the biggest issues faced by IT is the business clients' demand for all the latest and greatest technologies without consideration of compatibility requirements with existing network components, or the cost to support these new technologies. This demand is a significant cost driver. Often only the PC hardware and software expense is considered in the cost of a PC. The business client tends to selectively overlook, or just ignore the additional costs of general PC management; documentation; network operational support; change management controls; backup; disaster recovery; staff backup; database knowledge; knowledge of the legacy systems which they access; knowledge of company networks, and security. Companies without a plan to manage PC's in a coordinated and consistent manner will experience significant problems. The cost management function is very important in bringing resolution to these cost issues.

Implementation of the CPTOIA architecture and its support organization will have major impact on EUC and its business clients. It will provide value-added services to the PC user which will enhance partnerships between EUC and its business clients.

This management layer is always in constant motion because of the pressure of business clients to implement the latest innovations in technology; consequently, cost containment is a constant issue. The threat to IT is that company senior business management will not support IT in its efforts to contain business client demand for EUC resources. Because PCs, and PC related products, are located in the office environment the business client sometimes feels they can budget these resources in their own budget and by-pass the need to request them from IT. Failure to address this issue can be a real threat to IT's ability to effectively manage these resources on behalf of the company.

Architecture management layer:

IT architectural strategies, objectives, and major initiatives are generally supportive of increasing company effectiveness and assisting in the evaluation of new technologies for their fit with the business vision. A significant architectural challenge driven by the model is the support of the computer platform, technology and organization independent architecture (CPTOIA). Other architectural initiatives can include such things as working with the application development units in the development and publication of a formal business application systems architecture; creating a greater awareness of project work architecture; and making technical architectural reviews a regular part of every major system and technology development effort. Application systems should fit together in a management systems architecture. A project architecture should be clearly defined in which project scope and objectives do not overlap with each other and create redundant work efforts, or poorly defined project deliverables.

Expediency is a major threat to the development of IT architecture. It causes management to be impatient of developing long-range solutions, resulting in systems that don't always effectively interact with each other. Companies that are aggressive in acquiring new companies can significantly increase IT costs and decrease operating efficiencies by introducing incompatible architectures into the existing IT technical architecture.

Technology management layer:

Technology involves the development, maintenance, and use of computer systems, software, and networks for the processing and distribution of data. As related to the model, technologies apply to the four primary information processing areas of data, voice, text, and image. The Technology layer is closely aligned with the Architecture layer, and are often jointly owned and managed by the chief IT architect. Technology is probably the most forward looking management layer outside of the Vision/Business Plan Management Layer. A major function of the Technology layer is to assist the team creating the business vision by determining what technologies can best enable the business vision objectives. On an ongoing basis Technology should be the primary portal through which new technologies are evaluated and introduced into the company. The inability of the company to introduce new technologies can threaten the viability of a company by making it less competitive in the market place.

The introduction of new technology products have made many traditional IT organizational support structures obsolete. It used to be that technology fitted nicely into the individual support structures of classic computer services (data), telephones services (voice), copy/print centers (image), or records centers (text). Now technology must be managed across all computers and organizational structures in a consistent manner. Products like geo-positioning systems, social media, smart phones, workflow, document management, Internet, imaging systems etc. are difficult to fit to exact support structures. A problem in many companies is just keeping up with the basic knowledge of these new technologies, and coordinating their implementation and on-going support.

It is difficult for one individual to be skilled in all the technologies; therefore, although the technology layer owner is typically the chief IT Architect, a supporting committee should be established to partner with the IT Architect in leading efforts at this layer. The committee would be chaired by the architect, and composed of the technical managers representing the various technologies active in IT. It is this committee that focuses and aligns all the knowledge of the technologies towards the accomplishment of the business planning objectives.

Technologies are significant IT costs that are driven primarily by the business vision and the need for a company to remain competitive in the industry. Technology costs include not only the cost of acquisition, but the installation, training, development, and on-going maintenance of the technology. A real threat at this layer is that the company cannot afford the technology it needs to enable its business vision and plan. Many smaller companies face this very real threat.

Systems software management layer:

Systems software are the operating systems, system utilities (i.e. disk, communications, and print management systems), and other system programs and utilities that support the general operation of the computer and the business applications running on them. Any software that directly supports the application systems is generally classified as applications software. System software is often viewed as an extension of the computer hardware. Each computer and technology has system software (aka operating systems). The trend is that many computers and technologies are beginning to operate under similar operating systems and utilities: hence, there are many opportunities to leverage technical support staff across computers and technologies. This trend is a major enabler of the CPTOIA architecture.

Typical IT work and management activities at this layer are: installing new releases of computer operating systems and utilities; installing hardware upgrades to existing computers; acquiring and installing new computer facilities; working with vendors and the application developers in reviewing the potential applicability of new software utility products; and expanding the level of systems software support to technologies such as document/ image processing and telephone systems.

System software identified as *applications system support software* is often over-looked in planning, but it does play a significant role in application system development. This type of software does not directly support computers and technologies per se, but it provides system software support tools for the business applications systems development environment. It includes programmer productivity tools, program change management systems, and utilities used to enhance application system functionality (e.g. report enhancement, online report viewing, graphics, microfiche, etc.) The software products can be grouped into what are referred to as a "developer's toolkit". This type of software is often complex to use, or the application system developers don't use it enough to remain proficient in its use, or they just don't want to be bothered learning the use of the software. For whatever the reason, IT can establish a separate team within the technical services support division to assist the application system developers in the use and maintenance of these business application system software utilities. Such a support strategy is included in the model's requirement for a systems and services organization.

The number and diversity of the computer platforms and technologies that must be supported by the technical support division is a major IT cost driver. From this management layer down through the communication and network layers of the model, the CPTOIA architecture implementation will have the greatest impact. It is at these technical layers that the need to develop the necessary technical skills required to support CPTOIA are at their highest level of demand. A failure to acquire the necessary technical skills in the time required can prove catastrophic to a "best company's" overall IT plan objectives.

Database management layer:

The database plan layer includes the capture, storage, maintenance, access, and reporting of company information. Since the model has an objective to manage information, not just data, database refers to the information stored in the records centers, the data center, the telephone system, and all other text, graphical or pictorial representations of information, no matter where or in what media form the information is stored. IT business clients should not care where a data element is stored, or how it is accessed as long as their business requirements are satisfied. Why should IT manage data storage differently just because it is stored on a different computer or technology? It shouldn't. Such a view supports a computer platform and technology independent approach to the storage and utilization of information.

Database management provides significant opportunities to leverage IT staff and reduce costs. Database also shares the same concern with the other technical support areas as it relates to the continued implementation of CPTOIA - can they acquire the needed skills in the time required?

Computer hardware (operations) management layer:

This management layer refers to all types of computers, equipment, and hardware including their procurement, operation and maintenance. Other work activities at this management layer include operation of the business application systems; management of the data center's physical facilities; disaster recovery readiness; on-site and off-site back-up facilities; physical security administration; capacity planning and performance monitoring; help desk support; and general housekeeping and administrative duties associated with the production environment. References to hardware, computer operations, production, and the data center are often used interchangeably in the book. The computer hardware layer is greatly impacted by work initiatives in the upper layers of the planning model, especially new business application systems development and new technology implementation. New business applications normally demand more computer capacity, and potentially, additional operational staff support and training, new computer platforms, and new technologies.

This management layer has all types of significant opportunities for IT and the "best company" because of the implementation of several of the model concepts. The computer platform, technology, organization independent architect (CPTOIA) enables the consolidation and transformation of formerly disparate processing technologies of data, text, voice, and image into an information technology concept. The systems and services organization structure enables the seamless management of the information processing facility. These opportunities not only have the potential for significant cost savings, but provide staff improvement opportunities, and the development of more effective products for IT's business clients.

Costs at this management layer are normally driven by the demand for greater computer capacity to support the development of newer and better business systems. A concern (threat) is that IT operations could exert a negative effect on upward layers of the plan model by not providing enough computer capacity to support the development and support of new business application systems. This concern is exacerbated by the possibility that the company can't purchase the necessary equipment upgrades to satisfy the required computer capacity. Computer upgrades are normally associated with significant price tags which companies are sometimes reluctant to fund. This is a major concern in many companies. Frequent downtime, poor response time, and failure to complete production processing cycles on time are symptoms of the lack of adequate computer capacity.

Communications/networking management layer:

Communications/networking is the physical connector, the bridge, over which all information passes from application to application, no matter where it exists geographically. Logical connections of the applications that run on top of the network are normally considered an extension of business application systems architecture. Networking includes all types of networks, whether they are internal, wide-area, value-added networks, social networks, telephone, Internet, etc. The network must align with and support the business application systems operating across it, not constrain or limit them. Communications/networking can be a significant enabler of both the business and IT visions.

This is a critical management layer. It is very much impacted by the demands of e-commerce including online shopping and the support of warehouse distribution operations. Think of the enormous impact Internet, and the social media networks, have had on business systems and operations. These newer networks are truly "game changers". The requirements at this layer create significant opportunities, but they can pose serious concerns (threats), and expose IT weaknesses. The failure to acquire the necessary skills in the timeframe required to implement the new architecture is a real concern at this management layer.

Staff education, training and skills management layer:

This management layer addresses the skill sets, training, and education required to satisfy the requirements contained in the other model layers. It is very important to the delivery of the overall IT plan. If it is so important, then why is it at the bottom model layer? The reason is that until all upper level layer requirements are known, staffing skills, education, and training requirements cannot be effectively determined, nor scheduled. Support of planned work is concerned not only with the number of associates required to perform the work, but the skills and training these associates must possess. Once plan requirements are known and filtered down through the various management layers, the current skill inventories can be queried, and the gaps between the current staff skill levels and the required skills determined. The gaps are resolved by developing educational and training programs designed specifically to introduce the skills and training necessary to satisfy the planned work skill and training requirements, in the timeframe that these skills are needed. So often the training and educational resources are overlooked in planning, or are not targeted to specific planned work. The result is that critical resources must be diverted from other projects so that associates can get their needed training. Neither practice is a very effective use of training resources.

The model allows IT to focus on critical training and education initiatives. The layer owner works with all the other IT layer owners to ensure their education and training requirements get satisfied when they are required by the plan's work schedule (aka "just in time training").

IT education, training, and skills development costs are driven by the number and complexity of new hardware, software, application systems, and technologies. The concerns are twofold. The first concern is that there won't be enough time to install and perform all the needed education. Secondly, there is a concern that many associates "won't find the time", nor have the desire, to take advantage of the educational opportunities. To overcome this reluctance, education and training requirements must be included in the associate's plan and performance review. Training is not an option. It is a mandate.

Expansion of the Management Functions Structure

Accommodate Information Processing:

The management functions structure is the base chassis of the IT management model described earlier in (Figure 2) in this chapter. It is based upon a single computer (mainframe), a single function (data processing), and a non-networked computer environment. Just as the computer and technology have evolved over the years, the model and the required management structure and supporting organization evolved with it. The following sections describe the evolution in computer and technology development over the years, and its impact on the development of the model.

The symbols used in the discussion of the computer evolution are rather simple: a rectangle and a cube. There is significance in the selection of these two shapes. Both represent a computer processing platform and its supporting infrastructure. The rectangle represents a single dimension computer platform, one which primarily provides a single computer function classically identified as data processing services. The cube, with its added dimension of depth, symbolizes a multi-dimensional computer platform that can process information in any media form including data, text, image, and voice. The computer platforms are further classified as tiers. The tier 1 platform is the most powerful computer processor in a network of computers. It has the greatest scope of information management in the company. The size of the rectangle or cube is indicative of the relative power of the computer platforms. Scope relates to the "company-wide impact" of information processed and stored on a computer. The further the processing tiers are extended into the departments and divisions of a company, normally the less powerful the computer, the more local the scope of information.

Single dimension mainframe computer:

The original computer platform was the Tier 1 Mainframe computer. Figure 6 illustrates the mainframe model. It reflects a single dimension, data processing only computer. IT referred to these early computers as mainframes. The name was derived from the fact that they were the most important, and normally the only, computer in a company. Most companies could only afford one mainframe computer. Today there are literally thousands of computers in a given company, and these computers can be physically deployed to satisfy a myriad of requirements, in a variety of geographical locations, and over varying network topologies. Mainframes were, and still are, expensive. It was housed in a separate room surrounded by glass walls and installed over a raised floor. They were difficult to access both physically and from a data access perspective. Rarely did the business clients gain access to the "inner sanctum" of the mainframe computer. The physical environment in which the mainframe computers were maintained contributed to some of the undeserved mystique surrounding the early computers, and the "different type people" who programmed and operated them. This was the beginning of the era of the "computer geeks".

It may come as a shock to the reader how little the general functional architecture of the computer has changed over the years. Computers are all fundamentally alike in basic function and structure. No they don't look alike. They have different internal processing technology. They are much smaller and more powerful, but they are similarly architected. Keep in mind that the original computer had 6 major components: a central processing unit (CPU); main memory; external storage; channels (bus); output; and input.

Figure 6 Tier 1 (Mainframe) Processing Platform

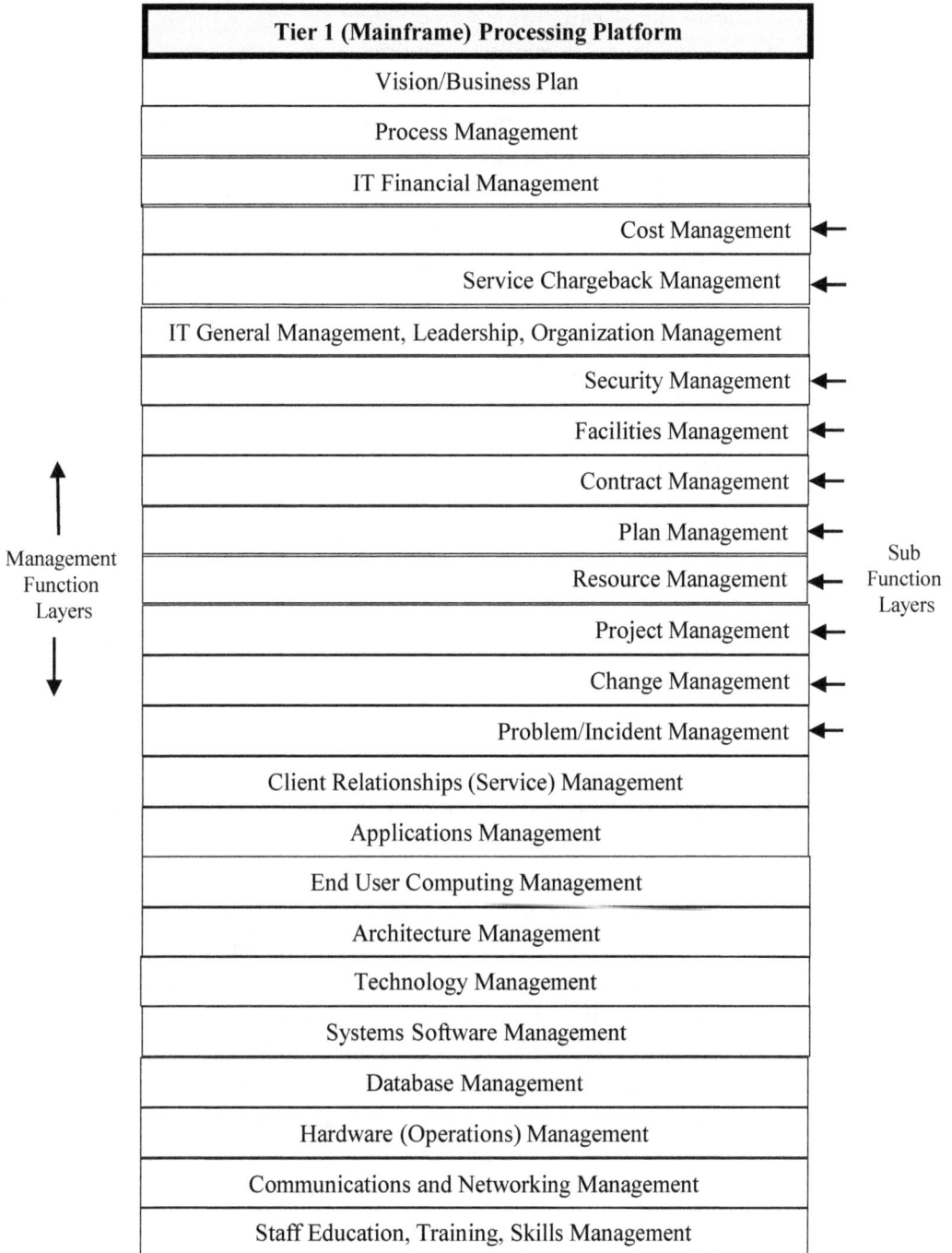

Tier 1 (Mainframe) Processing Platform
Vision/Business Plan
Process Management
IT Financial Management
Cost Management ←
Service Chargeback Management ←
IT General Management, Leadership, Organization Management
Security Management ←
Facilities Management ←
Contract Management ←
Plan Management ←
Resource Management ←
Project Management ←
Change Management ←
Problem/Incident Management ←
Client Relationships (Service) Management
Applications Management
End User Computing Management
Architecture Management
Technology Management
Systems Software Management
Database Management
Hardware (Operations) Management
Communications and Networking Management
Staff Education, Training, Skills Management

Management Function Layers (↑↓)

Sub Function Layers

Includes all Model Layers

The plan model assumes these same functions still exist on each computer in the network today, although they are delivered by newer, more powerful technologies. For example, the laptop computer used to write this book is probably more powerful than the mainframe computer utilized to support the data processing operations of a small to medium sized manufacturing company in the past. The laptop is definitely more software enriched. The functions required to manage a computer platform today have changed even less. These facts loom large in technology planning approaches taken with the subsequent introduction of the minicomputers, personal computers, and all other processing platforms imaginable.

The mainframe was not alone in being a single function (i.e. data processing), stand-alone processing unit. Voice processing was delivered by stand-alone telephone systems with a unique technology base. Likewise, text and image processing were stand-alone technologies and included such things as type writers, copy equipment, printers, facsimile, image and document processing facilities. The data staff, the records center staff, the telephone staff, and those working in the print shop normally worked in different technology worlds. It was in the early 1980s, that the technology base of these various information processes began to integrate around a common computer platform and communications network base. Internet and the advancements in computer operating systems accelerated the information integration process.

Mainframe computer gets company:

The mainframe computer platform was no longer the only computer on the block with the arrival of the Tier 2 Minicomputer (Figure 7) in the early 1970s. The introduction of the minicomputer was an important revolution in computers because it helped establish the components and principles of a distributed computer architecture. The question of what role each computer would play in the overall computer architecture had to be addressed once there was more than one computer in a company.

The industry began installing minicomputers at a rapid pace to alleviate many of the access and performance problems associated with the mainframe. The "mini", as it was called, was a full-fledged computer, just smaller in size, less expensive, and somewhat less powerful than the mainframe. Word processing, e-mail, some report writer applications, and other systems were delivered on this new platform. The mini actually ushered in the concept of office automation (OA) and management information systems (MIS). It could deliver fully-functional business applications, but in spite of this capability, there was a tendency to keep major business applications on the mainframe platform for performance and capacity reasons.

But guess what? The "mini" was fundamentally the same as the mainframe in function, management, operation, maintenance, and architecture. All the issues of backup, security, maintenance, responsiveness, capacity and performance were the same as those of the mainframe, although the business clients sometimes had selective memory when it came to the need for these functions. Those IT departments which properly deployed the minicomputer positioned themselves and the computer facility closer to the business clients. This was referred to as distributed computing. Of course,

Figure 7 Introduction of Tier 2 Mini Computer

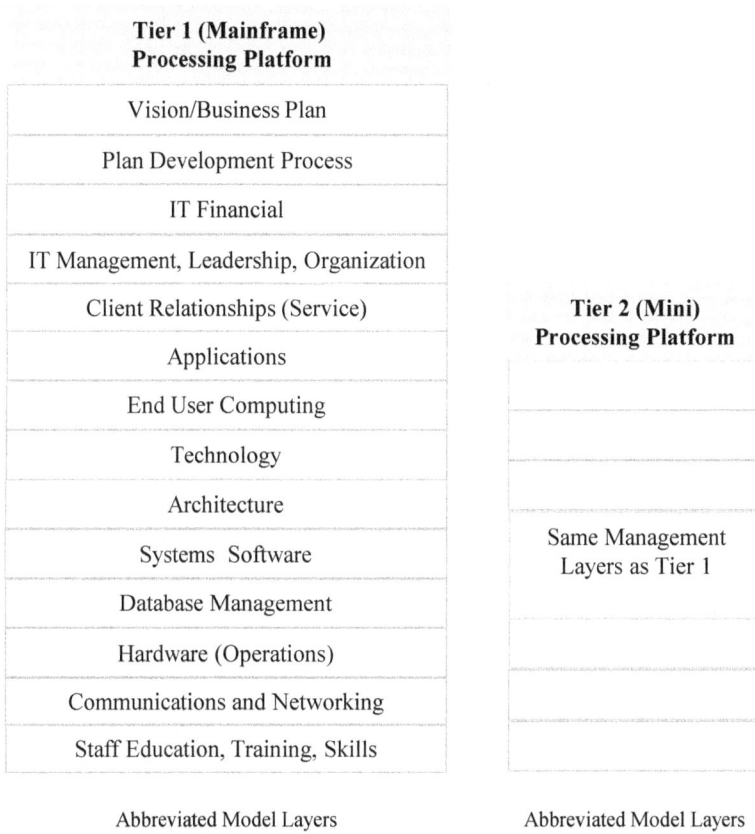

Tier 1 (Mainframe) Processing Platform
Vision/Business Plan
Plan Development Process
IT Financial
IT Management, Leadership, Organization
Client Relationships (Service)
Applications
End User Computing
Technology
Architecture
Systems Software
Database Management
Hardware (Operations)
Communications and Networking
Staff Education, Training, Skills

Abbreviated Model Layers

Tier 2 (Mini) Processing Platform
Same Management Layers as Tier 1

Abbreviated Model Layers

some companies went a little too far in distribution of the mini by allowing the business clients to treat the mini as a stand-alone computer (i.e. owned and operated by the business client) in order to bypass working with the IT's mainframe support groups. The belief in the distributed computer movement didn't eliminate the IT requirement of exercising management discretion in what functions and applications the business clients were permitted to access and execute independent of IT. Actually, those IT departments which viewed and managed the mini as a complementary extension of the mainframe computing facility positioned themselves well to take advantage of the personal computer revolution which was soon to follow.

Personal computer (PC) revolution:

The Tier 3 Personal Computer (Figure 8) appeared on the scene soon after the minicomputer was introduced. The PC got so much more attention than the minicomputer because its scope of impact was so much greater, but the issues were still the same as those associated with the mainframe and the minicomputers.

IT had to develop an architecture that accommodated a computer on every employee's desktop. This presented a huge IT management challenge.

Figure 8 Introduction of the Tier 3 Personal Computer

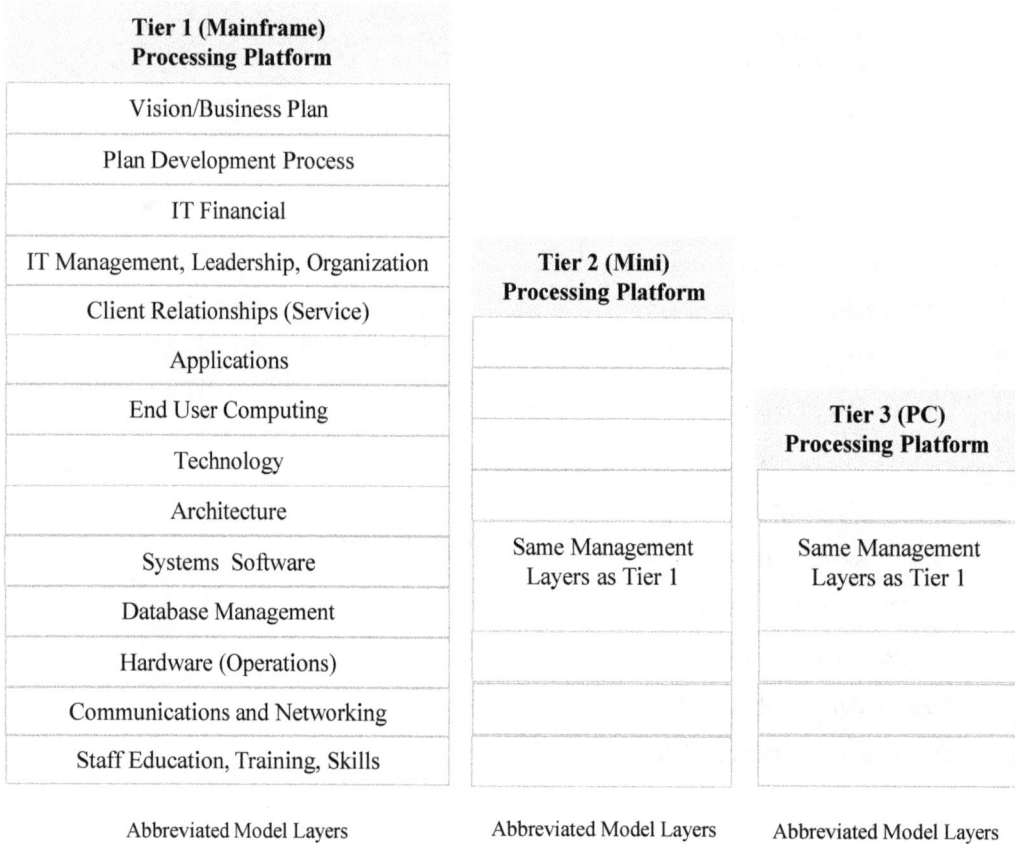

Tier 1 (Mainframe) Processing Platform
Vision/Business Plan
Plan Development Process
IT Financial
IT Management, Leadership, Organization
Client Relationships (Service)
Applications
End User Computing
Technology
Architecture
Systems Software
Database Management
Hardware (Operations)
Communications and Networking
Staff Education, Training, Skills

Abbreviated Model Layers

Tier 2 (Mini) Processing Platform
Same Management Layers as Tier 1

Abbreviated Model Layers

Tier 3 (PC) Processing Platform
Same Management Layers as Tier 1

Abbreviated Model Layers

The only difference in concept between the minicomputer and the personal computer was their number, size, enriched desktop applications like spreadsheet and word processing, and most importantly, their low cost. Business units could begin to put computers in their own budgets, often to the dismay of IT which was afraid of losing control of the total cost of IT. The PC had the same 6 major components or functions. It also required the application of the 24 management functions for it to be effectively used within the company. Many employees viewed the personal computer as a further escape from the IT's scope of authority, but they often failed to understand the issues of financial management, client support, required maintenance, software upgrades, security, proper application selection, installation and use, training, back-up, power protection, the value-added to their work by being a part of a company network, and the need to operate in a standard operating environment. The PC is much more than a small computer. It is a powerful information tool. Why should the PC be excused from management best practices? Without PC management best practices the integrity of the individual PC could not be maintained, nor could any guarantee that a PC would be able to effectively communicate over a computer network with other company computer users and applications be made.

Tier 4 and beyond:

The plan model works no matter how many platforms (tiers) you add to the architecture (Figure 9). Additional platforms could be smart phones, hand held computers, image scanners, etc. They are all computers. This distributed architecture allows computer processing power to be distributed to the location that the business application requires in order to be effectively utilized. No longer were system designers and business clients constrained to the use of a particular type of computer platform that didn't match the business application requirements.

Network enables a distributed computer architecture (aka *Distributed Processing* or *Cooperative Processing*):

The physical displacement of computers was enabled by the development of more sophisticated, computer-based communication networks. More options were made available to connect the physically dispersed computers because the networks were fast becoming more "intelligent" and flexible. The communication networks focused on the physical aspects of connecting computers, and the logical connections were a concern of business applications architecture.

Distributed business application systems:

It was great that computer platforms could be physically distributed all over the world, but if the business applications couldn't be designed to take

Figure 9 Tier 4 Computers and Beyond

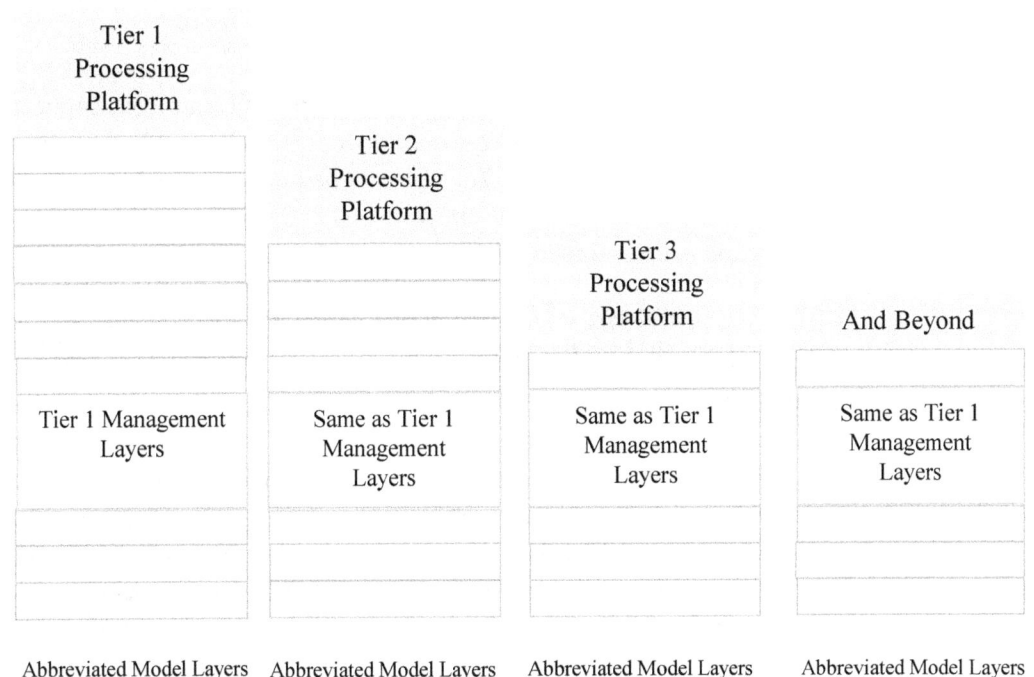

Tier 1 Processing Platform	Tier 2 Processing Platform	Tier 3 Processing Platform	And Beyond
Tier 1 Management Layers	Same as Tier 1 Management Layers	Same as Tier 1 Management Layers	Same as Tier 1 Management Layers
Abbreviated Model Layers	Abbreviated Model Layers	Abbreviated Model Layers	Abbreviated Model Layers

advantage of this distributed network of computer platforms, all IT really had was just a "bunch of computers" located in many places running stand-alone business applications. This led to the advent of distributed business application systems. The requirements of the business applications should dictate where and what functions are performed on what computer platforms. It was no secret that many business clients wanted business applications to be placed on platforms that they controlled regardless of what platform the applications required. The advent of distributed business applications provided IT a method of professionally addressing these "apparent power grabs" by some business clients.

The concept of distributed business application systems is based upon an architected view of the business application systems itself. Business applications have distinct software components which can be identified and distributed over the computer network to match business application requirements. The model identified four major business application components (data input; data output; application processing; and database), see (Figure 10). These four components can all be performed on a singular computer platform, or the various application components can be mixed/matched across the network of computers in order to best satisfy the business application requirements. Consistent business application development and deployment best practices must be defined to determine on which platform a particular application component is best deployed. The best practices amounts to a balancing act between how much system autonomy should be allocated to the business clients without compromising the integrity of company systems. Without adequate management best practice in place, development and deployment of distributed business application systems could become rather chaotic.

Network is the computer platform:

Today it is the network of all the computer platforms, all seamlessly connected via a value-added communications network, which must be managed as a singular processing entity. The vision of being able to instantaneously transact with systems across the entire globe has become a reality with the introduction and continued development of Internet.

Enter the concept of Computer Platform, Technology, and Organization Independent Architecture (CPTOIA):

Technology Independence (Figure 11) dictates that each computer platform can perform voice (telephones), data (traditional computer processing), text, and image processing. The individual technologies no longer need be processed on separate computer networks. A cube is now used to represent a computer platform with this added dimensionality. Even the mainframe computer assumes this new dimensionality. As stated earlier, the first assumption upon which the model is built is that all computers are fundamentally alike,

Figure 10 Distributed Business Application Architecture

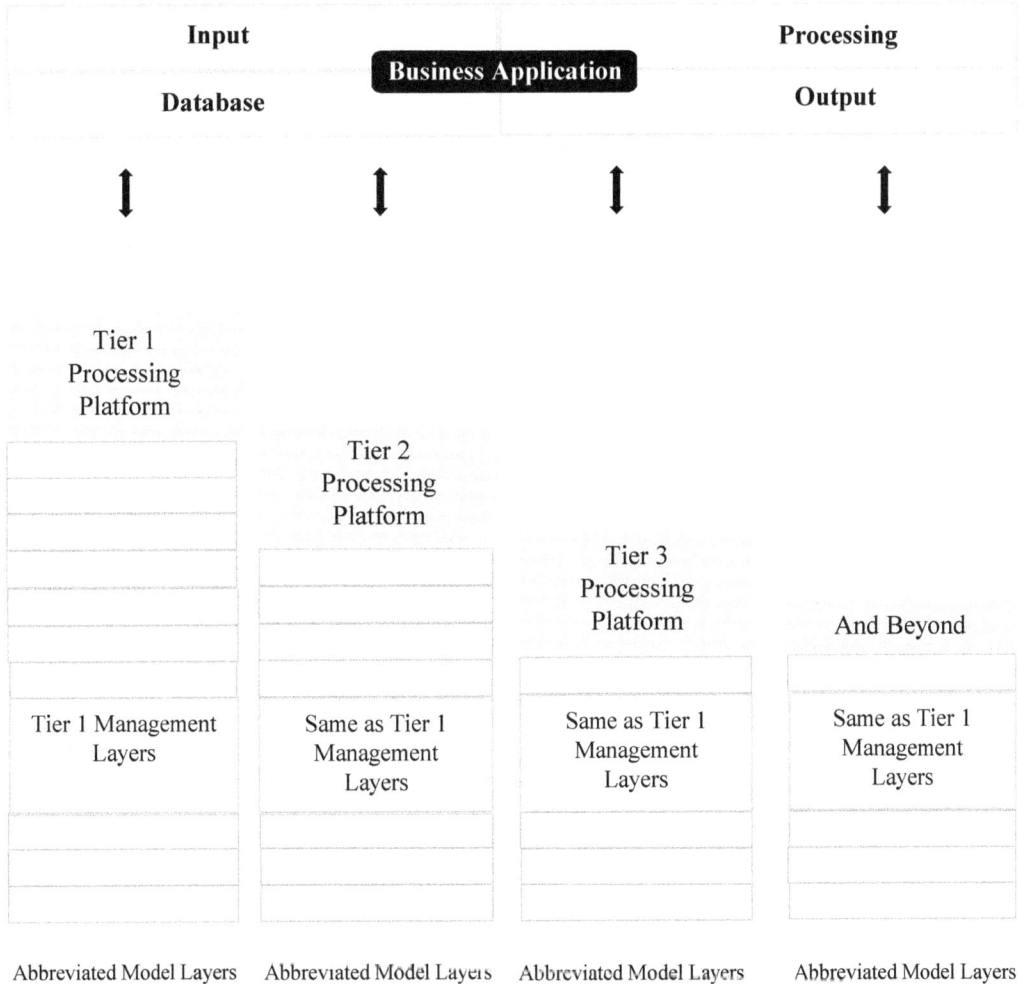

Input	Processing
Business Application	
Database	Output

Tier 1
Processing
Platform

Tier 2
Processing
Platform

Tier 3
Processing
Platform

And Beyond

| Tier 1 Management Layers | Same as Tier 1 Management Layers | Same as Tier 1 Management Layers | Same as Tier 1 Management Layers |

Abbreviated Model Layers Abbreviated Model Layers Abbreviated Model Layers Abbreviated Model Layers

and all new technologies, no matter from what processing technology they originate, can be delivered by a common hardware and network architecture.

The 24 management functions apply equally to all the technologies performed on a computer platform. The commonality of platforms, management functions, and technologies enable IT to achieve its leveraging opportunities. The decision where to place an application system is made independent of the platform since each platform is functionally equivalent.

Resource Leveraging Keys the Model's Payback

The relevance of the planning model's assumptions that all computers are fundamentally alike and are supported by the same basic management support functions allows IT managers to isolate and coordinate like management and support functions across platforms and technologies, thereby making more effective use of IT resources. It is this ability to leverage resources

Figure 11 Concept of Computer Platform, Technology, and Organization Independent Architecture

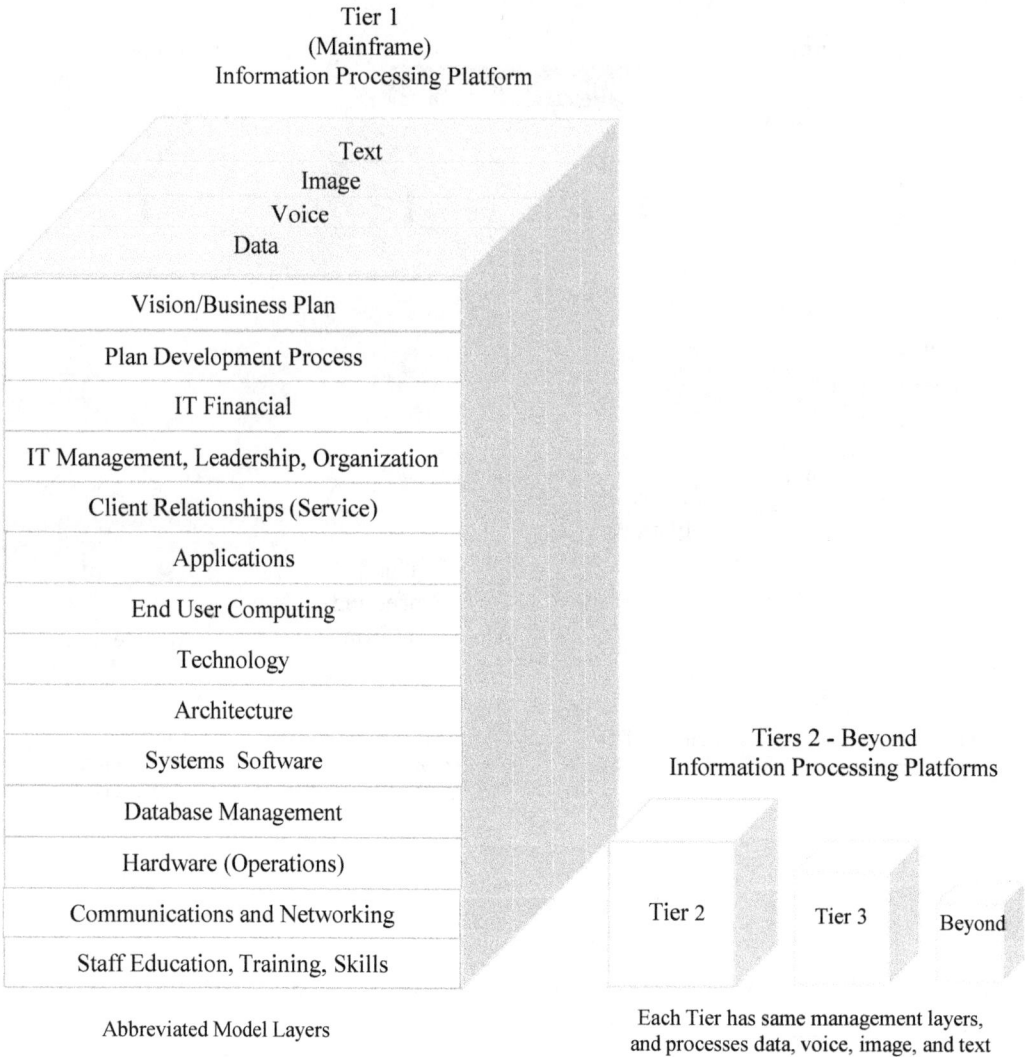

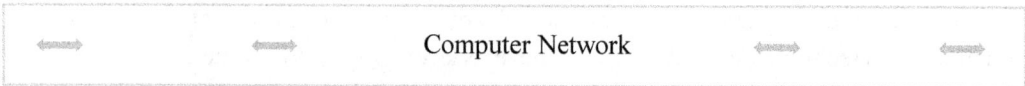

Tier 1
(Mainframe)
Information Processing Platform

Text
Image
Voice
Data

Vision/Business Plan
Plan Development Process
IT Financial
IT Management, Leadership, Organization
Client Relationships (Service)
Applications
End User Computing
Technology
Architecture
Systems Software
Database Management
Hardware (Operations)
Communications and Networking
Staff Education, Training, Skills

Abbreviated Model Layers

Tiers 2 - Beyond
Information Processing Platforms

Tier 2   Tier 3   Beyond

Each Tier has same management layers,
and processes data, voice, image, and text

Computer Network

that provides the opportunity to achieve significant IT payback on your investments in technologies; improve your system delivery effectiveness; and allow staff to learn new skills and increase their career opportunities.

Two graphics, Figure 12, Unleveraged Resource Management Model, and Figure 13, Leveraged Resource Management Model illustrate the differences between the two planning models.

The Unleveraged Resource Management Model represents a "silo" management structure on steroids. It is composed of four rectangles, each

Figure 12 Unleveraged Resource Management Model

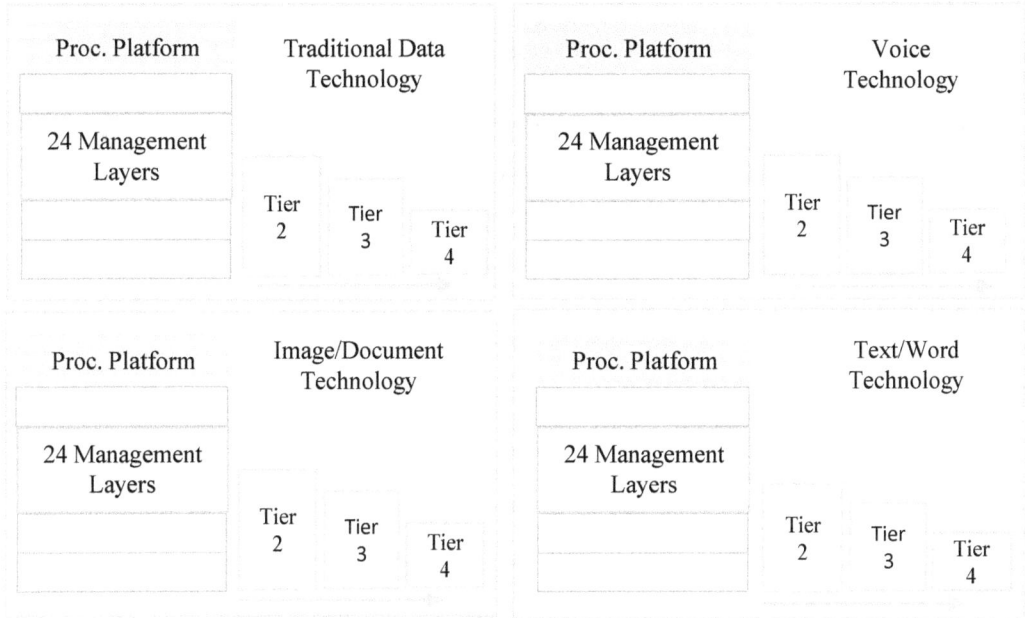

Proc. Platform	Traditional Data Technology			Proc. Platform	Voice Technology		
24 Management Layers				24 Management Layers			
	Tier 2	Tier 3	Tier 4		Tier 2	Tier 3	Tier 4

Proc. Platform	Image/Document Technology			Proc. Platform	Text/Word Technology		
24 Management Layers				24 Management Layers			
	Tier 2	Tier 3	Tier 4		Tier 2	Tier 3	Tier 4

representing one of the four information technologies (data, voice, text and image). Each rectangle arbitrarily includes four tiers or computer platforms. Any number of platforms could have been selected for demonstration purposes. In the unleveraged model all 24 management functions are duplicated over all platforms for each of the technologies. This situation represents the worst possible case of managing resources. Imagine how difficult and cumbersome it would be to coordinate and plan all of these IT components?

A glance at the Leveraged Resource Management Model (Figure 13) illustrates an intuitively less complicated resource model, one that should be far easier to coordinate and plan. It should be easy to determine after reviewing the graphics that a leveraged model can significantly reduce the requirements for staff resources. The leveraged model is based upon the simple idea that the same business plan, financial management, general management, client relationships, business applications, technologies, architecture, etc. apply to each computer platform and technology. It should also be clear from review of the two models that traditional organizational structures can't be effective in managing the work of the leveraged model. If the leveraged resource model is adopted, the systems and services organizational strategy to deliver and support it should be adopted. This organizational strategy is explained in detail in Book 2.

Non-Financial Management Model Benefits

Conservative expense reductions of 10%-15% can be realized by leveraging staff resources across computers and technologies, by focusing and aligning the IT plans with the business plan objectives and vision, and by

Figure 13 Leveraged Resource Plan Model

Leveraging management functions and resources across the information processing
platforms

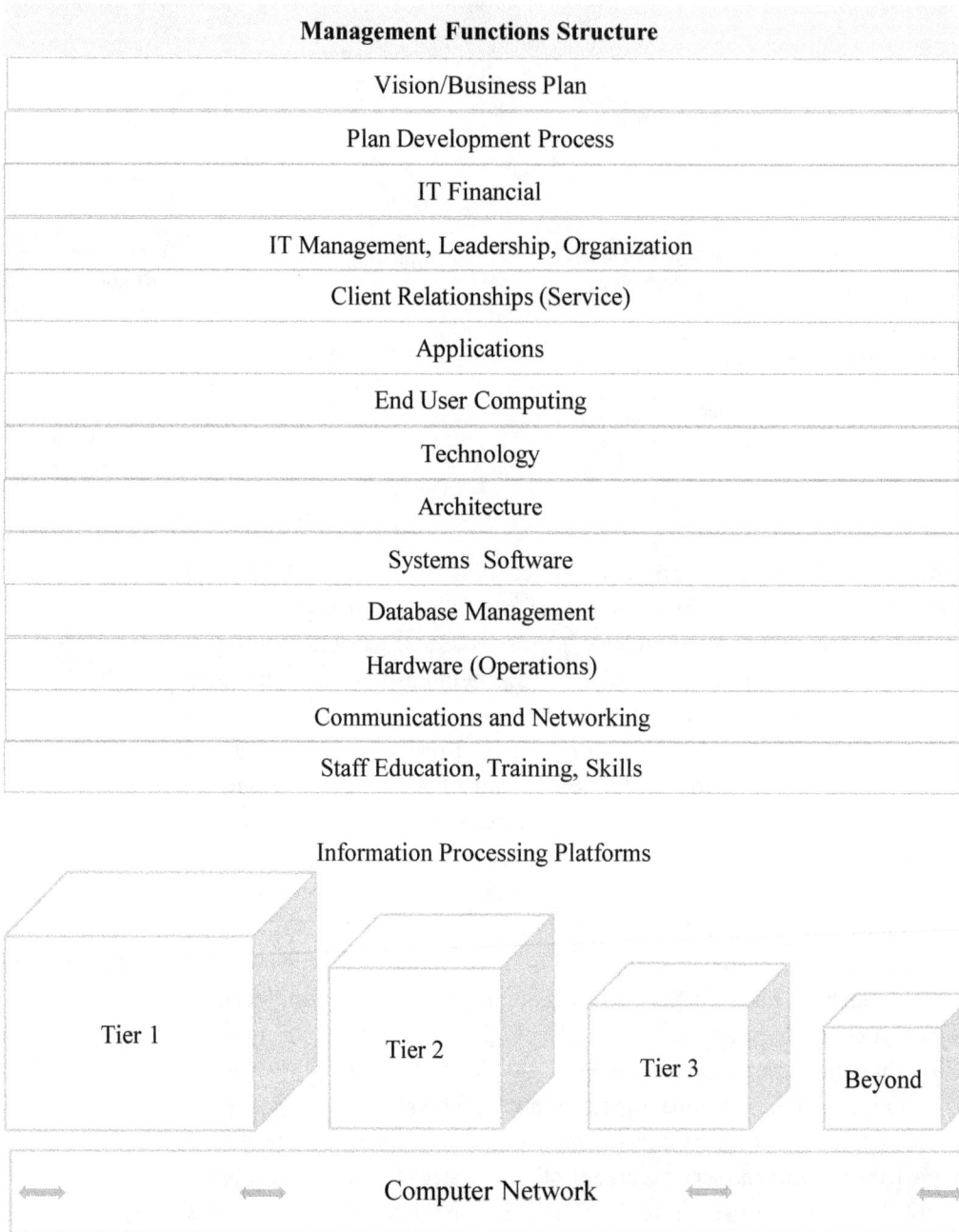

Management Functions Structure
Vision/Business Plan
Plan Development Process
IT Financial
IT Management, Leadership, Organization
Client Relationships (Service)
Applications
End User Computing
Technology
Architecture
Systems Software
Database Management
Hardware (Operations)
Communications and Networking
Staff Education, Training, Skills

Information Processing Platforms

Tier 1

Tier 2

Tier 3

Beyond

Computer Network

right-sizing requirements with budgeted resources. What follows are some
of the non-financial benefits that can be realized by using the model and
supporting processes.

The model enables IT to target training to specific plan objectives and projects. A basic "just-in-time" training, education and skills delivery capability

can be created by focusing on the critical training, education, and skills needed to support the requirements of the planned work, at the time when the training, education, and skills are required. This capability can positively impact the on-time delivery of projects.

The associate's annual performance review process can be enhanced by aligning associate planned work with personal performance objectives established by the IT manager. In actual practice they should be relatively the same, but work planned for an associate six-eight months in advance won't always match perfectly with the actual work performed by the associate during the course of the year. It certainly is an objective well worth pursuing. Plan reports from the work management system should be included in the associate's performance folder at the beginning and end of each review period, including planned education and training. Inclusion of these items enhances the review process for both the associate and the reviewing manager. Variances of planned to actual work performed by the associates provides valuable feedback on planning accuracy to the associate, manager and IT plan administrator. If a significant number of work initiatives performed during the performance review period did not appear in the plan, then these discrepancies can be used as the basis of improving the plan for next year by revising the associate's current year plan. This entire process assists the manager and associate in internalizing the plan into the manager's and associate's daily activities which is one of the overall IT objectives. The plan is no longer tangent to the performance review process, it is at the core of it. Why go through all the effort of planning and tracking planning activity and not use it? This process represents a key step forward in management best practices.

A plan can increase the sense of job fulfillment, job empowerment, and job enrichment. Associates want to feel their efforts are worthwhile. How better to tell that story than to demonstrate how an associate's efforts are aligned with planned business objectives. Because plans have been right-sized to the expense budget, the projects duly prioritized, and responsibility for the completion of the project assigned, the staff has truly been empowered to do the work. They are working on projects most significant to the company, and they have the authority to act.

The computer, technology, and organization independent architecture (CPTOIA) provides associate job enrichment opportunities to develop new skills and work in support of different types of projects and non-data technologies. But the opportunity must be seized by the associate. Too often IT associates complain about wanting to work with new technologies and systems, but when confronted with the learning opportunity to obtain new skills required to perform this newer type work, they never seem to find the time to attend the necessary training sessions, even though the time was offered by management. Maybe there's a little bit of that *Escape from Freedom* in the associates' response to opportunity.

Strategic Management Plan Worksheet Develop and Manage the IT Management Model Process

Objectives:

Some of the objectives are repeated over the processes, but a particular process may have unique strategies to achieve them. Major objectives for the Develop and Manage the IT Management Model Process are:

- Establish the role of the company business plan in the IT management process
- Reduce overall IT expense
- Operate IT as any other business unit
- Create an information processing complex
- Provide capability of creating multi-tech products delivered by diverse service options
- Expand career opportunities for staff

Strategies to Achieve Objectives:

The strategies are the action plans concerning how the management model will achieve its objectives. Note that strategies can align with multiple objectives.

Establish the role of the company business plan in the IT management process:

- Develop a layered model with management functions hierarchically arranged in priority sequence
- Place the business plan as the highest layer in the model
- All lower layers must be aligned with attainment of business plan objectives

Reduce overall IT expense:

- Align and focus IT work on accomplishment of planned business objectives
- Manage and leverage IT resources
- Implement the computer platform, technology, organization independent architecture
- Implement the systems and services organizational structure
- Right-size required resources to available resources
- Promote the use of a common plan model and process for both IT and the business units
- Allocate responsibility for expense and revenue management to IT managers

- Identify, classify, and prioritize the work IT performs

Operate IT as any other business unit:

- Promote IT's mission statement of contributing to the company's bottom-line
- Establish a work management system
- Establish a cost management system
- Establish a service chargeback management system
- Establish a planning and resource management system
- Balance IT technical management functions with IT management functions
- Tightly integrate IT financials with company financial practices and procedures
- Expand view of IT as both technical and business partners
- Form closer partnerships with the company's financial and accounting functions

Create an information processing complex:

- Merge the disparate technologies of data, voice, text, and image around an IT information pro:cessing concept and unified organization structure
- Implement the computer platform, technology, organization independent architecture
- Implement the systems and services organizational structure

Provide capability of multi-tech products delivered by diverse service options:

- Implement the computer platform, technology, organization independent architecture
- Implement the systems and services organizational structure
- Emphasize re-engineering of the staffs' technical skills

Expand career opportunities for staff:

- Implement the computer platform, technology, organization independent architecture
- Implement the systems and services organizational structure
- Align education and training with planned work requirements
- Introduce education and training to assist in re-engineering staff skills base

Strengths, Weaknesses, Opportunities, and Threats (SWOT):

The SWOT analysis presents the strengths, weaknesses, opportunities, and threats which illustrate the attributes of a "best company" in which the process can be most effectively implemented. It lists the typical strengths to be exploited, opportunities to be seized, and weaknesses and threats that need to be reduced. Most characteristics of a "best company" environment repeat across the other processes presented in the book; therefore, the SWOT analysis presented in this section should be referenced as the detail SWOT analysis for each subsequent process presented in the book.

Strengths:

The following items list qualities of a company that increase the probability of a successful process implementation:

- Business plan plays a central role in the company management
- Company is financially sound
- Strategies and work are aligned to the plan objectives
- IT and company moving forward from a project mentality
- Commitment to managing IT as any other business unit
- Company accounting and financial reporting have high presence in company
- IT has excellent working relationship with company's financial staff
- IT is service oriented
- IT management is sensitive to the impact of greater financial controls placed on its staff
- Culture that isn't content to accept things as they exist today (i.e. a vision-driven company)
- Relies on objective measures of success or failure
- IT is viewed as a technical, financial, and a business partner
- Value-add partnerships exist between IT and its business clients
- Architecture plays a major role in IT development activities
- Strong base of business application systems and underlying computer network architecture
- IT associates are committed to obtaining the proper skills and training to perform the work required of the new IT management model
- Disciplined, responsible, and knowledgeable staff
- Distributed management is promoted throughout company
- Information processing driven

Weaknesses:

Weaknesses are for the most part the absence of what are seen as company strengths. If left unaddressed these weaknesses will compromise the ability to successfully implement the process. If weaknesses go unaddressed they can become threats.

- Company's size and its ability to compete with larger companies in the acquisition of new technologies to remain competitive with other companies
- A potential weakness, and again a very real threat, is that IT associates may not be able to acquire all the skills required by the new management model in the timeframe required.
- Business clients fail to deliver on their responsibilities in the system development process
- Difficulty working in multiple planning years
- Inability of some managers to think in a strategic or visionary manner

The "best company" is headed in the correct direction to address these potential weaknesses by introducing a new business plan driven management model which tightly aligns IT work, training, and skills acquisition with business plan objectives.

Opportunities:

There are many significant opportunities that can be seized by the implementation of the process.

- Reduce overall IT expense
- Increase the effective use of IT resources using leveraging techniques
- Create a professional business view of IT
- Create an information processing complex by combining the processing technologies of data, voice, text, and image under a common management umbrella
- Introduce multi-tech, multi-platform support organization
- Introduce multi-tech products and services delivered by multiple service options.
- Develop enriched partnerships with business clients
- Develop better, more comprehensive decision making process by adding a financial element to the process
- Job enrichment
- Just-in-time training
- Staff Empowerment

Threats:

Threats can result from factors outside or inside the company. These must be mitigated to reduce their potential impact.

- Satisfaction of business plan objectives could require resources far beyond IT's budget, and the gap in resources could be perceived as a lack in IT effectiveness, not the aggressive nature of the plan objectives.
- Politics can be a significant threat to IT.
- Inability to overcome IT's negative reaction to more stringent financial controls, especially time reporting
- Business associates may react negatively towards new service billings
- Major inaccuracies in the business vision
- Assumptions of model may prove false
- Company business management may continue to view IT as a technical partner only, not a business partner
- Training requirements of associates in the new skills required to support the process may not be realistic, or acquisition of new associates with the proper skills cannot be accomplished in the timeframes required.
- Company may balk at supporting the requirements of the new management model

Cost Drivers:

If properly implemented the model should result in *lower* costs, improved service, and a more motivated staff. Drivers of IT cost that the process can specifically address are those associated with fragmented management structures, organizations based around a "silo" view of information technology management, and a failure to adopt a computer platform, technology, organization independent architecture (CPTOIA), along with its systems and services support organization.

Deliverables:

The deliverables are witnessed in the statement of the objectives.

Critical Success Factors:

What events or actions must occur in order to successfully execute the process plan?

- Effectively "sell" and gain acceptance for the process concepts from company and IT senior staffs
- Development of effective business partnerships
- Ability to develop or acquire the skills and training necessary to implement the process's major concepts and facilities
- Ability to *execute* the work driven by the process

Management Function Impact Analysis:

The purpose of this section of the strategic management plan worksheet is to assess the potential impact of the new process on the 24 management functions listed in the management functions structure. This ensures that all areas of IT responsibility will be assessed for impact. The process owner makes the initial impact analysis based upon their judgement of impact on each management function. Since there are potentially 23 other stakeholders who have a need to make their own assessment of impact, the strategic management plan worksheet is distributed to them for review and comment.

Reference the section titled *Strategic Management Plan Worksheet* discussed earlier in this chapter for a more detailed discussion of the *Management Function Impact Analysis* if necessary. The *Management Function Impact Analysis* procedures are common to all processes presented in the book; therefore, further explanations for the completion and use of the *Management Function Impact Analysis* will not be repeated in the discussions of the other processes.

The illustration of process impact on each management function layer is of necessity only representative of the potential impact a process can exert because we are dealing in principles, not an actual company.

Business plan management:

A process should align with the business objectives listed in the summary business plan example presented in chapter 1. This process aligns with, and is supportive of, the following business objectives listed in the summary business plan example.

- Continuous improvement initiatives
- Effective organizational structures
- Cost awareness
- Plan driven
- Embrace Quality
- Empower staff
- Career development opportunities
- Fair compensation
- Increase skills and training opportunities
- Exceed expectations
- Customer-focused solutions
- Cost effective products
- Bottom-line oriented
- Financial awareness
- Cost management
- Introduce new technologies and systems in support of business plan

Process management:

The process to develop and implement the model is led by the process owner, but requires a team structure much like that required to build the business plan. Its impact on IT and the company is very pervasive. The support teams will include the company's senior business management team, the IT senior management teams, and ultimately most of the IT and business managers. The process will require many meetings and presentations just on educating and "selling" IT and the company on the idea of the model.

IT financial management:

The process owner's commitment to the financial management function is reflected in the model's emphasis on being driven by business plan financial objectives, and its role in increasing company profits. IT intends to be managed and operated as any other business unit. Expense management procedures are enhanced by installing a cost management function, and revenue management procedures are likewise enhanced with the introduction of service chargeback management. Both of these functions are tightly integrated with the company's financial systems so that company financial ledgers will report IT revenue and expense. A greater push is being made to have IT managers assume responsibility for their expense and revenue management functions.

IT general management, leadership, organization management:

A major component of the model that affects this management function is the implementation of the computer platform, technology, and organization independent architecture (CPTOIA). It provides the opportunity to totally reengineer management and organizational structures around the information management concept. Traditional hierarchical organizational structures based around the "silos" of data, voice, text and image processing technologies do not fit with the model. The supporting management and organizational structure required for successful implementation of the model is delivered by a *systems and services organization* structure. The model uses management techniques of staff leveraging, plan alignment, focusing, gap analysis, and right-sizing to maximize the use of IT resources.

Plan, resource, cost, and service chargeback management:

The process owner determined that the work management functions of planning, resource management, cost management, and service chargeback are components integral to the successful implementation of the model because the work IT performs is a major part of the model. A system is required to plan, cost, manage, and recover the costs of this work.

Client relationship (service) management:

The business client's access and use IT products and services will definitely be impacted by the model's introduction of the systems and services organization. The model also promotes value-add IT/client partnerships based upon the model's objective of adding a business dimension to the technical dimension of the current partnership. The relationship must be two-sided with the business partners accepting equal responsibilities with IT.

Application management, end user computing management, architecture management, technology management, systems software management, database management, hardware (operations) management, and communications and networking management:

The model is based upon the importance of implementing the computer platform, technology, and organization independent architecture (CPTOIA) and its support organization. The requirement to support this architecture will be significant at these management function layers. The impact in these areas is probably best stated by the owners of each of these functions. At a minimum, the type of products they deliver, the manner in which they interact with the business clients, and the way they manage their areas of responsibility will all be impacted.

Education, training, and skills management:

The model requires a significant reengineering of staff skills. Education and training of the staff is important to the success of the model's implementation. Many programs must be developed to introduce IT and the business community to the concepts and facilities of the model.

Potential impact on other management functions:

Use this section to solicit the potential impact of the new process on the process operation of the other management function process owners.

CHAPTER 3

IT Work

The basic IT management processes, and the other miscellaneous processes that IT manages, provide the structures used to organize IT work, but all IT work is not the same. Work must be decomposed into specific work types by defining and classifying it at a level of detail that satisfies IT's management and reporting requirements. The Work Classification Scheme (WCS) is the vehicle used by IT to identify and classify its work.

Once the basic management processes have been defined and the objectives and strategies aligned with them, it's time to take the next step and align the detail projects and work initiatives necessary to accomplish the objectives and strategies. In order to include and align the work to the processes a scheme for consistently identifying and classifying work must be developed. The key word is consistent. You can liken this scheme to a chart of work. The scheme is referenced as the Work Classification Scheme (WCS). It is a major component of the Information Technology Management Process.

Ownership

Overall ownership of the work classification scheme is probably best assigned to the IT plan administrator. A plan is composed of the work IT must perform to accomplish the plan objectives; therefore, placing ownership under the IT plan administrator seems logical. The owner of the work classification scheme must work with nearly all the other IT managers in establishing the classifications scheme. The IT plan administrator will play a particularly dominant role in creating the initial work classifications because the process and issues will be so new to everyone. As the work classification scheme matures, scheme activity will lessen and maintenance becomes more a joint partnership between the IT managers and the IT plan administrator. The most significant changes occur to the work classification scheme during the plan development process, and in the first several weeks after the new plan is put into production. A major emphasis must be placed on educating both the business and IT staffs in the work classification concepts.

Work classification requires the IT plan administrator to play significant roles as an architect and chemist. Work classifications must have a consistent set of guidelines for establishing the new work items. The work classification scheme is an architecture. As an architect the IT plan administrator must be able to decompose work into clearly defined elements to avoid overlap in work classifications. *Tenacity* is a strong character trait to have, especially in the early years of system growth. The IT plan administrator is going to be continually "pushed" by the IT managers and associates to add new work classifications "right now" so that associates can satisfy their time entry requirements on schedule. Managers don't have time to wait until a proposed new work item is properly researched and classified. Expediency is typically the driver of this push. Expediency can't "rule the day" because if it does there will be total inconsistency in classifying work, and this will lead to a loss of integrity in plan status reporting. In all these roles the IT plan administrator must be able to facilitate large groups in making work classification decisions.

Terms, Concepts and Approaches

Work specificity must match management requirements:

A work classification scheme (WCS) identifies, defines, organizes, classifies, and reports the work IT performs. It demystifies IT to the extent that it clearly identifies its work. If work performed today can't be described, how can the work planned for tomorrow be described? Without such discipline and structure, IT work could become viewed as some amorphous, mysterious activity. Establish a work classification scheme that specifies work to a level of granularity that allows a manager to satisfy their management responsibilities. IT may be OK with just tracking and reporting production versus development work. Does IT want to account for work at a systems level, or a business unit level, or a combination of both? Does it care about "break/fix" work? Does it want to define work down to the level of application systems, projects, tasks, business units, and associate? The answer is dependent upon IT's objectives. One of the major objectives promoted in the book is to use information to isolate areas of inefficient operation. With this objective in mind, the WCS should be taken down to at least the level of application systems, projects, tasks, business units, and associate. Using the WCS at this level of granularity makes it a true management tool.

Over-looked work categories:

Certain types of work are often over-looked or under-estimated in establishing a WCS. Most of the over-looked work categories relate to non-project work. Examples of these work types are: administration; general management; operations; production support; required maintenance; security; general program enhancements; on demand reporting; and regulatory changes. Projects are much easier to identify, and tend to draw more attention and visibility. In cases where certain types of work are ignored, under-estimated, or just over-looked in planning, the IT business clients are going to experience significant frustration because resources that they thought were available for their projects aren't going to be available.

Work identification:

A unique identifier must be established for each WCS work item. An example of a work classification scheme is one in which work records are uniquely identified with a four level index number formatted as 99.99.99.99. The first three levels of the index are primarily used to classify WCS work categories. WCS work categories are summary header records used primarily for clarity in online viewing and reporting. Only one summary header record is required to identify a WCS work category, the other two are optional. As many of these summary header records can be created in a scheme as are needed to track and manage the work at the level of granularity required. The fourth index level is coded as blank to identify a summary record, or 99 to specify a WCS work item record (i.e. task, project, non-project work) to which activity can be posted. The 99 record type can contain an additional, detailed work description (e.g. install a new personal computer) to describe the work item.

The following example illustrates an associate using the scheme to record work. The associate is a computer operator and works in a data center running the nightly accounting cycle. Time spent on this work item is recorded to a WCS record with an index value of 01.02.01.99. The first index (01) is a summary descriptor for Non-Discretionary. The second index (02) is a summary descriptor for Production Support. The third index (01) carries a summary descriptor of Computer Operations, and the fourth index (99) has a detail descriptor indicating the work involves operating the nightly accounting system production cycle.

A typical medium sized company could have hundreds or even thousands of WCS work items. The WCS structures among companies can, and will differ. It all depends upon what type of information, and at what level of granularity, a company wishes to track and report work. The WCS should reasonably reflect the type of work performed in an IT department. The importance of the WCS to the overall success of IT's technology management efforts cannot be over-emphasized.

Start-up considerations:

Early in the system development and implementation phases there will be a requirement to control the process using a top down approach in which the IT plan administrator exerts significant control on the overall approach to the work. Expediency and the lack of an architectural approach to the situation are usually factors contributing to the requirement for tight control of the process. Everyone seems to view work in slightly different ways. Senior level IT managers can support the IT plan administrator in these earlier stages, but once the work classification scheme matures and refines, things will settle into the routine of daily management activities in which the IT plan administrator interacts with the line IT managers in maintaining the scheme.

Critical link of time entry and the work classification scheme:

Time entry is a critical work function used in planning, resource management, costing, and service chargeback. Without a realistic and responsive work classification scheme process, time entry cannot be effectively executed. Work classification is at the core of effective time entry. The WCS has significant impact on the appearance and operation of the timesheets.

A typical time entry scenario begins when an associate is entering time and a project or work item is not available on the associate's timesheet. The associate informs their manager that they require a work item to be added to their timesheet in order to satisfy their time reporting requirements. Since the work classification scheme is centrally controlled, the IT manager engages the IT plan administrator to get the work item placed in the scheme so time can be entered. Sometimes the issue is just a matter of the associate and the IT manager being unaware of the work that is currently in the classification scheme, and in this case, the IT plan administrator simply informs the IT manager of the work item's identity. If the situation truly requires a new work item to be added, the IT plan administrator would probably confer with other line managers to gain agreement on the classification of the new work item so that the same work item is not defined with another name. Another associate may already be working on the work item using a different name.

Keeping everyone informed:

Work categories and work types should be constantly evaluated for inclusion in the WCS. Many times a work item is established that proves to be unneeded (i.e. unused). These items should be deleted from the system as long as no planned or actual activity have been recorded to them. A good time to delete unused or duplicated work items is during next year's plan development process when most interested parties are available to make decisions on the work item's status. When any type of change is made to a work item, a notification indicating the name, the change made, and the purpose of the work item should be broadcast to all IT managers, and possibly business managers.

Common work classification scheme for data, voice, text, and image technologies:

The manner in which traditional data technology project and non-project work are classified and organized in the WCS is easily adaptable to the other technologies of voice, image, and text. It is recommended that the other technology work types be merged with the traditional data technology work types. Merging the technologies facilitates consolidated technology reporting. The major work categories for the other technologies should remain relatively the same, but the individual work items, projects, and tasks will vary with each technology.

Work Classification Scheme
Non-Discretionary Work

Non-discretionary, as the name implies, is work that must be performed by IT to stay in business. This type of work is sometimes referred to as the work which "keeps the lights on" in the company. Choose your name. It consumes a significant part of IT resources. Relative to IT, this is work that is generally performed in the operational or production environment. The volume of this work should be one of the first useful bits of planning information communicated to management. It's one of those "I never realized" type of numbers.

A question a Chief Information Officer (CIO) may be asked by the Chief Financial Officer (CFO) is - "What if IT discontinues all developmental work? What would be the cost to maintain IT operational work?" The work classification scheme could assist in identifying this type work. It's not a "stretch of imagination" to discover 65% of the work is operational when considering total IT expense. This doesn't mean that IT could immediately reduce its expense by 35%, but it does provide a good ballpark number to begin a further analysis. The entire 35% reduction cannot be realized because of fixed or "sunk" expenses for certain equipment, software and facilities. Just stopping the discretionary work doesn't automatically eliminate the expense.

Management and administration:

These non-discretionary work categories are generally considered IT overhead work. Most of this work is reallocated to the business units as an administrative charge based on a formula of choice.

General Management and Administration:

This work is in-office work that cannot be associated directly with specific projects or other work items. Examples are general administrative duties (creating reports, scheduling meetings, updating charts, etc.), and conducting or attending general staff, team, or status meetings. Obviously managers record a higher percent of their work to this category than non-managers. The exact percent depends upon the work mix of the managers. Some managers are "working managers" in that they record time to detail work initiatives, others are more pure managers/administrators in which case they may record as high as 100% of their time to the general management/administration category. This category can become a catch-all in time reporting. It can easily be abused. It must be a closely monitored by the IT managers. A typical percent allocated to IT non-managerial associates is in the range of 3%-5%.

Paid-Time-Off (PTO):

Vacations, sick days, personal days, leaves of absence, and holidays comprise this work type. The percent of time allocated to associates is normally determined by the payroll/human resources division working with the IT managers.

Companies that do not pay overtime, but instead provide compensation time-off (aka "comp time") to associates who work overtime may want to consider a work type identified as Paid-Time-Off – Compensation Time

Personal Training and Education:
Time allocated for personal training and general development of associates and managers is recorded to this work type. If the training or education is required for a particular project, the time should be recorded directly to the project.

Mentoring and Tutoring of Associates:
Time associated with assisting, directing, mentoring and instructing associates in performance of their work assignments is recorded to this work type. Some managers may enter this activity under the general management category. That's not a problem unless a manager clearly wants to track mentoring time as a unique work item.

Production support:

This non-discretionary work type is used to record time spent in performing system and operational support activity designed to keep production systems running to successful completion. There are numerous sub-work types contained within this work type. The majority of this work is performed in the data center environment.

Operations:
This is work associated with operating the computer equipment and running the daily production system cycles. It not only includes the operation of traditional computer facilities, but the other technologies of voice, text and image.

Abnormal System End (aka ABEND) resolution, trouble-shooting, on call support, and "break/fix work":
Activity associated with fixing and recovering from problems that occur in the daily operation of production systems is recorded under this work type. Most production support work is further classified by major application system (e.g. accounting, order entry, sales reporting) or business unit such as payroll or accounting. Recording work at the application level helps determine the quality and integrity of the production performance of the various application systems. If a system requires significant support time, maybe it is time to replace the system.

Customer Support:
A help desk normally provides this work type. It tends to be related to general inquiries, service requests, incidents, problem identification and resolution work.

General Business Unit Support including IT:

Work such as trouble-shooting, answering questions about production status, assisting in submitting work requests, answering questions about equipment or just things in general about IT operations is recorded to this work type. Many of these questions can be funneled through the help desk. Some companies have a group identified as business analysts assigned to specific business units to assist the business users in the performance of this work.

General Systems Software Consultation and Assistance:

Work here includes IT's response to questions/issues concerning the operation or support of application systems and their various system software components. Requests can be made by a business unit or IT support unit. The questions submitted tend to be technical in nature.

Required maintenance:

Required maintenance refers to the IT resources that are regularly required to install changes to business application software, system support software and utilities, and even to equipment of all types to ensure the latest enhanced system features are included in these IT components. Updates can be in the form of vendor-supplied software releases, internal software patches, internal release updates, or other types of regular system maintenance. They guarantee the continued enrichment of new functionality in the IT components, and ensure the components integrity. Some companies stop taking required maintenance on their products to reduce expenses. Decisions like these must be carefully considered because a time may come when IT needs to take a new release of required maintenance and the cost could prove prohibitive to bring the current system up to specification so that the new release can be installed.

Regulatory and Compliance Support:

This is a particular type of system maintenance designed to keep business application systems current with new governmental, professional and association type requirements. Audit support, compliance reporting, rating surveys, market conduct studies, standards organizations are some of the types of specific work included in this category. Requests can originate from internal or external sources.

Required Services:

This work type refers to the access and utilization of existing IT products (e.g. PC's) and services, not problem calls. It includes the installation, movement, reconfiguration and/or addition of these products in the client base. Services normally relate to desktop and server type facilities, and can include hardware, software, networking, communications, security, or access services. Other required services provided are training in the use of IT products, and some operational services. These services are typically recorded at the business unit level.

Regular Software Release Installations:

This is work required to install software releases associated with in-house business applications, or fixes/patches/major releases from 3rd party vendors.

Equipment Installations, Moves, Upgrades and Repairs:

The work here relates to equipment typically installed in the data center. Equipment utilized at the desktop is covered under Required Services or Customer Support depending upon a company's organizational structure. If the work is significant enough, a project can be established to record the work. Many companies use the company's facilities management group to do some of this work. In these cases the work recorded would include only IT's work participation.

Systems Housekeeping/Administration:

Regular IT system support activities such as compressing and moving files for optimum performance, moving, deleting and replacing files upon various storage devices, and maintaining system tables and other system control files are included in this work type. Time is typically recorded to IT or a particular business application system.

Security:

Security work involves services and network controls required to provide secured access to the IT computer network. Today this is a very significant work type in all companies. Work related to securing the IT facility, as well as work securing individual application systems, fall under this work type. Work is typically charged directly to a business unit or application system, or it can be charged to the company security office and reallocated to the business units as overhead.

Discretionary Work

The second major classification of work is Discretionary work. It is work which the company chooses to perform. It is concerned with creating new projects or systems and enhancing or adding functionality to existing systems. Even though development is considered discretionary, it is foolish to think that a company can stay in business for a very long period of time if some level of discretionary work isn't performed. There are two major sub classifications of discretionary work: Tactical Development and Enterprise Development.

Tactical development:

Some IT managers describe tactical development as work which "supports the business". It is work that generates changes in the existing operational environment. It normally doesn't cut across organizational boundaries. Most tactical work is allocated directly to a specific business unit or business application.

General Program/System Enhancements:
This work is commonly referred to as system modifications or system enhancements. It adds new features or functions to an existing program or system. It is another of those often used, and abused, work types. The work is planned and tracked as a "bucket of work resources", in which multiple work initiatives are recorded to a common work item. It is used by the IT managers when they don't choose to track their work as a tactical project. .

Tactical Projects:
Tactical project work is much like enhancement work except that it is managed as discrete projects. The project may or may not be managed by the Project Management Office (PMO) using its project management system (PMS). IT can provide the option of managing a project outside the PMO using a non-PMO project leader assigned from the normal IT support teams, but using PMO project development methodology. Management of tactical projects all depends on the call of the project sponsor/champion.

On Demand Reporting (aka one-time or unscheduled reporting):
This work type includes work in support of unscheduled report requests. An aggregate number of hours can be planned for this work type knowing these types of reports are requested throughout the year. This work category is also planned as a "bucket of work resources". This type of work is typically charged to a business unit or business application. On Demand Reporting is one of those functions "power users" of IT's services can take onto themselves. That's OK if they inform IT and their business mangers what they are doing. A caveat is that when non-IT system users create reports using company data as input, there is a real possibility that their results could differ from results reported from company financial reporting systems. Non-IT users must use control data to ensure they are reporting data consistent with company reporting.

Enterprise development:
Enterprise Projects are those projects determined by senior business management to be of critical importance to the company. These projects have the full attention of company's senior staff. They are normally managed by the Project Management Office (PMO). Enterprise projects are reported individually in plan reports. These projects by definition have company-wide impact, and are significant in cost and scope. They can change the way a company conducts its business. They are subject to a strict system development methodology, and are led by a project sponsor/champion and formal PMO project leader. They can include significant IT infrastructure type

projects in addition to major business applications systems. If the projects are directly sponsored by a business unit, allocation of resources goes to the sponsoring business unit. If the project impacts multiple business units, the project is normally charged to the sponsoring business unit and then reallocated back to the other business units. Enterprise projects can cause many resource conflicts with other, more operational type projects. Typically enterprise projects can consume as much as 45% of a company's planned IT application development staff resources.

Other work type classification considerations:

Business-owned versus IT infrastructure projects:

Projects can be classified as those in direct support of a business unit's re-quirements (the project owner is a business unit manager) and those that are designated as IT infrastructure projects (the owner is an IT manager). IT infrastructure projects are overhead. They reduce available resources for the business units. They function like projects in the municipal world where sewers, streets and utilities are available for all to use. All pay their fair share of the infrastructure utility even if they don't utilize it. The reallocation of the charges for IT infrastructure projects can be likened to the assessment of a tax in the governmental world. IT manages and owns the infrastructure work even though it is being done on behalf of the business users.

Carryover Projects:

These are projects that are active in the current year, but are expected to carry over to the next plan year. IT managers are often surprised at the number of projects that carry-over from year-to-year. It is important to highlight these projects because they have a way of "crowding out" new project work. Their presence in the current plan does not guarantee their inclusion in next year's plan. If the volume of these projects is significant, the situation may be symptomatic of some underlying planning or project management deficiencies.

Work Programs:

A *program name* provides a higher level of group reporting flexibility by reporting individual projects and non-project work items under a collective name. For example, a company could use a program name of "Investigate New Manufacturing Technologies". Projects such as "Investigate the Impact of Robotics in Automating the Production Lines", "Install Supply Change Management System", and "Investigate Impact of GPS Technology on the Transportation Division" could all be included under this program name. Grouping by program name permits the total cost of all the projects in a program to be reported. Company senior level business management doesn't always want to deal with individual projects. They sometimes require a higher level of report grouping. The use of a program name can also help manage situations in which large projects are submitted for evaluation in smaller project segments in order to disguise the larger scope of a project.

Alias project names:

Some projects and work initiatives are identified in their development stage with a name arbitrarily assigned by the project leader or programmer. These names may be changed to more formally assigned names when the project or work initiative is moved into production. An alias name can be assigned to the production name to avoid having to change all the places where the original name is encoded in systems or programs.

Project classifications are not mutually exclusive:

The project classifications just described are not mutually exclusive. In other words, an IT infrastructure project can be designated an enterprise or a tactical project. Business-owned projects can be classified as tactical or enterprise. Classification is all about scope, size, impact, and cost of the project.

CHAPTER 4

Information Technology Management Process

This chapter contains the main topic of the book. It is about 10 pages long, and represents about 5% of the book's total text. There's a message in all of this.

Information technology management is probably the most significant IT management process. Its objectives are to manage IT work and technologies in support of the company business plan objectives, and provide IT products and services to its business clients. It is driven by the company business plan and managed consistent with the model. Its components are: the company business plan; the model; the work IT performs; the work management system; and the processes of planning, resource management, costing, and service chargeback.

Its deliverables are:

- Business plan driven technology management process
- Expense reductions
- Identification of areas of operational inefficiency
- Technical and business based IT/business client partnerships
- Multi-tech business products and services delivered by multiple service options
- Plan management
- Resource management
- Cost management
- Service chargeback management
- Business client invoicing
- Operational, strategic, and information technology plan development
- Integration of IT's management and financial reporting with the company's financial and accounting procedures
- IT managed as any other business unit
- Information based computer architecture and support organization
- Work classification scheme

Too good to be true? Not in this case. If it can be imagined, it can be accomplished. "Why not?"

So what is the message alluded to in the theme statement for this chapter? A company can't just implement an information technology management process and expect to be successful. It's not chance that so much information had to be presented in the intial chapters of the book. The preliminary information relates to the initial infrastructure that must be implemented to support the development of the information technology management process. It includes the role of the company business plan; the IT management model; the work IT performs; the work classification scheme; the supporting computer architecture and organizational structure, and the other work management processes involved in the information technology management process. The remainder of the book concludes the discussions of required infrastructure. The development of an information technology management process is a significant initiative taking on the appearance of a major IT reengineering effort. If a company is not committed to developing the required infrastructure, success is highly unlikely.

Ownership

Who should own the broadly-defined technology management process? There certainly are many options to choose from, and most of these options are dependent upon the company's culture, management structure, organization, and most importantly, the availability of individuals with the proper experience and skill sets. The Chief Information Officer (CIO) is the titular owner of the overall technology management process, but as in other cases of major IT ownership issues the CIO will probably assume the role of champion and designate another individual(s) to lead the actual development and implementation of the technology management process. Suggestions of ownership are mainly conjecture because there isn't an actual company or individuals to reference.

Possible candidates to consider/eliminate from ownership are:

- Consider – Vice President of IT Systems or Vice President of IT Services
- Eliminate - External consultant since technology management process is a critical, on-going process, not a one-time review and install process
- Consider - Owner of the IT management model process if that individual is not a consultant
- Consider - Senior business manager who happens to possess the skills and traits necessary to head the technology management process
- Consider - The IT plan administrator because the planner is involved with, or aware of, most of the "moving parts" of IT. The planner knows the business plan and the vision upon which it is based; the work that must be completed to achieve business objectives; and the connections of the plan to budgeting, resource management, costing and chargeback.

- Consider- The chief IT architect seems a logical choice just from a title perspective, but is typically more involved with technical architectures and the technologies. A "just technology" view of IT is not a comprehensive enough view. There's more to technology management than technology.
- Consider – Any other individual in IT who seems to possess the proper skills and traits, and is available for reassignment

Even though ownership of technology management is referenced here as a singular matter, the technology manager requires extensive support from a variety of teams. Creation of the proper support teams will require the technology manager to be a facilitator. The support teams will most likely be the IT senior management team, IT senior technical support team, and the IT senior administrative support team. The IT teams will work closely with both the senior business management team and other business management teams to make sure IT is closely synched to the business objectives. The technology manager must also play the roles of visionary, strategist, opportunist, and architect. Ultimately technology management will involve nearly everyone in IT. It's that big. Collectively the technology manager and the various support teams will be referenced in the book as "the" technology manager. This is done for simplicity's sake in presentation of the material.

Information Technology Management Process

Establish a fit with company culture and management best practices:

One of the worst things a technology manager can do is to assume that things that worked in their past professional experiences automatically will work in their current environment. The company and IT environment and infrastructure into which technology management is implemented is often overlooked, or worse yet, not considered. Not addressing disconnects or gaps between model concepts and assumptions and the existing company's environment and culture can have a significant impact on the effectiveness of the proposed technology management solution. If the disconnects are left unresolved it can result in a technology-only approach to solving technology management issues. Merely throwing technology and money at a problem won't always provide a satisfactory solution to the problems. The gaps, and specific strategies to reduce them, must be included in the technology management plan presented to the company's senior management teams.

Develop a plan:

Since information technology management is a process, the plan to present the process should be contained in a strategic management plan worksheet developed by the process owner. The plan should initially be presented to the board of directors, the senior business management team, and the IT senior management teams. As such it should contain a statement of technology management objectives, strategies, major work initiatives, objectives, SWOT analysis, cost drivers, critical success factors, and an impact analysis of the process upon both IT and the company. It's a hybrid process as contrasted with a basic IT management process. Other components included in the process are: the company business plan; the model process; the strategic management worksheets; the work IT performs; the work management system; and the basic IT management processes of planning, resource management, costing, and service chargeback. The plan communicates what IT and the company must do to prepare for a successful implementation of the information technology management process; the cost of developing and maintaining the process; the funding strategy; the benefits; and the factors instrumental to the success of its implementation?

Selling the concept, presenting the plan:

Senior level sponsors and champions of the information technology management process plan must be identified. Relationships with these individuals must be nurtured and enhanced. Creating and implementing a major process using a new model is a very challenging task. The plan will have its skeptics whose concerns must be addressed. The information technology management process represents a major reengineering of the way IT plans and manages its work. It will significantly impact the manner in which the business units relate to IT. Business and IT management groups aren't going to "blindly" accept the proposed concept of developing a technology management process. Just the aggressive list of objectives will get a lot of attention and push back. The process is going to have to be sold to the senior business management team, select business department heads, with review by the Board of Directors. They will want to know what is "broken" in the current environment, and what solutions will the new process provide to resolve the apparent problems? There'll be many questions. Answering these questions, educating management on the concepts, and gaining buy-in to the ideas will take a lot of time and require a specific IT management marketing strategy. A good person to obtain as an ally and sell the concept to is the Chief Financial Officer (CFO). The CFO will especially like the discussions concerning proposed expense reductions.

Operational support requirements:

The operational requirements of the Information Technology Management Process are reflected in the operational requirements of the components which comprise the process. The process owner works with each of the component owners to ensure that each process component is planned and managed to achieve the Information Technology Management Process objectives. The component process owners can report to a manager other than the technology manager. They provide their management functions independent of the Information Technology Management Process. In this case a matrix organization structure can be implemented. According to Wikipedia.org "a matrix organizational structure is a company structure in which the reporting relationships are set up as a grid, or matrix, rather than in the traditional hierarchy. In other words, associates can have dual reporting relationships - generally to both a functional manager and a product manager". In the case of managing the Information Technology Management Process, the managers of planning, resource management, costing, and service chargeback are the functional managers and the technology manager is the product manager. Each company must decide on the exact reporting relationship between the Information Technology Management Process owner and the component process owners.

Strategic Management Plan Worksheet
Information Technology Management Process

Objectives:

Some of the objectives are repeated over the processes, but a particular process may have unique strategies to achieve them. Major objectives for the Information Technology Management Process are:

- Maximize the utilization of information technology resources in best achieving business plan objectives
- Increase the effectiveness of the technology products and services delivered to IT business clients.
- Achieve the business objectives within the resource limitations (budget) established for IT
- Reduce IT expenses

Strategies to Achieve Objectives:

The strategies are the action plans concerning how the Information Technology Management Process will achieve its objectives. Note that strategies can align with multiple objectives.

Maximize the utilization of information technology resources in achieving business plan objectives:

- Business plan driven
- Implement the management technique of plan alignment (focus resources)
- Information processing driven, consolidate management of technologies
- Implement the CPTOIA computer architecture

- Implement the systems and services support organization
- Balance IT technical and management functions
- Identify areas of inefficient IT operation
- Implement the management technique of staff leveraging
- Implement the management technique of gap analysis
- Implement the management technique of right-sizing
- Promote the use of a common plan model and process for both IT and the business units.

Increase the effectiveness of the technology products and services delivered to the business clients:

- Information processing driven, consolidate management of technologies
- Implement the CPTOIA computer architecture
- Implement the systems and services support organization
- Service mentality and attitude

Achieve the objectives within the resource limitations (budget) established for IT:

- Business plan driven
- Manage IT as any other business unit
- Implement the CPTOIA computer architecture
- Implement the systems and services support organization
- Support work management (i.e. planning, resource management, costing, and service chargeback)
- Emphasize architecture, ownership, responsibility, and partnership
- Balance IT technical and management functions
- Identify areas of inefficient IT operation
- Distribute expense and revenue responsibility to the IT managers
- Form working relationships with company accounting and financial reporting

Reduce IT expenses:

- Successful implementation of the strategies will result in a substantial reduction in expenses.

Strengths, weaknesses, opportunities, and threats (SWOT):

Because the "best company" is the same for each process, the SWOT analysis for this process will not be repeated here. Reference chapter 2, *IT Management Model, Strategic Management Plan Worksheet to Develop and*

Manage the IT Management Model Process for the details of the "best company" SWOT analysis.

Cost drivers:

If implemented properly this process should result in reduced expense levels and improved service.

Deliverables:

Reference the list of process deliverables in the beginning of this chapter. The list is quite significant.

Critical success factors:

What event(s) must occur or strategies be successfully completed in order for the process to achieve its objectives?

- Buy-in by all major partners to the IT management model concepts
- Ownership and responsibility allocated for all management functions
- Acquire skills and training necessary to implement required concepts and facilities
- Successful implementation of the CPTOIA architecture
- Successful implementation of the systems and services organization
- Successful implementation of the information processing concept
- Successful execution of the required IT work

Management Function Impact Analysis:

Business plan management:

A process should align with the business objectives listed in the summary business plan example presented in chapter 1. This process aligns with, and is supportive of, the following business objectives listed in the summary business plan example.

- Continuous improvement initiatives
- Effective organizational structures
- Cost awareness
- Plan driven
- Embrace Quality
- Empower staff
- Career development opportunities
- Fair compensation
- Increase skills and training opportunities
- Exceed expectations
- Customer-focused solutions

- Cost effective products
- Bottom-line oriented
- Financial awareness
- Cost management
- Introduce new technologies and systems in support of business plan

Process management:

The Information Technology Management Process will be developed by the leadership of the technology manager working with the IT senior management team, the IT senior technical support team, the IT senior administrative support team, select members of the senior business management team, and departmental/divisional business management teams. The process will impact all areas of the company that provide and use IT products and services.

IT Financial management:

Impact at the IT financial management layer is basically the same as described for the Develop and Manage the IT Management Process. For this process the issue is more about implementation of the strategies and work initiatives to make it all happen.

Plan management, resource management, cost management, and service chargeback management:

The process owner has determined that plan management, resource management, cost management, and service chargeback management are major components of this process. These management processes are described in detail in chapters 6, 7, and 8.

IT general management, leadership, and organization management function:

IT associates will add a business dimension to their technical image. There will be a continued movement towards a more distributed management style. The systems and services organizational structure will support an information processing capability by managing the technologies of data, voice, text, and image under a common organizational structure. CPTOIA architecture, besides supporting a critical technology requirement, will provide opportunities for career enhancement and improvements in staff morale

Application management:

The computer platform, technology, organization independent architecture (CPTOIA) will have a major impact on business application systems delivery and operations. The supporting systems and services organizational structure will impact the manner in which the applications are developed and serviced.

Business application systems can now be developed as true information systems, not just data systems, by including in the systems design the integration of data, voice, text, and image technologies. Business clients will be provided more comprehensive solutions to their business requirements. System designers must reengineer their design skills, and become knowledgeable in the concepts of information processing.

Client Relationship (Service) management:

Business clients will definitely be impacted by the implementation of the Information Technology Management Process. Its introduction will fundamentally change the way business clients interact with IT and the products and services they access and use. Each service area will have to determine the exact impact.

Architecture management:

The computer platform, technology, and organization independent architecture (CPTOIA) will definitely impact this management function layer. It basically overhauls the entire technical base of IT. Other architectural issues driven by this process's influence are an increased emphasis on developing a formal business systems application architecture, and a project or work architecture.

End user computing management, technology management, systems software management, database management, hardware (operations) management, and communications and networking management:

The model is based upon the importance of implementing the computer platform, technology, and organization independent architecture (CPTOIA) and its support organization. The requirement to support this architecture will be significant at these management function layers. The impact in these areas is probably best stated by the owners of each of these functions. At a minimum, the type of products they deliver, the manner in which they interact with the business clients, the way they are organized, and the way they manage their areas of responsibility will all be impacted.

Staff education, training, and skills management:

The implementation of the Information Technology Management Process requires a significant reengineering of skills, especially in the areas of the CPTOIA architecture; its supporting systems and services organization; knowledge of company financial management practices and reports; information processing concepts; and the use of modeling techniques in managing technology. Other major training initiatives involve developing better IT/business client relationships, and training in the concepts and impact of service chargeback.

Potential impact on other management functions:

Use this section to solicit the potential impact of the new process on the process operation of the other management function process owners.

CHAPTER 5

Work Management System

The work management system is the information technology management process engine. It manages the IT base work functions of planning, costing, service chargeback, and resource management which enable the achievement of the process objectives. Work is managed in what is referred to as the "work management loop". It begins with the budgeted expenses maintained in a company's accounting and financial reporting systems; it flows through the IT costing, planning, resource management, and service chargeback functions; and it ends in the company's accounting and financial reporting systems with the posting of IT financial transactions to the IT and business client account ledgers.

The IT work management system ensures that the work (i.e. projects, tactical enhancements, production support, system maintenance, etc.) required to achieve the objectives of the company business plan are planned, costed, resource managed, and billed to the IT clients. It is a major component of the Information Technology Management Process. It is a system architecture which includes four tightly integrated sub-systems - planning, costing, resource management, and service chargeback. These sub-systems operate in an IT work management "loop" that begins and ends in the company's financial reporting systems. Note that these sub-systems are basic IT management processes.

What distinguishes these four management processes, and why they are included in the Information Technology Management Process, is their primary purpose is to manage work. The other management functions included in the model are more involved with the development and delivery of IT products and services, or in providing ancillary support services.

Figure 14 illustrates a graphic depiction of the work management "loop". The company's financial systems provide the initial IT expense budgets (expense management) to start the "loop". They set the bounds within which IT must develop and manage its work. The simple objective is that IT must recover all its expenses through the deployment and utilization of its resources. The *cost* management process identifies the cost components that comprise the IT products and services; assigns both the IT direct and indirect expenses to each product and service from the expense budgets; and determines the number of IT product units available to perform planned work. From this data a unit cost rate is calculated for each IT product and service. *Planning* is initiated by the plan development process which identifies and organizes next year's planned work; determines the products and services required to

Figure 14 Graphically displays the work management loop.

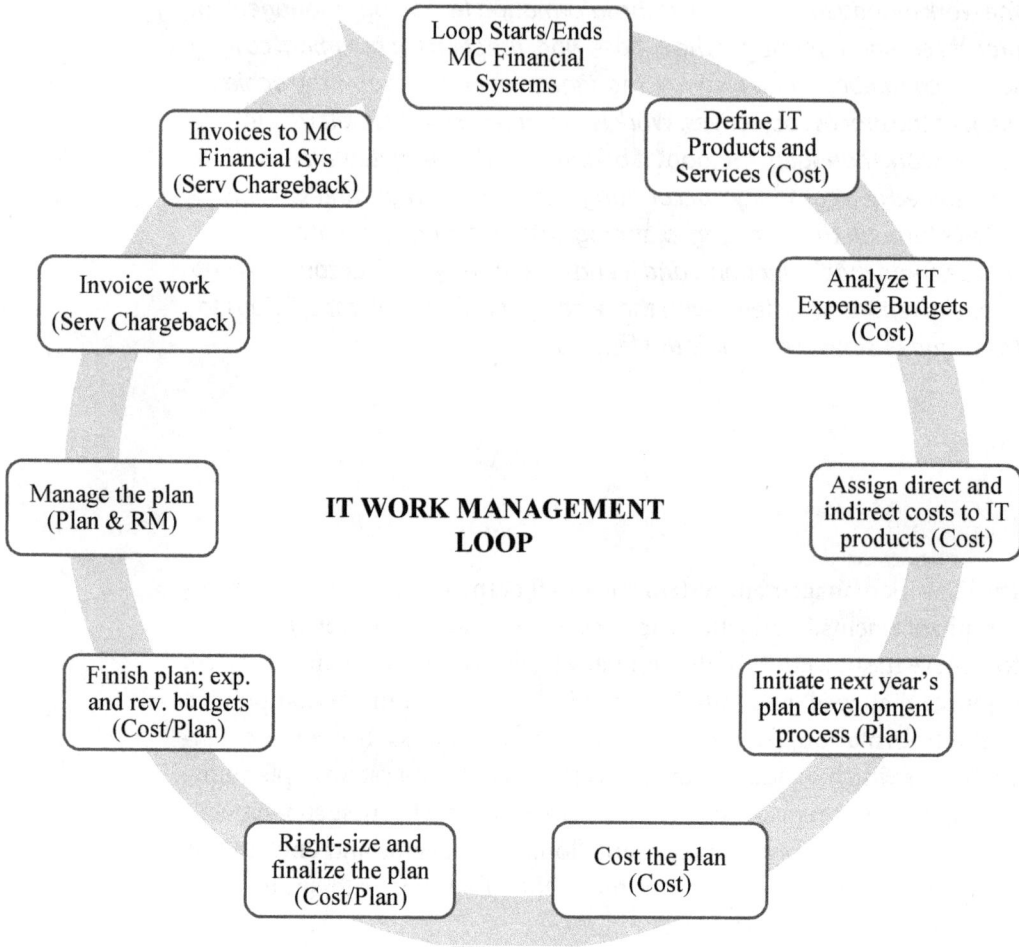

deliver the work; costs the work; assigns the work to the IT business clients; and finally right-sizes, approves, publishes, and implements next year's final IT plan. Next year's IT expense and revenue budgets are based upon the new plan. These budgets are posted to the company's financial reporting systems. The planning resource management processes manage the plan in next year's production cycle to ensure the plan is delivered, on-time and within budget. The *service chargeback* management process reports actual utilization of the IT products, and charges back (i.e. invoices) the business clients for the work performed on their behalf. Invoices generated by service chargeback are imported into the company's financial reporting systems completing the loop. Both IT revenue and expense are now in the company's financial reporting systems allowing IT and business units to manage IT's revenue and expense in the same financial reporting systems, and in the same manner in which they manage all their other financial transactions. This marriage of the IT financial management systems to the company's financial reporting systems is a significant achievement.

Ownership

The question of ownership of the work management system is sometimes difficult to determine. Three components (cost, service chargeback, and the interface with the company financial systems are clearly under the ownership of the IT financial manager; therefore, the recommended choice of ownership of the system is the IT financial manager. Without specific individuals to address, specific recommendations are difficult to make. Clearly the IT financial manager should partner closely with the planner, and the various IT senior management, technical, and administrative teams. Business managers will play a significant role in this system because they are a basic user of its services.

IT Work Management System

System classification:

Architecturally the work management system is best classified as a cybernetic system. As defined by Whatis.com, "cybernetics" is the science or study of control or regulation mechanisms in human and machine systems, including computers. The system is designed to maximize the effective use of IT resources in order to satisfy the planned resource requirements of a company's business plan. It monitors resource cost and business client utilization of the resources to make sure that costs and revenue are staying within the bounds of the expense and revenue budgets. The system continually monitors for variances between planned resource requirements and resource availability, and between expense and revenue. It attempts to resolve the variances by reporting them to IT management for corrective action. It must constantly react to variances in order to remain within IT resource limits.

The system, through its four sub-systems, maintains both IT strategic and operational information. The strategic information items are the visions, objectives, and strategies which were developed from the strategic management plan worksheets. The operational information contains the detail work and projects that enable the delivery of the objectives and strategies. Without the ability to link work to strategic management objectives and strategies the system would be just a system of projects. It can be linked, and share information with, select company legacy systems (e.g. the project management, payroll, human resources, accounting, and budgeting systems). This sharing of information increases the system's functionality; provides value-added information to the legacy systems; and increases data integrity of all the systems so integrated.

From a business application perspective, the system is likened to a *project portfolio management system*. A project portfolio management system is both system software and a set of management practices that facilitates the selection and management of the projects and work initiatives that best enable the company to achieve its vision and business objectives within the constraints of the company's technology budget. Sound familiar?

Company considerations:

A company considering installation of a robust portfolio management system, or some other type of work management system, needs to answer the questions - Does the company require such a system? Can it afford to acquire/build and maintain the system? Can it fully utilize the capabilities of such a system? Does the company and IT have the aptitude, experience, and skills required to effectively operate the system? Will the existing management practices, organization, and systems environment into which the system would be introduced support the system? Will the business and IT resources required to support and maintain such a system be available? A project portfolio management, or like system, can cost hundreds of thousands of dollars to acquire, and it can generate significant system support and maintenance costs. All these requirements and constraints impact the success of a system implementation. What works for one company, may not work for another company. There are few perfect system solutions.

For whatever reason, some companies that are not positioned from a company or IT management perspective to implement such high-powered systems attempt to implement them anyway. The system gets installed, but the anticipated positive results associated with its implementation are never fully realized. The point to be made is that merely throwing technology and money at a problem won't always provide a satisfactory solution to your work management requirements. The key to achieving a positive system implementation is to know your resource limitations; clearly establish the problems that need to be solved; establish specific implementation objectives; and prepare the environment into which the system will be installed and maintained.

Tightly integrated system:

The development of the overall system, and each sub-system, places importance on cooperative development, management, and operation of the system. Cost management has to cost the products and services that the IT system developers use to build their systems or complete their projects. Planning needs to know how the products and services will be combined to deliver the work that has been planned. Service chargeback needs to bill for the IT products and services the business client utilizes. These products must be billed at the rates agreed upon by the cost manager and the various IT providers of the IT products and services. Finally, IT must interface with the company's financial systems to complete the cycle. Sounds complicated, but it isn't.

System development considerations:

The system has an architecture which integrates the sub-systems of planning, resource management, costing, and service chargeback. Any development work is performed on the sub-systems using normal system development methodologies. Any proposed system changes must be approved by the system owner.

System operational considerations:

Production support and regular system maintenance is provided to the system by the normal operational support teams assigned to the system.

Production Cycle:

The system production cycle has a daily, monthly, quarterly, and yearly processing cycle. Posting of information to the system can occur on a daily basis. Time entry and the maintenance of timesheets comprise most of the daily activity. Service chargeback is most active at the end of each month and at year end. Other monthly reporting can be provided dependent on IT and company requirements. IT product and services costing occurs throughout the year as new product and services are added, but the majority of costing activity takes place just prior to, and during, the plan development process. Most IT and business unit management reports are produced on a quarterly basis. During the annual plan development process there is a heavy demand for all types of ad hoc (i.e. unscheduled) reports to support planning efforts.

Legacy system connections:

The system connections to company legacy systems are a very important part of the overall IT architecture. These connections enhance the information content and integrity of the system. Each company will most probably have a variety of legacy systems and configurations.

Examples of legacy systems considered for integration and their potential use within a work management system type architecture are:

- Project Management System (PMS), targeted to manage, initiate, and track planned projects
- Payroll/Human Resources system, targeted to supply supplemental associate information, and provide a control function for associate file maintenance
- Help Desk Service Request System, targeted to initiate and track planned work related to production problems, incident reporting, and miscellaneous service requests
- Work Request Management System, targeted to initiate and track planned work related to tactical projects and system enhancement work requests
- Accounting/Budgeting systems, targeted to exchange budget and financial information.

CHAPTER 6

Cost Management

"Cost management is one of the most powerful information weapons with which you can arm IT management. It gets business management's attention and provides a solid base for making technical decisions. If you don't value the cost of a product, what incentive is there to take care of it and utilize it wisely?"

Cost Management is a very powerful management tool. It arms IT managers with information that augments technical analysis and decision making. Cost management identifies and assigns IT expenses as recorded in the company financial reporting systems to the cost components of the IT products and services IT sells to its business clients. It assigns these expenses in order to determine the total cost of each product or service. Cost management is one of the first IT management functions that must be addressed in developing and managing the work management system. Costing uses the model and its concept of management function layers to ensure that each management function manager knows the proper products and services to use in recovering the expenses related to the operation of their particular management function. Use of the management function layer concept also ensures that all the IT managers are using the same products and costs.

Ownership

Most IT departments of the size to install a formal cost management function probably have an IT financial manager who is a member of the CIO's staff. This individual is a part of the IT senior management team, and works as a team member in planning, resource management, and service chargeback. If there is no such person on the IT staff, then someone in the company's accounting department should be assigned dual responsibility for this function with a manager in IT appointed by the Chief Information Officer (CIO). In either scenario the IT individual assigned responsibility for the cost management function should have an associate in the company accounting department who will partner with them.

The cost manager must definitely have the mindset of a chemist and an architect. A major part of building the cost management function is to identify the various elements (cost components) and the manner in which they are architected to build the compounds (IT products). Some imagination is required to assist the IT managers to view their products in unique ways, but significant visionary skills aren't required. There is an element of strategy involved in the manner in which costs are developed, and the cost manager definitely should be able to facilitate the interaction of managers and associates in the resolution of cost issues. The cost manager is an opportunist who uses reports of excessive costs to isolate areas of ineffective IT product utilization.

Some Basic Terms, Concepts and Approaches

Difference between cost determination and cost allocation:

Cost determination is the assignment of expenses to a product or service. Normally the cost of a product or service is charged directly to the business client who exclusively utilizes a product or service. Cost allocation is an accounting procedure. It doesn't affect the cost of a product or service. It allocates the cost of a shared product or service, or the cost of a product or service in which multiple business clients share in the benefits of its operation with other organizational entities. Allocations can be based on some simple, equitable formula, or a sophisticated algorithm. Sophisticated cost allocation procedures are often used to spread the utilization of online systems that are concurrently used by multiple users

Putting things in perspective:

Voltaire is quoted as saying that "The perfect is the enemy of the good". There's a lot of truth in that statement. The book takes a reasonable and practical approach to the development of the cost management function. A company doesn't have to delve deeply in the theoretical aspects of costing to gain significant returns on their investment in cost management. Significant results can be achieved with a practical approach. The primary focus of the book is about technology management, not accounting methods.

Standard cost accounting versus other costing options:

A standard costing system, which is based upon budgeted or anticipated expenses, is at the basis of the costing methods used in the book. Instead of using a standard costing system, some companies accumulate monthly expenses into one cost center, and allocate all the expense to the business units on some equitable percentage basis. This manner of cost allocation defeats the purpose of using cost management as a management tool used to reduce company expense and improve overall efficiency. It treats the process as an accounting tool, not a management tool. Such a system is not a cost system, but an expense allocation system.

Personal computer - an unshared desktop computer or a shared computer server:

The book's reference to a personal computer as a PC denotes it as an unshared, desktop computer. A personal computer referenced as a server in a client/server network denotes it as shared computer server.

Cost, plan, and budget periods:

The terms *cost*, *plan*, and *budget periods* are frequently used. In the standard cost method presented herein, costs, plans, and budgets for a given year all reference the same period of time.

Billable units, productive units, and unit capacity:

Billable units are the same as productive units. Billable units tend to be used in discussions of the planning, resource management, and service chargeback processes. Productive units are used in cost management. Both are net unit numbers calculated by reducing the total number of units a product produces in a given period by the units that are unbillable or unproductive (i.e. scrap, inefficiencies, paid-time-off, or units utilized by IT).

Capacity is just another term to indicate the maximum number of productive or billable units a particular IT product or service can generate in a given period of time. It is most often used in relationship to computers and other types of equipment.

Relationship of IT Expense Budget, Costs, and Plan:

Costing starts with an analysis of IT expense budgets reported by the company's financial reporting system at the beginning of a fiscal year. The expense budgets are the cost basis of the IT plan currently in effect. Expense budgets and the plans "go hand-in-hand". The costing objective is to allocate the entire IT expense budget to the defined IT products and services, and plan the utilization of these products by the IT business clients in order to recover the IT expense budgets. As the next year's plan is developed, the expense budget evolves accordingly to reflect changes in the plan's utilization of the IT products. Costs must be adjusted to reflect expense and plan changes. When next year's plan is finalized, next year's IT expense budget, costs, and the plan should all be in synch.

Cost Management Process

Figure 15 illustrates a summary overview of the costing process. The process starts with the company financials. The IT products and services are defined,

Figure 15 Overview of the Cost Management Process

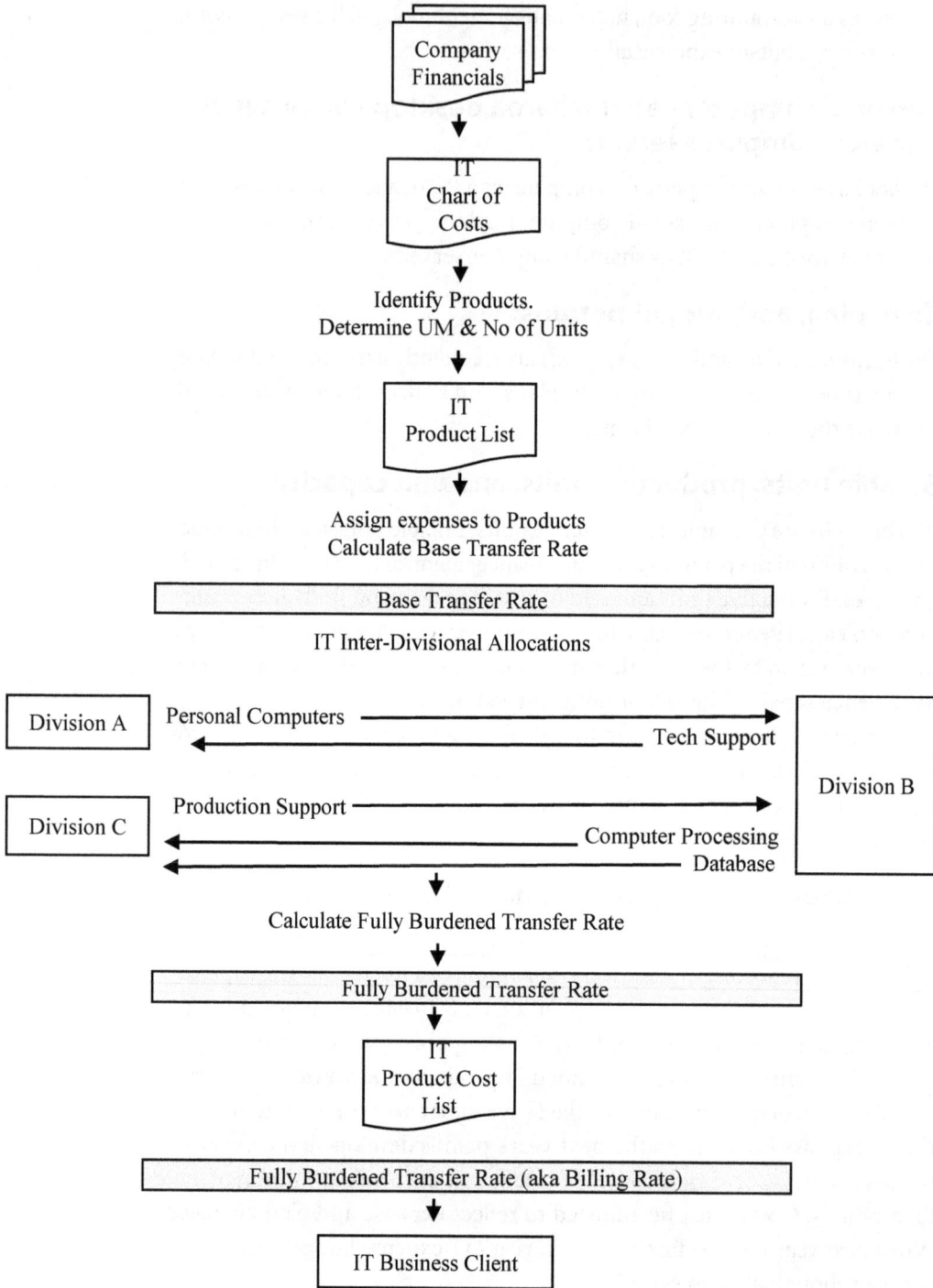

```
                          Company
                          Financials
                              │
                              ▼
                             IT
                          Chart of
                           Costs
                              │
                              ▼
                      Identify Products.
                  Determine UM & No of Units
                              │
                              ▼
                             IT
                         Product List
                              │
                              ▼
                   Assign expenses to Products
                   Calculate Base Transfer Rate
```

| Base Transfer Rate |

IT Inter-Divisional Allocations

Division A	Personal Computers ────────────────────►	
	◄──────────────────────── Tech Support	
		Division B
Division C	Production Support ─────────────────────►	
	◄──────────── Computer Processing	
	◄──────────────────── Database	

```
                              ▼
                   Calculate Fully Burdened Transfer Rate
                              ▼
```

| Fully Burdened Transfer Rate |

```
                              ▼
                             IT
                         Product Cost
                            List
```

| Fully Burdened Transfer Rate (aka Billing Rate) |

```
                              ▼
                       IT Business Client
```

and the expenses are allocated to the products. A unit of measure and the number of productive units a product can produce in the cost period are determined. Dividing the product expense by the productive units produces a base transfer rate. Each IT division allocates costs to each other using the base transfer rate and the IT inter-divisional allocation process as the vehicle to transfer the costs. The IT inter-divisional allocations represent the support costs provided to each division by another IT division. The IT inter-divisional allocation costs, when added to the base expense budgets of a division, equals the fully burdened cost of operating a particular division. Dividing the fully burdened cost of operating a division by the standard number of productive units produces a fully burden transfer rate which is used by the division to bill its business clients for product utilization.

Define IT products and cost components:

Each IT manager who owns a budget needs to work with the cost manager to define the IT products and services that they develop, deliver, and support. Figure 16, *Sample IT Product List*, illustrates an example of a limited product list. Products and services must be costed and assigned a client billing rate. Each IT manager is responsible for recovering the total expense of their budget by billing their clients for utilization of their products and services. Both a costing and product pricing strategy for each IT product or service must be carefully developed upfront in the costing process. This is where the cost manager plays the role of a product chemist (identifying the cost components) and the role of the architect (assembling the cost components into products and services). If a division has no business client products, and is considered overhead division, the division must ensure its expenses are fully allocated to other IT divisions that have products and services.

Assign expense to IT products:

Each new budget year the IT manager who has an expense budget must allocate their annual IT budgeted expenses to their individual IT products and services. These expenses will be used as a part of a calculation to determine a standard cost for each of the division's products and services. The entire process is overseen by the IT financial manager, but each manager must internalize this process into their monthly activities. Once the annual budget has been analyzed and the initial standard costs have been determined, it is the responsibility of each IT division manager to monitor the company's monthly financial reporting system to determine if there are any unanticipated expenses, or any changes in existing expenses, which are not reflected in the initial standard cost rates. When variances occur, and assuming the variance is significant enough to appreciably change the current standard costs, the IT manager and the cost manager must work together in addressing the situation.

A cost structure should be established so that expenses can be consistently classified and allocated to products. The manner in which IT classifies expenses for cost management purposes will vary among companies. The cost structure used in this book is based upon a mixture of IT experience,

Figure 16 *Sample IT Product List* **illustrates a sample of a limited product list**

Information Technology Department 20XX Sample Product List		
Product	Unit of Measure	Rate Per Unit
Application Systems Software		
IT Developed Systems	Staff hours	$$$/Hour
	Dev computer proc	$$$/Hour
3rd Party Acquired Systems	Staff hours	$$$/Hour
	Dev computer proc	$$$/Hour
	Application software	Cost of software
	Vendor support	$$$/Hour
System Staff Services		
Design & Program	Staff hours	$$$/Hour
Enhance	Staff hours	$$$/Hour
Demand Reports	Staff hours	$$$/Hour
Tactical Projects	Staff hours	$$$/Hour
Enterprise Projects	Staff hours	$$$/Hour
Production Services		
Application Production Support	Staff hours	$$$/Housr
Application Required Maintenance	Staff hours	$$$/Housr
Customer Support	Staff hours	$$$/Housr
PC Support	Staff Hours	$$$/Hours
Technical Consulting	Staff Hours	$$$/Hours
Computer Processing		
CPU Time	CPU Minutes	$$$/Min
Main Memory	Memory/Time	$$$/Min/Memory
Input	No. of Inputs	$$$/per Input
Output	No. of Outputs	$$$/Per Output
Channels	No. Commands	$$$/Per Command
External Storage	Residency	$$$/Storage/Time
Onlibe Business Transaction System	No. Transactions	$$$$/No, Transactions
Development Computer processinging	Hours	$$$/Hours
Pass-Thru Expense		
Equipment	Each	Quotation
Training	Each	Quotation
Other	Each	Quotation

standard costing techniques, and references to cost definitions contained in such websites as Wikipedia and Investopedia. The way costs are defined and applied to cost components can vary among companies. Differences in costing techniques across companies makes comparative cost studies difficult to analyze. With that said, Figure 17 represents the basic cost structure used in the book.

Figure 17 Base Cost Structure

IT Cost Types

Direct Costs: These costs are directly attributable to the creation of the IT product or service.

> *Staff Expenses:* Salaries, salary taxes, benefits

> *Non-Staff Expenses*: Any equipment, software, facilities, etc. directly attributable to a product or service.

Indirect Costs: These costs are not directly attributable to the creation of the IT product. Indirect costs are sometimes referred to as overhead costs. Indirect costs are typically allocated to the product on some equitable basis.

> *Non-Staff Expenses:* These costs relate to the costs of system development software, travel, employment fees, moving expenses for staff, office equip, supplies, general training & education etc.

> *Non-IT divisional overhead expense*: These costs relate to such items as security, power, utilities, and office space, legal services, and are typically allocated from other, non-IT company departments.

> *IT inter-divisional support cost allocations:* These are the costs allocated for support services received from other IT divisions. The majority of these allocations relate to staff support services, but can also be for computer processing services, general training, and consulting, etc.

Pass-thru expenses: These are expense items incurred on behalf of a specific business client, and for a particular purpose. They are directly expensed (passed-thru) to the client's accounting ledgers via IT service chargeback. They are not included in any rate calculations. They can include such expense items as the acquisition of third-party business application software, specialized training for business users, and specialized computer equipment, etc.

It is assumed that the budgets and other company financial reports used in the expense assignment process are as they existed at the beginning of the current year. Standard costs are normally calculated at the beginning of each new fiscal year. At this time the budget, plan, and costs should all be in synch. The budget contains all expenses budgeted directly to the division, including any overhead expenses charged by non-IT divisions for such things as office space, utilities, security, etc. Pass-thru expenses are not included in any rate calculations, but must be noted so that they can be charged directly to the business unit which requests the product. IT is acting merely as a "caretaker" of the IT budget in the instance of a pass-thru expenses.

If some budgeted expenses are not listed on expense budgets or other financial reporting system reports at a level of detail required to allocate the expenses to a particular IT product, the IT manager must seek more detailed information sources to allocate the expense. This situation normally occurs with budget expenses for large computer equipment purchases. For example, the budget expense for a large computer could be $2,000,000, but from an IT costing perspective the expense needs to be broken-down to the IT sub-component products of central processor, channels, and/or the various input and out devices. Alternative sources of this more detailed information are the original equipment purchase order, or a call to the vendor of the product.

Determine productive units for each IT product and service:

Staff products or services:

Staff expenses are assigned a *unit of measure* (UM) of hours. The number of *productive* hours that an associate can generate in a given costing period are the hours the associate records to all work types except *Inefficiency* and *Paid-Time-Off (PTO)*. Productive units (net hours available) is a key number used in developing an associate's cost and billing rate, not total hours available (i.e. gross hours). The best source of this staff information is a review and analysis of IT's time reporting system, if one is available. Without a time reporting system, you'll have to improvise either by doing extensive interviews with IT managers and associates, or by creating staff profiles. The model company discussed in Book 2 reverted to the use of profiles because the model company, being a fictitious company, had no supporting time entry data. The profiles do not demand that much of a compromise in cost integrity since the profiles develop a standard set of productive units, and cost standards are what IT is trying to manage. Profiles allow IT to start from "scratch", and establish standards to which they want to manage.

Since the cost of an associates' time is based upon a standard number of productive hours worked per costing period, associates who record hours in excess of the established standard hours, yet do not receive overtime compensation for such work, can cause a costing and billing issue that has to be resolved. Resolution of this billing issue can have an adverse effect upon an associate's work habits if not properly resolved. It's right that IT managers encourage their associates to work hard and do whatever it takes to get the job done, but in the instance of overtime and standard costing, the work ethic and the costing best practice can become conflicted. The standard costing practice needs to accommodate this situation. Either pay the overtime; provide compensatory time-off; eliminate overtime work; or continue the practice and charge the time to some type of variance account. This example again illustrates the point that costing and service chargeback can have a significant impact on IT behavior and performance. It also illustrates the point that IT wants costing to isolate areas requiring management action.

Shared computers and other equipment:

A computer's unit of measure (UM) and the number of productive units (aka *capacity*) it can produce in a given costing period will vary depending upon how the cost components of the computer product are decomposed, if at all. If the computer product is viewed and costed by its sub-components of central processing unit (aka CPU); main memory; input; output;

channels (aka bus); and external storage, then a unique UM and number of productive units must be calculated for each sub-component. The sub-components can be decomposed even further if that achieves costing objectives. For example, external storage could be expanded to include tape/cartridge, disk, and imaging. Output could be decomposed into printed reports, microfiche, or online report viewing. The decomposition of cost components can go even further if the cost manager wants to cost storage and memory usage activity by actual access of the storage component (*number of inputs and outputs*) and the time the storage component is occupied (*residency*). On the other hand, a cost manager could just say computer cost is so inexpensive that it will be singularly costed including all its components. It all depends upon what objectives are established for cost management.

If the option is taken to cost at the component level, then the cost manager will require significant assistance from the technical service support teams. Equipment utilization (especially computer utilization) statistics are produced as a normal course of equipment operation. Computers love to report on their activities, all of them. Reports are normally used to assist the technical support staff in isolating areas of inefficient use of the computers. Additionally these reports can be used to provide the cost manager with unit data they need to develop unit cost rates.

A *theoretical* calculation of a computer's capacity to generate productive units for its sub-components is almost impossible to calculate because of limitations that may be imposed by IT's particular implementation of a computer in the current computer environment. Some companies use what is referred to as a *relative capacity* to accommodate these implementation specific limitations. Under the relative capacity scenario the capacity to produce productive units is established at a level the product has been witnessed to produce under the current configuration.

Special consideration should be given to the concept of *scrap factors* when establishing the number of productive units. IT is in the business of manufacturing products and services, and in any manufacturing operation, not all products produced are usable by the business client. In IT, "scrap" is normally created by the requirement to rerun computer systems because of some IT error. It could be caused by a program going into a logic loop, a "bug" created in a critical program, or an equipment failure in the middle of a production job. An estimate of "scrap" needs to be made for each of the IT components that have been identified for cost determination. This number reduces the number of productive units used in calculating a rate. IT shouldn't bill its business clients directly for "scrap", but they can't "eat the cost" either, so the scrapped units are recovered by charging a higher rate for the productive units. The scrap factor is normally established for each product as a percent of the total units produced, and is usually based on experience. The scrap factor percent can be viewed as a measure of IT effectiveness in the development and delivery of its products. Be careful in establishing the percent used in costing because it has the ability to create significant variances between actual cost and the charge billed to the client.

Computers also perform IT internal housekeeping work. Jobs are run which backup operating systems and business application databases. They perform system administration jobs which maintain system tables and control files. Some jobs are run to provide computer resources which support the development and testing of new systems and programs. There are security jobs, disaster recovery jobs, and many other internal support jobs that are run for IT purposes. The sum total of the computer resources used for these internal functions can be very significant. They can't be directly charged to the business clients, nor to IT acting as its own client. Most of these computer resources are allocated to various IT products or services and become part of the products and services burdened billing rate. For example, backups of the operating systems and system utilities are allocated to the CPU cost component of the computer. The allocation of these resources is accomplished via the *IT inter-divisional cost allocations*. The computer resources that aren't billed to a product or service are referenced as non-billable jobs which reduce the overall productive units used in the calculation of a product's rate, and thereby increase the billing rate to business clients.

Calculate the base transfer rate:

Once the budgeted expenses have been assigned to the products and services, and the productive units have been calculated for each product, a base transfer rate can be calculated for each product by dividing the product's budgeted expense by the product's productive units. This rate is used to enable an allocation of expenses for resources provided by one division to other IT divisions in support of their operations. The base transfer rate at this stage of the process is considered to be a division's initial billing rate.

Calculate IT inter-divisional cost allocations:

Calculation of the final base transfer rates for all IT products and services initiates the IT inter-divisional cost allocation process. These allocations represent the costs associated with the services and support IT units provide to each other. The support resources can be any product or service a division provides. Inter-divisional cost allocations can be viewed as an "internal billing" of IT products among IT support units. They do not affect the division's direct salary expense budgets, or the base transfer rate. They function to burden a division's overall budget to reflect a division's fully burdened cost of operating their division.

Planning can assist in the determination and calculation of these inter-divisional cost allocations because planning contains the associates' plans for general support work provided to the other IT units and cost centers. An inter-divisional cost allocation can be calculated for the associates in each IT unit by multiplying the number of planned hours in their general support work categories by the base transfer rate of the IT unit. The client in the case of these inter-divisional cost allocations is the IT unit receiving the support service. Work related to specific projects or work items owned by another IT unit are not included in these inter-divisional cost allocations because this type of work is charged directly to a specific project or work item.

These inter-divisional cost allocations, when allocated to an IT unit's expense budget, increase the transfer rate for services provided to IT business clients, and they provide a truer cost of what it takes to operate a particular IT division. The costs allocations not only apply to staff expenses, but are equally applicable to non-staff expenses. The new transfer rate is referenced as the fully burdened transfer rate, or billing rate, for the IT unit.

Calculate business client billing rates:

The billing rates are used to create an IT division's charges to business units for the utilization of their IT products and services. The rates are higher than the base transfer rates because they include the IT inter-divisional cost allocations. Billing rates can be a blended or unblended rate. A blended billing rate is the average of billing rates within, or across, IT organizational units such as departments, divisions, groups, and teams, etc. Using a blended IT departmental rate is a common practice for many companies in the early stages of cost management implementation. It's much less complicated, and it tends to create less controversy with the business units. A caveat of using a blended departmental rate is that it can hide individual areas of high cost and inefficient operations. An unblended rate (i.e. individual rate) is based upon a particular associate's fully burdened expense. Associates who are billed at an unblended rate are isolated from the general population of associates based upon special skills and knowledge the associate possesses.

Products and Services Requiring Special Consideration

The following products require special mention because of their extensive use, priority, complexity, unique processing requirements, and cost. Three such products will be discussed: computer processing; interactive or online systems; and personal computers (PCs).

Computer processing:

Computer processing as an IT product deserves special mention because it represents one of the most complex, expensive, and pervasive of the IT products. It is a product that is used by nearly every IT division, business unit, and associate in a company. The term computer processing describes the work the computers perform on behalf of the multitude of jobs submitted to the computer. Jobs are a collection of computer programs that instruct the computer to perform a specific business function or task.

Computer processing is a composite IT product consisting of the computer hardware, the operating systems and system utilities, the power, security and physical environment in which the computer is housed, backup and disaster recovery capabilities, and any ancillary supplies and equipment the computer requires. The staff required to operate and maintain the computers are not directly expensed to the computer processing product, but are all allocated to it as a part of the inter-divisional cost allocation process. The bad news is that costing computer processing requires the capture of voluminous amounts of processing statistics to measure its utilization. The good news is that computers track and report these processing statistics for IT.

Computer Classes:
Computer processing is typically a product of IT's computer operations division. The book identifies three computer processing products within the IT operations division. Some companies define more computer processing products, others less. These computer products are consistent with three types of computer classes (aka computer platforms) commonly used in IT. The three computer classes are:

- Tier1 computers (mainframe class computers)
- Personal computers (PCs)
- Client/server network.

Shared and Unshared Computers:
Within each class the computers are further classified as shared or unshared computers. The designation unshared basically treats the computer as having one owner. Unshared computers are normally treated as a pass-thru expense requiring no rate calculation. Unshared computers can belong to any of the three classes. The most obvious example of an unshared computer is the desktop personal computer (PC) even though a PC can be used as a shared computer when it is utilized as a network server device which allows multiple users to share its services. The shared computer designation relates to a computer which can be used concurrently by multiple clients. References to a PC in the following discussions relate to an unshared desktop PC.

Because a computer is shared, a rate must be developed, and a measure of client utilization determined, so that a user's utilization of the computer can be tracked and invoiced. The large and most powerful computers in a company (Tier 1 computers) are very expensive and are typically utilized as shared computers because of their cost, power, and capacity. The entire client/server network can be collectively considered by IT as a singular shared computer facility. It can even be viewed as a differently configured mainframe computer.

Figure 18 illustrates a view of the three computer classes consistent with the Model's assumption that each of these computer classes are functionally alike in that they have the same basic components of a central processing

Figure 18 Architecture of the three major classes of computers used in costing.

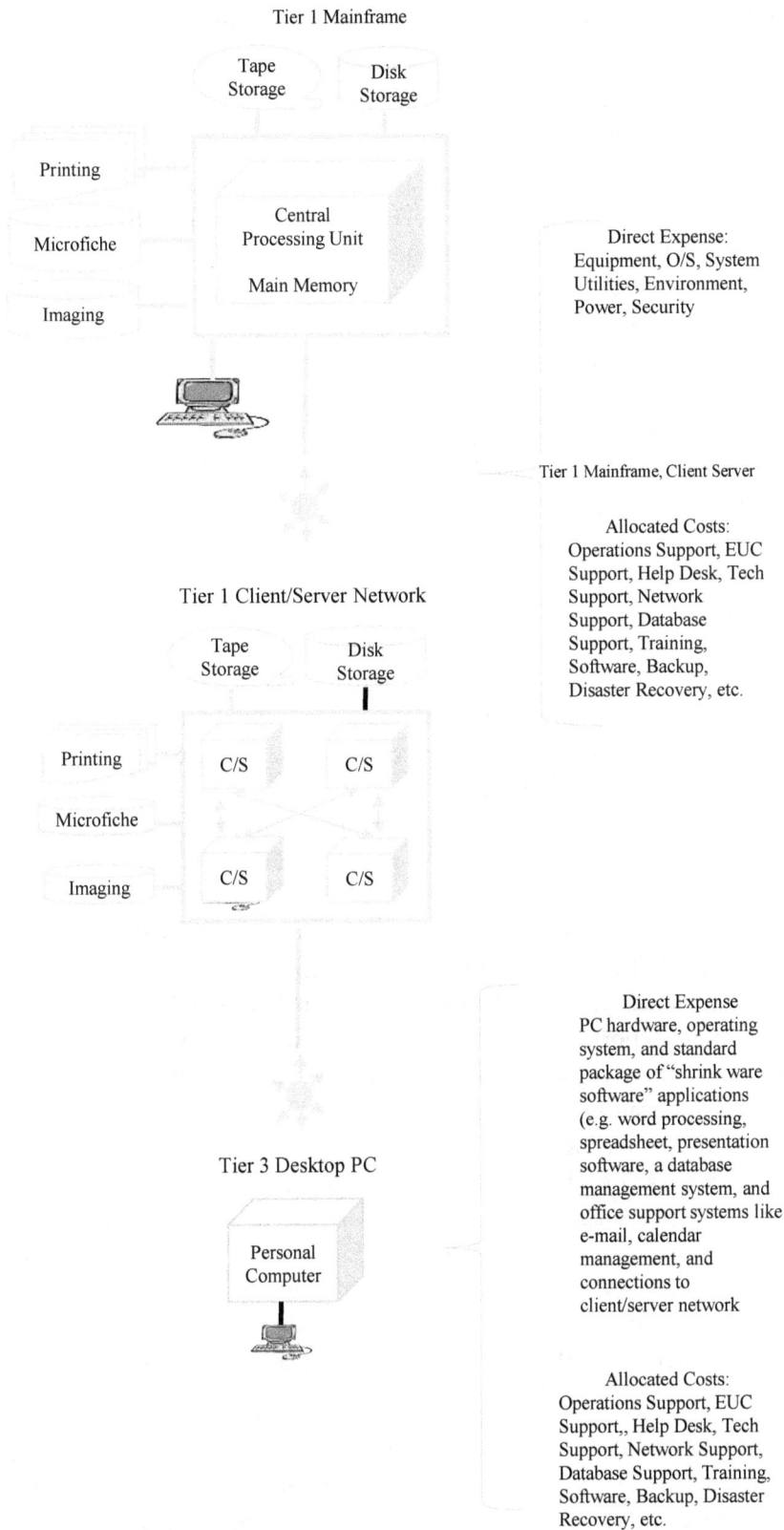

Tier 1 Mainframe

Tape Storage

Disk Storage

Printing

Central Processing Unit

Microfiche

Main Memory

Imaging

Direct Expense:
Equipment, O/S, System
Utilities, Environment,
Power, Security

Tier 1 Mainframe, Client Server

Allocated Costs:
Operations Support, EUC
Support, Help Desk, Tech
Support, Network
Support, Database
Support, Training,
Software, Backup,
Disaster Recovery, etc.

Tier 1 Client/Server Network

Tape Storage

Disk Storage

Printing

C/S

C/S

Microfiche

C/S

C/S

Imaging

Direct Expense
PC hardware, operating
system, and standard
package of "shrink ware
software" applications
(e.g. word processing,
spreadsheet, presentation
software, a database
management system, and
office support systems like
e-mail, calendar
management, and
connections to
client/server network

Tier 3 Desktop PC

Personal Computer

Allocated Costs:
Operations Support, EUC
Support,, Help Desk, Tech
Support, Network Support,
Database Support, Training,
Software, Backup, Disaster
Recovery, etc.

unit (CPU), main memory, channels/bus, input, output, and external storage. Note in the figure that each class of computer can be linked to any of the other computer classes and thus provide a networked computer facility. Note also the sample of the direct and allocated expenses associated with each computer class.

Desktop PC:

The PC is not illustrated at the level of detail as the other two computer classes even though it shares the same fundamental functions as the other two computer classes. Why? The PC is a relatively inexpensive computer from the perspective of direct expense, and is typically a single user computer. Utilization of its sub-component resources is not normally a cause for concern; therefore the PC is treated differently from a management and cost perspective. It's sufficient to manage the PC as a single unit. Normally there is no need to collect extensive statistics about its sub-component utilization. The PC user usually tells IT to get them an upgrade or new PC when performance of the PC begins to degrade. An analysis of the PC's sub-components may be made before an upgrade is made.

Like the other computer classes, the PC has direct and indirect (allocated) costs assigned to it. These allocated costs must be included in the unit price of a PC, and therein lies a cause of many a heated debate between IT and its PC business clients. The "true" cost of the PC is often significantly understated because of the failure to consider the allocated support costs. The following scenario highlights a PC cost issue.

A business client requests a PC. IT quotes a selling price of $3,000. The IT business client goes ballistic, and replies that they can go to the local computer store and buy a PC for less than $1,000. They are correct. The direct cost of the PC including the hardware and base office software is very inexpensive, but the PC they purchase from the computer store does not include value-added IT services and features including training, on-going production support, Help Desk, technical consultation, back-up, disaster recovery, connectivity and compatibility to the company network and other business applications, etc. The company and IT promotes these services because they want the PCs to be effectively utilized within the company. The PC user can't achieve this objective if they do "their own thing" with the PCs. Cost management helps add objectivity to the discussions about PC cost because it provides the information to make informed decisions. Experience shows that in many companies the cost of the PC hardware and software amount to only about 30-35% of the true PC cost. IT has a responsibility to educate the PC users in these matters, and cost management is a tool that assists them in this effort.

Tiered and Client/Server Computers:

The tiered and client/server computer classes are nearly identical except that the central computer in the client/server configuration is actually a network of servers (computers) all sharing attached network devices including even the larger tiered computers. The complexity of these two computer classes originates in the fact that they have many "moving parts", and the effort required to manage, cost, and measure the activity generated by utilization of these parts is a significant, but worthwhile effort. The client/server network appears to be the more difficult class to manage because in contains multiple computers/servers.

The tiered and the client/server computer classes are jointly discussed because they are so similarly architected. Each computer/server maintains an operating system and system utilities which capture performance utilization statistics for each of the computer/server sub components used on behalf of the computer work (jobs) the computer is executing. The *job* is the basic unit used to capture and report computer processing utilization. The computer job is linked to a business client by its job name. The performance statistics recorded to a job are cost management's source of capturing the units of measure required to recover the costs of each computer/servers' sub components. The same statistics are used to invoice (charge) IT clients for the utilization of these components.

IT can chose to capture a myriad of computer processing utilization statistics to track for any given computer job executed upon a tiered or client/server computer class. A sample of some of the more frequently used statistics are:

- Amount of time used by the central processing unit (CPU) to execute the job's instructions
- Amount of main computer memory storage used, and the length of time it was used
- Volume of activity used by the channels/bus to access attached devices
- Accesses to external devices (e.g. disk drives, tape drives, printers, communications)
- Input device accesses to the computer (e.g. terminals of all types)
- Volume and type of external storage used (e.g. disk, microfiche, e-reports, e-documents, tape, etc.), and the length of time the storage device is occupied

A caveat about costing at the more detailed computer cost component level is that each sub-component is a product, and because they are products, a standard cost, unit of measure, and an estimate of the standard number of productive units the product can produce in a given cost period must be developed and maintained. If a major objective of costing is to assist in ensuring that computer equipment is effectively utilized, then costing at the computer cost component level is the way to proceed.

Computer jobs can use significantly different components of a computer, and since the costs of computer components vary, the cost of running jobs on a computer can vary. IT typically wants to manage and effectively utilize the central processing unit (CPU) as a major component because it is a very expensive component. It's a good practice to isolate CPU intense computer jobs, but a computer job can use little CPU time, yet make excessive accesses to files on the external storage devices. Excessive accesses to the files can significantly degrade computer performance. Conversely, a computer job may place a significant amount of data on external storage devices, store it for an extended period of time, but infrequently access it. If IT has no mechanism to analyze the utilization of external storage, it could think a computer was out of storage capacity when in reality the storage wasn't being properly utilized. Failure to recognize the inefficiencies of computer jobs can influence IT to make a decision to upgrade its computer capacity when none is required. The proper procedure is to look at the computer jobs executing on the computers and isolate jobs that are utilizing significant amounts of computer resource components, and improve performance by reengineering the inefficient system design, program code and/or programming techniques. A worst case scenario is to completely rewrite a poorly performing system or computer job.

Experience demonstrates that it can be difficult convincing system designers and programmers to relook at their programs on the basis of reports listing and ranking computer jobs by their performance statistics only. Add the total computer processing cost of the jobs to the same report, and rank the jobs from highest to lowest costs, then see what type of response the report generates. The use of cost management in this manner truly assists IT in achieving the cost management objectives. "Dollars do talk."

Equating Performance Statistics of Different Computers:

Exacerbating the complexity of using computer performance statistics is the issue of equating the units of measure across each computer. A CPU minute in a PC is not the same as a CPU minute in a tiered or networked server computer. A CPU minute in one vendor's computer may not equate to a CPU minute in another vendor's computer. A mainframe computer can process significantly more work in a CPU minute than a server or personal computer can process in a CPU minute. The reason this may become an important issue in some companies is the business client may not want to see the cost of their computer processing charges increase for the same mix of jobs just because IT replaced computers or moved the processing of their jobs to another computer. This is a valid argument. Cost should be somewhat predictable over various computer platforms. Some method of equating the statistical measurements has to be developed if a company's ultimate costing objective is to equate the costs of running a computer job on any computer. This is a noble objective, but one not recommended, and frankly, the cost and effort to develop and maintain such a costing technique would probably exceed any benefits that could be realized by its implementation.

Avoiding Computer Processing Costing Complexities:

Many IT departments avoid computer processing costing complexities by choosing to view all computer processing as a singular IT product. All costs for computer processing are summarized into one cost center. The costs are allocated to the business clients and IT by using a simplistic measure such as assigning an arbitrary percent to each client which allocates a share of the aggregated computer processing cost component to the client. This idea doesn't work for those IT departments wanting to use cost management to assist in effectively managing its computer resources. Analysis of computer sub-component utilization can isolate areas of inefficient use in order to achieve maximum computer throughput, and thus reduce expense. Each company must balance the cost of creating and operating a cost management methodology with the benefits that costing may return.

Batch jobs:

A batch job is the dominant type of non-online computer job. It runs from start of job to end of job with no in-between operator intervention. It is typically run on a regularly scheduled basis by IT computer operations. There is only one business unit owner of the job. The purpose of running a batch job is to process a given business application function, such as creating a report or processing invoices.

In the "good old days of data processing" with its dependence on batch processing techniques, there were no big cost allocation issues. The main issue was how to cost the job. It was "one computer, one job". Get in the queue and await your turn. Each batch job used to develop or test programs charged its usage to the owner that was coded on the job card. Production batch jobs also ran with a job name that reflected the owner of the system. If for some reason there was the need to allocate a batch job to account codes different from the account code in the job card, some off-line process could perform the required allocation. If "push came to shove" the allocation of a batch job could be done manually in the accounting department.

Online systems:

An online system, in comparison to a batch job, is a computer program or system of programs that is initiated when the overall computer is started each day. It is alternatively referred to as a real-time or interactive processing system. It runs continually in the computer in a monitoring mode until it is interrupted by a system user wanting to process a computer work request (transaction). The system provides coordinated access to various system facilities. At the end of the work day it is shut-down.

Types of online systems:

There are any number of online systems operating in an IT department on any given day. Most online systems have more in common than not. The book will discuss two types of online systems that are most frequently observed.

- Online System Development Tool (hereafter referred to as the *Computer Development System*)
- Online Business Transaction System

The *Computer Development System* is used by the system designers, programmers, technical support, and other IT associates as a system development and maintenance tool. The system provides its users the ability to perform all system development and testing functions they formerly performed using manual and disparate methods. All system development functions can be performed at the desktop with the tool. The other type of on-time system is the *Online Business Transaction System* which provides real-time access and simultaneous business transaction processing capabilities to multiple business clients. It provides a computer platform and network which connects the business client to other system users and their applications; a common connection to application databases; and an umbrella of system services used to develop and share transactions with other users in a consistent manner. Without an online system executing business transactions under a common processing umbrella, each business application would have to be developed and operated independently. This practice would not only result in an inefficient use of scarce resources, but would result in a business applications "Tower of Babble".

Both the Computer Development System and the Online Business Transaction System are conceptually similar. They differ in their purposes. In addition to the significant computer processing resources used by these jobs, they also require many software support utilities and priority support by the technical support units. Online systems in most IT departments have high visibility, and require significant technical support at peak hours of processing time requirements.

Both use similar cost and allocation techniques. Commonalities in the basic approach to cost allocation of online systems are:

- Both look like any other computer job executing in the computer
- Both operate under some type of system software control monitor which coordinates user access to the system and its resources
- Both have some type of logging mechanism which tracks transaction activity and captures user defined data
- Both have the ability to track and report key utilization statistics
- Both have performance monitoring capabilities to indicate system load and response time

Costing of online systems:

If the reader looked at a computer operator's console they would observe that the online system looked like any other job executing in the computer, although the amount of resources it was consuming would probably stand-out. The jobs are sharing the computer cost components of tape, disk, terminal and communications access, print, CPU time, and memory, or any other component for that matter. They actually compete with each other for resources and can impact each other's performance. Online systems are normally given priority access over batch jobs for the use of computer processing components. Each job executing on the computer is producing component utilization statistics which are used to create a total cost for each online job. Note in Figure 19 that the real-time system and the batch job are both "just" computer jobs running on a computer. The job used to initiate the online system has one owner, just like the other jobs. The owner is most probably the IT operations division. It is their product. Costing of an online system job is fairly straight-forward because it looks like any other job, and it has a single owner. It will generate all the statistics about its performance just like any other job. These statistics will be used to cost the online system, just like any other job. Costing of online systems is not the issue, it is the allocation of online system cost that is the issue.

Figure 19 Illustrates a computer schematic depicting a batch and real-time system running on a computer.

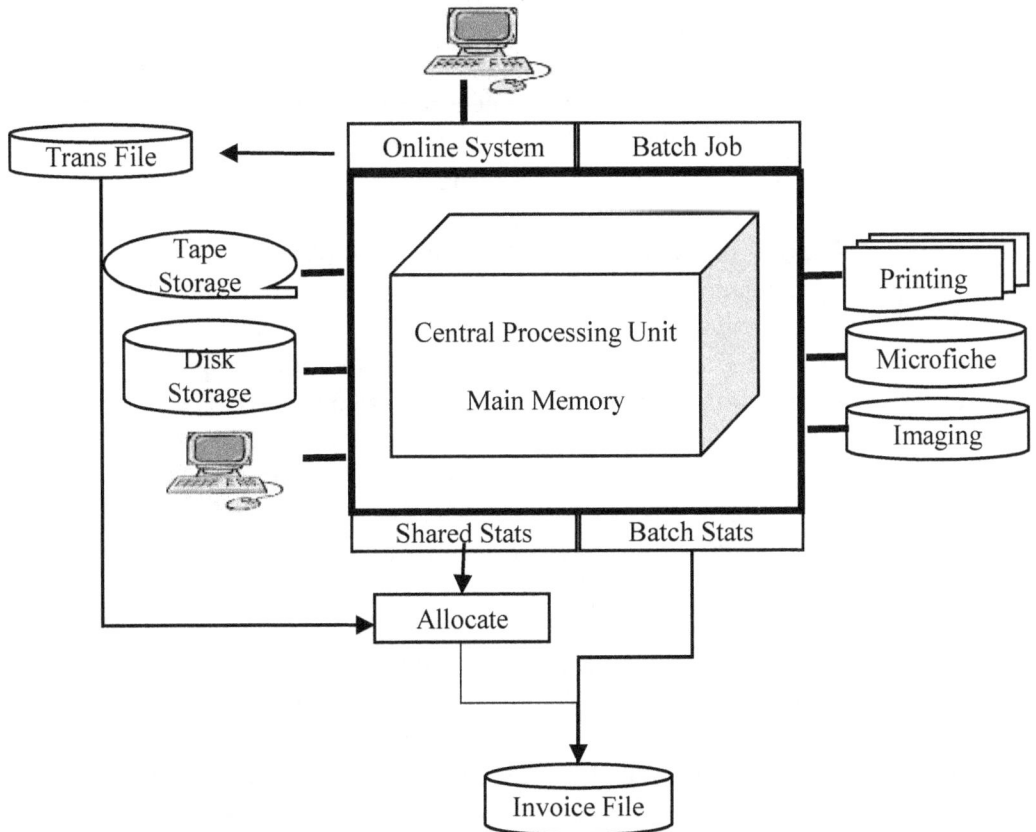

Allocating the cost of online systems:

Online system cost allocation presents some different, and more challenging, issues not witnessed in allocating the cost of batch jobs. The basic issue is based upon the fact that the computer job running the online system is being simultaneously utilized by multiple system users. Each online system user utilizes a unique mix of computer resources. The challenge is to create an online system allocation procedure which equitably distributes the total cost of the online system to the various system users who are utilizing the system, yet a procedure in which the benefits accruing to the allocation of the resources exceed any costs incurred in creating and maintaining the cost allocation procedure. It's another instance of the cost accounting "balancing act".

Common steps in the online system allocation process:

Just like there are commonalities between the system attributes of the two online systems, there are commonalities in the cost allocation procedures for the two systems.

- Both are products of the computer operations division
- The standard rate/cost of the resources required to operate the online systems are determined by the operations division and IT cost management.
- The operations division creates a budget for each IT division/business client who will utilize the systems in the next planning period.
- The IT division managers and IT cost manager determine how charges for utilization of the online products will be managed and allocated to the IT divisions and business clients
- IT divisions and business clients are billed for actual product utilization.

Allocate the cost of Computer Development System:

The computer development system product is used by nearly all IT divisions. The IT operations division supplies each IT divisional manager with an estimate of the total cost to utilize the product for the coming planning period. Each IT division manager must develop a costing strategy to recover the cost of the product being allocated to them. All types of options to recover the cost of the product are available for consideration. The option used as an example in this book assumes two views of the product's utilization. Each view requires a unique approach to its cost and allocation management.

The primary view of the product is as a direct support tool for developing, testing, and maintaining computer systems. A secondary view of the product is as a tool to provide a general IT administrative work support capability. For those divisions using the system for general administrative support, the cost can just be considered a divisional overhead cost. On the other hand, associates using the system for development work normally don't want to have this cost included in their normal staff services product rate for several reasons. First, they want to keep their staff services rate as low as possible so as not to discourage use of their services. Second, exclusion of the cost from the staff services rate provides a more realistic view of a project's true cost structure.

For those IT divisions using the computer development system product as a systems development tool, a more sophisticated cost recovery approach must be taken. Again, there are many options from which to choose. The example used in this book is based upon these assumptions:

- The system development and testing tools delivered by the computer development system product are mostly used when the developers are working on projects, or other work items, for business clients

- For every developer hour worked on a client billable project, or other work item, a corresponding hour of computer development system processing time is utilized.

- Each transaction processed in the computer development system utilizes an equal amount of computer resources.

Caveats to these assumption are: there is no guarantee that for every hour a developer is working on a billable project, they are using the computer development system; and, transactions are probably not equal in resource utilization. To some readers these may be a good assumptions, to others bad assumptions, yet to others they are practical assumptions. The cost manager, working with the appropriate IT support teams have to decide whether it is cost effective to develop a more sophisticated costing method, or use a more practical, but realistic measure of computer resource utilization. A practical approach is recommended.

The next step is to allocate (bill) the cost of computer development system product utilization to the IT divisions and/or business clients. For each IT division making general administrative support use of the computer development system product, the cost of the product would normally be included in their budget as an overhead item, and be included in the cost of their other IT product rates. Nothing more need be done for these system users. No rate need be calculated for the utilization of the product.

The IT divisions which make significant use of the computer development system product as a system development tool, and want to keep the cost of this product out of their other product rates, need to take a different approach to managing the cost and allocation of this product. Specifically, a billing rate must be created for the product. The plan file can be used to assist in the calculation of this rate. In this approach the plan file is used to calculate an estimate of the total billable hours planned for projects and other work items in the planning period. It also identifies the IT business clients for whom the hours are planned. In order to calculate an overall hourly rate for use of the product, simply divide the total cost estimate of the product provided by the operations division at the beginning of the planning process by the total estimate of billable hours for the planning period as contained in the plan file. This rate will be used by all IT divisions in recovering the cost of the computer development system product.

Each billing period the IT business clients will be billed for their use of the computer development system product based upon the actual hours recorded to them in the plan file. A billing record is created by multiplying the overall rate for a billable hour of product utilization by the actual project or work item hours recorded in the plan file. The billing record should include:

- Business client or unit requesting the work
- Billable hours recorded to the work
- IT associate who performed the work
- Associate's IT division
- Project or work item

This detail billing record can be grouped to any level for invoicing purposes. The procedure is not perfect, but it is reasonable and best matches the cost management objectives that were established.

Allocate the cost of the Online Business Transaction System:

Allocation of costs for this system follow closely along the lines of the cost allocations for the Computer Development System with the following exceptions:

- Allocation is based on different assumptions

- It uses the statistical file produced as a part of online system utilization and system login procedures to provide cost allocation information

- Passes cost allocations directly to the business units utilizing the system

The cost allocation assumption for this type of online system is that each business transaction executed in the system utilizes the same volume and mix of computer resources. In other words it assumes an average transaction is executed in the system. IT regularly reviews transaction statistics of most online systems for reasons of performance review and impact analysis of the transaction on the rest of the system; therefore, IT knows this assumption of an average transactions is not perfect by any means, yet it could be a reasonable assumption from a cost allocation perspective. Experience dictates that transactions which use significantly more resources than the average online transactions will eventually get isolated, "weeded-out", or fixed because they show-up on IT system performance monitors, usually because of degraded system response time.

IT operations normally manages this allocation process. IT operations determines the standard cost for the product and a standard cost per transaction when developing its plan for the coming plan period. Each month during the production cycle's normal billing process a statistical file is produced by the online system and is used to allocate the total online system job cost for the billing period to the various users of the online system. The allocation program merely takes each transaction and multiplies it by the standard cost per transaction to arrive at the allocated cost. The procedure minimally requires the transaction ID, the business associate performing the transaction, the business unit to which the associate is assigned, the business application system, and the number of times the transaction was executed during the billing period. Unless requested to the contrary, the transactions in the statistical file are normally grouped by the business unit. This results in charges for the online system reported at a business unit level on invoices. Other levels of grouping can be provided as long as the information is captured in the online statistical file. Since this is an operations division's product, the operations division will bill the charges for the product using the standard cost per transaction it developed. It will export the resulting billings to service chargeback for posting to business client invoices.

Strategic Management Plan Worksheet Cost Management Process

Objectives:

The following objectives are established for the Cost Management Process in a "best company" environment. Some of the objectives are repeated over the processes, but a particular process may have unique strategies to achieve them.

- Reduce expenses
- Develop a culture of measurement
- Account for, and report, the total cost of information technology
- Tightly couple IT's cost management function to the company's financial and accounting practices:
- Create an awareness of the importance of the cost management function

Strategies to Achieve Objectives:

The strategies are the action plans concerning how the process will achieve its objectives. Note that strategies can align with multiple objectives.

Reduce expenses:

- Create an awareness of the cost and utilization of IT products and services to promote more effective use of IT products and services.
- Use cost management information to manage technology on a business as well as a technical basis.

Develop a culture of measurement:

- Develop reports and scorecards indicating performance against standards for key IT products and services
- Augment subjective and intuitive evaluations of technical matters with fact-based objective measurements

Account for, and report, the total cost of information technology:

- Charge all technology expense to IT, and either pass thru the expense to the IT client, or allocate it back to the client on a product utilization basis
- Obtain senior business management's sponsorship and support of IT's objective to manage all IT costs
- Promote the concept of total cost of ownership of individual IT products and services

Tightly couple IT's cost management function to the company's financial and accounting practices:

- The company's financial reporting and practices must "drive" the IT cost management function:
- Form close working relationships with company cost accounting staff which will add credibility and integrity to IT's costing efforts
- Advance IT towards objective of being managed as any other business unit
- Integrate the cost management function with the other management functions of plan, resource, and service chargeback management
- Add a financial dimension to IT decision making
- Cost management advances IT objective of contributing to the bottom-line

Create an awareness of the importance of the cost management function:

- Education, education, and more education of both IT and business management in the objectives, concepts, and benefits of cost management

Strengths, weaknesses, opportunities, and threats (SWOT):

Because the "best company" is the same for each process, the SWOT analysis for this process will not be repeated here. Reference chapter 2, *IT Management Model, Strategic Management Plan Worksheet, Develop and Manage the IT Management Model Process* for the details of the "best company" SWOT analysis.

Cost drivers:

The three primary cost drivers of cost management are: the number of IT products and services that must be costed; the difficulty in collecting the productive units generated by the products; and the complexity of the products in terms of the number of cost components.

Deliverables:

The deliverables are witnessed in the statement of the objectives.

Critical success factors:

What event(s) must occur or strategies be successfully completed in order for the process to achieve its objectives?

- The company's acceptance of the role of IT to be managed like any other business unit
- The business and IT associates' acceptance of the importance and relevance of cost information
- The ability to identify, capture, and process the required utilization data
- Availability of qualified IT staff required to develop and manage the cost management function

Management Function Impact Analysis:

Business plan management:

A process should align with the business objectives listed in the summary business plan example presented in chapter 1. This process aligns with, and is supportive of, the following business objectives listed in the summary business plan example.

- Continuous improvement initiatives
- Cost awareness
- Plan driven
- Cost effective products
- Bottom-line oriented
- Financial awareness
- Cost management

Process management:

This layer addresses the participants, processes, and procedures required to ensure the proper flow and interchange of information amongst the key managers involved in development and maintenance of an IT cost management process. Clearly the IT financial manager, as the owner of the process, leads the development process. The manager will be assisted by members of the IT senior staffs, and members of the company's accounting staff.

IT financial management:

Cost management shares in the financial management objectives listed in the summary business plan example described in chapter 1. In addition, costing of IT products and services creates some very powerful information which can add a financial dimension to technical decision making. The business clients need to realize that IT cost and other IT financial management functions are dealing in real company dollars that affect the "bottom lines" of the business clients just like any other company expense does. IT division managers are similarly expected to manage their "bottom-lines" to ensure their expenses remain in line with their budgets, and billings cover their expenses.

Plan, resource, and service chargeback management:

The process owner has determined that plan management, resource management, and service chargeback management are major components of this process. These management processes are described in detail in chapters 7 and 8. The cost management process has a significant impact on the plan, resource, and service chargeback management functions because it defines and costs the IT products and services that these other management functions plan, manage, and bill. Ultimately the cost management process costs the entire IT plan which is the base for the IT budget.

IT general management, leadership, organization management:

Cost management is supportive of both the information processing concept and the supporting systems and services organization that enables it. Both of these concepts may add complexity to the costing of IT products and services. Other process objectives and strategies are to seek and establish excellent working partnerships with the company's accounting and financial divisions. Sponsors and champions of the cost management function must be developed. Cost reporting methods and reports must become an integral part of normal IT management activities. Cost information can be a significant measure of the success or failure of the model's implementation.

Change management:

The "best company" uses a standard costing system which is based upon budgeted or anticipated expenses. Change management is an important part of the cost management system and procedures. Changes to standard costs must be carefully made in this environment. The use of standard costs can create variances during the course of the year between the planned and actual expenses of an IT product. Variances can be caused by differences in units utilized, or by differences in cost of the product or service. These variances must be carefully monitored and adjusted as required because under service chargeback, cost variances can have a significant impact on the client's business operation.

Facilities management:

This is not a major issue for cost management's normal operations, but cost management does get involved with the company's facilities management group in the process of allocating the expenses associated with office space, utilities, office furniture and equipment etc. to the costs of IT products and services.

Client relationships (service) management:

Cost management does not normally deal directly with the business clients. Costing's service relationships are with the various IT division managers who work with cost management in the development, maintenance, and cost of IT products and services.

Application management:

The cost management system will provide IT managers and business clients the ability to develop comprehensive costs of business application systems and services. Knowledge of business application costs positions both the IT manager and business client to make more informed decisions about their applications and their use because a new financial dimension is added to the analysis and decision making process.

Architecture management:

The computer platform, technology, and organization independent architecture (CPTOIA) and the systems and services organization are major sources of anticipated expense reductions. Costing of these two initiatives to verify the success or failure of them is very important. The cost management process only calculates and reports the costs. The architecture must deliver the expense reductions.

Technology management:

Cost management is normally involved in the financial analysis of new technologies required to support business plan objectives. From a costing viewpoint new technologies can be problematic in the fact that there is sometimes limited "track record" or statistical type information that can be used to assess the potential cost of introducing new technology.

End user computing management, systems software management, database management, hardware (operations) management, and communications and networking management:

Cost management mainly gets involved with these technical layers in costing their IT products and services. The hardware or operations area of a company probably contains the majority of IT products and services. Cost management spends much time in this area identifying and costing the products and services, determining how to recover their expenses, and gathering the voluminous statistics required to measure utilization of the products and services by the business clients.

System Software is basically an extension of the operating systems that manage the computers. Costing of these products and services can pose some problems because they are overhead products and services that are shared across many other products. Communications & Networking is another product or service that poses similar problems as Systems Software. Traffic on networks is very voluminous and constantly changes. It's very difficult to "get a picture" of the network at any given point in time. These characteristics makes costing more difficult. Database Management is a little more straight-forward. Depending upon your company's costing objectives, costs for access to the data and costs for occupying the storage facility (residency) should both be considered.

End User Computing's (EUC) support of the desktop personal computer (PC) and its connections to the company network creates a significant involvement of cost management with EUC. It's not only the costing of the EUC products that consumes so much time and effort, it's the education of the PC users in concepts of true PC costs of ownership that involves so much work.

Staff education, training, skills management:

Cost management should work with the professional IT education and training staff to develop the programs to educate company management and IT managers on the why's and how's of cost management. This education is especially important in the area of desktop PC use.

Potential impact on other management functions:

Use this section to solicit the potential impact of the new process on the process operation of the other management function process owners.

CHAPTER 7
Planning and Resource Management

If you wake up each day and don't have a plan for what you want to accomplish that day, why would you expect to accomplish anything?

Costing identifies the elements and compounds that comprise IT products and services, and assigns cost to them. Planning determines what products and services are required to deliver the planned work. Resource management ensures the IT products and services (i.e. resources) are available to perform the work when required. If IT doesn't know what work is to be accomplished; who is requesting the work; who will pay for the work; what resources are available to do the work; or how many resources are required by the work, none of the other IT management functions have much meaning.

Keep in mind that the plan model is an implementation of the IT management model. The terms IT plan model and IT management model are sometimes used interchangeably in this chapter. Planning uses the IT management model and its concept of management function layers to ensure that each management function has the proper work planned so that management function objectives can be achieved. Planning also assures that the impact of plans in one management function layer are communicated to other management function layer owners in order to share the potential impact of a given plan on all other planners. The resource management function is tightly coupled with the plan management function. A reference to plan management includes resource management. A plan without a system to ensure the resources are available to deliver the planned work is not a plan but rather an IT project wish list.

Ownership

The ownership of the IT planning and resource management functions should reside with the IT plan administrator who typically reports to the Chief Information Officer (CIO) in a staff function. The IT plan administrator is assisted by the IT financial manager, and members of the IT senior management, IT senior technical, and the IT senior administration teams. Obviously these teams will interact with complementary business management teams at all levels of the company. Planning eventually reaches every level of the company organization.

IT plan administration is a critical management function. The IT plan administrator cannot be a pure administrative type person blindly processing managers' requests to create more and more detail work items. The IT plan administrator must demonstrate leadership capabilities, and create a broad coalition of IT and business managers who are involved in the planning process. In this role the plan administrator is very much a *facilitator*. The planner needs to use their *imagination* to envision the potential of future technology to shape the world, the company, and IT. They should participate on the team which develops the IT management model which shapes the entire IT management process. This is the *visionary* role to be played. In a *chemist* role the IT plan administrator needs to assist the IT technology manager in identifying and classifying all the technical elements and compounds IT wants to plan and manage. In the role of the *architect* the IT planner needs to assist in defining the primary and secondary roles for each of the elements and compounds within the overall technology architecture. The planner needs to know where IT and the company "wants to be", and recognize when an *opportunity* to get "there" presents itself. The planner assists in developing a plan of action, a *strategy*, which enables the company to achieve its vision and accomplish its major business objectives.

Some Basic Concepts and Approaches Taken

The IT planning infrastructure establishes the management environment within which the actual plan is developed. It includes the "selling" of the planning approach to company and IT senior management teams. Once senior management approves of the approach, then the rest of the company and IT managers should be presented with the "sales pitch". Feedback from these meetings should be included in the final rollout of the planning approach to the entire company. Topics to be discussed and actions to take place in this rollout process include:

- Education of IT and business management in the concepts of the IT plan model
- Assemble, organize, and create role definitions for planning team members
- Synchronize the planning and budgeting processes.
- Discuss and promote the idea of combining business and IT planning processes under a common plan model and development process
- Develop a comprehensive conflict resolution model
- Enhance work estimation skills
- Establish IT planning objectives, strategies, and supporting initiatives

Education of IT and business management in the concepts of the IT plan model:

Before anything can really happen in planning, the company's Chief Executive Officer (CEO), the Board of Directors, and the senior business and technology management teams have to be convinced of the need for a formal plan and resource management system. This need should be presented in the context of the model. Once the need is established, the objective is to obtain general agreement among senior management concerning the model; the basic planning approach; a list of plan objectives; management best practices; samples of the types of information to be provided, and a schedule of planning events and milestones.

Assemble, organize, and create roles for planning team members:

The planning process has to be comprehensive in scope and inclusive of the majority of company associates and managers. The requirement for comprehensiveness and inclusiveness places a premium on creating representative planning teams. The plan is truly a process, a journey, and if the published plan contains too many surprises for its readers, then the planning teams have probably failed in developing a process that effectively gathered and communicated ideas. Planning is a company-wide effort, not something done in the CIO's office.

Planning team architecture:

How should the individual planning teams be arranged to most effectively carry-out their mission? One way would be to have a benevolent dictatorship approach in which senior IT management dictates the process, but this is the antithesis of teamwork. Some dictatorial management style may be needed in the early stages of launching the planning process, but over the "long haul" the plan process will probably fail if this style of leadership continues throughout the process. Development of an effective plan requires buy-in, teamwork, and effective communications. Planning must become a part of IT's normal management activities.

There is an architecture to almost everything, and the planning team structure is no exception. A common planning team implementation is based upon a federated type team structure in which planning process teams are viewed at the local level (division, group and team); the state level (department) and then the federal level (senior management). A federated team architecture is likened to the organization of the local, county, state and federal governmental agencies that operate to manage the business of the country at the lowest level of government possible. Issues that can't be resolved at lower governmental levels are escalated to the next higher level in the federated approach.

The planning process needs to ensure that business and IT planning teams don't work independently of each other. The process can become dysfunctional without some unifying objective. The unifying factors are the business plan objectives. The IT plan needs to balance business requirements with available IT resources; in other words, stay within its budget. It needs to balance the needs of the departments and divisions with those of the overall company. There must be a synergy created which balances the challenge for new ideas with available resources limitations. An overall driving philosophy of the company should be to drive down the level of plan management and conflict resolution to the lowest organizational level from which management functions can be effectively executed.

The initial stages of the planning process requires strong direction and policy making decisions; therefore, the company and IT senior level planners are often designated as the groups that champion most of the initial stages of the process. Department, division, group and team level planning teams are normally involved in further planning stages as the situation requires. Business units and IT should have similarly structured planning units, not necessarily identical units. The coordinated and synergistic relationships between business and IT teams is absolutely crucial to the success of the planning effort.

Roles and functions of each planning team:

There are many options available for identifying and structuring the individual teams. The choice of team structure depends upon the company and its culture, but a requirement no matter how the teams are established is that a team architecture is required to ensure that multiple planning teams act in a coordinated and cooperative fashion. The planning functions performed by each team are basically the same. They differ mainly in the scope and impact of the planning functions performed. Common planning process functions performed by all the teams are:

- Develop/suggest guiding policies and best practices
- Initiate and/or sponsor work/project requests
- Align the work initiatives with business objectives
- Develop cost justifications for the initiatives
- Suggest work priorities
- Size the initiatives to the allotted resources
- Assist in resolving any resource conflicts
- Track and report status of the planned work

The further down a team is in the planning team hierarchy, the more limited the team's scope of authority. Company and IT senior management can give unqualified direction to lower planning teams, but the lower level planning teams have to influence the higher planning levels by working up the chain of command. Senior management that doesn't listen to its lower level managers may be the ultimate losers in the process.

Typical individuals and groups participating on the planning teams are: board of director members; senior business management team including CEO, CFO, COO and company planner; IT senior management teams; IT and business department, division, planning teams; and the project management office (PMO).

Synchronize the planning and budgeting processes:

In the "best practices company" the budgeting and planning process are synchronized between the company business planning team and the IT senior management team. This typically indicates that the plan is driving the budget. As plans are cut, budgets are cut, as plans are increased, budgets may or not be increased depending on the merits of the project driving the need to increase the budget. Too often what happens is the budget is established before the planning process is initiated, and no matter what projects are planned the budget remains the same. The planning process becomes a series of meetings to see what projects we will be cut from the plan to satisfy budget limitations.

Promote the idea of combining business and IT planning processes under a common plan model and development process:

Think how nice it would be if the business community and IT not only worked together in a common planning process, but also used a common plan model. Too often the individual business units, and the IT planners are out of synch with each other in both approach and scheduling of planned work. Coordinating all the company planning initiatives and procedures is a real possibility if all the groups agree upon a common process and plan model. Imagine the IT payback associated with the development of such a coordinated planning effort? The feasibility of using a common process and model are discussed in Chapter 1.

Develop a comprehensive conflict resolution model:

If a manager never experiences any resource conflicts, it may be indicative of the fact that the manager has too many available resources. Some amount of resource conflict is inevitable in IT operations, just don't let it get to the level where it has a general debilitating effect on work performance. The IT department, as a general statement of management practices, attempts to resolve resource conflicts at the lowest possible organizational level consistent with its management best practice of a distributed management approach.

Source of conflicts:
The source of resource conflicts is unplanned work. It could be un-planned because:

- The IT manager did not manage to a plan
- The business unit manager did a poor job of planning
- New, priority work was requested

IT's role in addressing unplanned work:
IT has a significant responsibility in the resolution of resource conflicts since IT is the "gate keeper" of IT resources. IT must manage their resources to the plan requirements to comply with this responsibility. As a management best practice IT must discipline itself not to let unplanned work "creep" into the plan. Failure to adhere to this practice could result in compromising the completion of planned projects. IT needs to emphasize the point that, within reason, *work should only be initiated by a specific work order linked to an approved plan work item.*

If a request for unplanned work is submitted to IT, and it results in a conflict of resources with other planned work, it is the responsibility of the IT manager to identify the exact nature of the conflict including the business units and other IT support groups involved in the conflicting work. Accurate identification and reporting of resource conflicts by associate, support group and project allows IT to push back at users and make them assume respon-sibility for their lack of planning. It is the responsibility of the individual requesting the new work to resolve the conflict with the other business users involved in the conflict. IT can assist in resolution of the conflict by identifying all interested parties, and present alternative courses of action.

The conflicts resulting from unplanned work are exacerbated because a typical IT division supports many business units, and a change in plans in one business unit can have impact on the completion of another business unit's work. It gets even more involved if a business unit's work requires the support of multiple IT units, which again is a common occurrence. Work can have many "tentacles" to IT resources.

Too often IT puts itself in the position of trying to resolve the conflict on its own. The IT manager who wants to come across as "the good guy" by accepting the new work and assuming responsibility for the conflict "digs a deeper hole" for themselves and their staff. An option for the "good guy" manager is to work their staff overtime to remain on schedule with the other projects. This might be an OK move in the short-run, but over an extended period of time such actions can cause serious staff morale problems. It is rather easy to go from that "good guy" to the "bad guy" image. There is not much sympathy for the IT manager who complains how over-worked their staff is, but continues to accept unplanned work. Planning is a value-add service to IT managers providing them a management tool which they can use to push responsibilities back to where they belong.

Business Units' role in addressing unplanned work:

Unplanned work, and the resulting conflicts, can be the result of a business unit not doing a good job of creating their plans. Business requirements significantly determine how IT resources are deployed. Poor business requirement definitions can create resource conflicts by causing IT to create unrealistic system requirement definitions which aren't discovered until after the work has been initiated.

In fairness to the business units there are situations in which unanticipated, priority projects arise in the course of business. If these situations regularly occur, it could again be symptomatic of poor planning. The plan should provide for some resources in anticipation of these unplanned projects, but experience indicates that resources put aside for contingency have a habit of being used for other projects.

A situation that all too frequently creates conflicts in IT occurs when senior business management sponsors major projects which they want completed in the current year, but the projects were never identified in the plan development process, for whatever reasons. Accommodating these projects causes major problems for business units and IT planners. Those most impacted by these senior business management imposed projects are the individual business units whose general enhancement and/or tactical projects are often sacrificed to accommodate these senior management sponsored projects.

Resolving Conflicts:

If a conflict occurs within a division, and only one IT support unit is involved in the conflict, the matter can probably be resolved at this level by mutual agreement of the managers involved. These conflicts normally don't involve any escalation procedures. Situations that typically require escalation procedures are ones that cut across business organizational lines or involve multiple IT support units.

Escalation Procedures:

A first level of escalation typically occurs at the business department level. Assuming the conflict is contained within a department's own divisions, the department head could easily deny the new work request outright, and the matter would be considered closed. If the department manager can be convinced to transfer the needed resources from one of their own divisions to another within its department, and if the IT associates with the proper skill sets are available in the timeframe required, and the transfer would not compromise the completion of other departments' projects, then the matter could again be settled at a department level by simply transferring resources among its divisions. IT of necessity would have to be involved in negotiations and approve any transfers of resources.

On the other hand, the business department head could consider the escalated request worthy of consideration, yet not be in a position to request transfer of resources within its own department. In this situation the department head, working with appropriate IT managers, could attempt to negotiate with other business department heads to obtain a transfer of resources from their business units to resolve the conflict. If this attempt at obtaining resources fails, the department head could just drop the matter altogether, or escalate it to the second level of escalation if the project in question has possible enterprise scope and impact.

A second-level of escalation requires the requesting department to gain support from the other departments to share in the funding, and assist in a senior management team presentation which includes a full business case proposal; a project cost/benefit analysis; and an impact analysis of requested project on current plans. The company senior management team can:

- Deny the request outright, case closed.
- Approve the request without the addition of any new IT resources. This decision of necessity results in plan resizing and rescheduling issues for all parties concerned. These issues would have to be worked out amongst the various department heads and IT. This decision requires the transfer of resources from previously planned work of a lower priority than the requested work. This action is not always a well-accepted solution because it typically means some divisions lose tactical resources that they believe are important to their divisions.
- The senior management team could accept the requested project for inclusion in the plan, but allow for the acquisition of additional outside IT resources to staff the project. This is the preferred option. The cost of these resources would be allocated to all departments with the thought that each department that shares in the funding of it should have future access to the project's deliverables. Procurement of additional resources must be done through, and with, IT's involvement. IT owns the new resources, but directly assigns them to the requested project. IT makes the final disposition of the additional resources when the project is completed. The choice of what happens to these resources should not be determined by the department that initially requested the project. Acquisition of outside resources must be closely managed. If left unmanaged, it is an area that can cause great concern for IT.

Major IT infrastructure projects are processed in the same manner as major business-driven projects. The only difference is that IT is the initiator of the request, and it negotiates primarily with the company senior management team. It's really not up to the business units to determine the need for IT infrastructure. The IT senior management team has a responsibility to communicate the need to the business units.

Enhance work estimating skills:

The first important step in planning is to identify the work to include in the plan. The next important step is to estimate the effort and cost of doing the work. Estimating is a critical skill, and it includes not only project work, but the work necessary to perform production support, enhancements, and required maintenance of the on-going systems. Inaccurate estimates provided to business managers can result in poor business decisions. There are all kinds of aides to assist associates in estimating work, but in the end, work estimation is as much based upon experience as anything else. It requires significant work experience with the type of work being estimated. Under and over-estimates of requested work could be the result of:

- Unqualified IT associates making estimates
- Business managers providing incomplete or inaccurate business requirements
- Failure by IT to challenge and reasonably scrutinize the business requirements
- Inability of IT to say "no" to a business manager requesting work
- Failure to involve IT in the work planning discussions

Business managers must accept their responsibility for creating clearly defined project specifications and business requirements. Likewise, IT needs to push-back on business clients who are sometimes lax in specifying their business requirements, and much less enthusiastic about putting them in writing. It's easier to orally communicate requirements, but just talk can gloss over some of the critical details and get IT locked into one of those "I thought you said" situations. Obtain the business requirements upfront in the work definition process, and get them in writing. No one likes to say "no" to others, and IT is no exception, but there are times when IT has to say they need better requirements definitions, and reject a work request. It is better to say "no" upfront in the process than to create a project that will be late to complete, over-budgeted, and doesn't satisfy the business requirements. Business requirements should be viewed as a contract between the IT and the business client. IT has a corresponding responsibility to provide a detail description of the work to be delivered including a firm delivery date and the cost of the work.

In some Project Management Offices (PMO) there can be a reluctance on the part of some project leaders to plan project work in any sense of detail beyond a year's planning horizon. This reluctance can be the result of the project leaders' need to develop very detailed project schedules. The further a project extends into the future, the more difficult it is to estimate the details of a project. There are two ways to address this reluctance. A separate project proposal file can be developed that doesn't require as much structure and rigidity as a project management system requires. The project in the proposal file can be converted to a formal project schedule when, and if, the proposal is accepted for implementation. A second option is to use the project management system (PMS), but plan at the division or group level, not the associate level, for projects scheduled beyond next year's planning period. The use of a project proposal file is recommended. In either option, the objective is to get the proposed project in a job queue which creates a future requirement for planned resources.

IT non-project work is typically not as difficult to forecast into future planning periods. The work can be annualized and rolled-over into future planning periods. Only if the IT managers know of some significant event that will impact non-project work would adjustments have to be made. For example, if a production system with high maintenance and enhancement costs is being replaced with a new, more efficient system, changes in annualized support costs should be expected.

Making no attempt to estimate the full extent of a work initiative's requirements in future time periods can result in initiating a project which should never have been initiated in the first place.

Phase 2 projects and "Shoe Box Systems":

The term Phase 2 project is commonly used in IT to refer to the practice of moving system deliverables that were originally planned to be operational in the initial release of a system to a follow-on project (Phase 2) because the work could not be completed in the time scheduled for the initial system release. This practice is sometimes done so that both the business sponsor and IT can say that the initial release of the system met its target completion date. Phase 2 projects often originate from projects sponsored by company senior business management who by-passed the normal planning protocol. The promised system functionality left out of the initial release is included in a Phase 2 project which is promised to be delivered at a later date, but like "tomorrow", the Phase 2 implementation date never comes.

This practice results in a business administrative unit support team being delivered a system that doesn't satisfy the business requirements of the support unit. But life must go on in the business world, so the new system is installed in production and a big deal is made about the success of the project. Meanwhile a shoe box system, basically a manual system designed to support the business functionality that was moved to the Phase 2 project, is quietly installed in the business administrative area, and is supported by an increase in staff. Meanwhile the Phase 2 project sits in the work queue waiting for implementation. Everyone suffers. The business and IT costs escalate, and sadly, client service declines until one day a company senior manager asks why the system service costs are so high and the service so poor. It's the result of too many Phase 2 Projects that result in too many "shoe box systems".

Funding general research and development initiatives:

A generalized research and development work category can be provided in a plan. The budget for this type of work should be approved by the company's senior management team and communicated to all business units. The issue is typically centered about how the R&D budget is funded and allocated. Senior business management needs to make the funding decisions. In line with the IT objective of developing a total cost of IT, funding should be provided to IT, and the cost should be allocated as IT overhead to all business units utilizing IT products and services as a cost of doing business. IT will continuously argue with business clients why they are working on general R&D type projects, and not on business-sponsored projects, without such a known general funding strategy.

Information required to perform a management process:

IT managers need to identify the information they require to manage their area of responsibility. Some IT managers are not always sure what information they need to satisfy this responsibility. They surround themselves with many detail reports containing lots of data, but little information. To be effective, a manager needs probably 4-5 major information items related to their area of responsibility. For example, if a manager knew the average cost per hour for their associates, they could determine much about the support unit's work efficiency. High rates of cost, as compared with similar industry rates, can reflect work inefficiencies.

In order to identify inefficient performance of application systems or improperly installed system software, a manager of IT operations may want to know equipment utilization rates; measures of systems up-time; counts of production system abnormal endings, and the number of times the online system was late for business client use. This type information enables IT to initiate appropriate management action to eliminate problematic areas, and to request follow-up information after corrective action has been taken to determine whether the problem has been addressed. If new plans are introduced to cut costs, provide the numbers to prove cost reduction expectations.

The work management system is an information system. It is comprehensive because it includes all technologies (i.e. data, voice, text, and image), platforms (i.e. mainframes, PCs, network servers), and work types (i.e. projects and non-projects). Since most management functions involve multiple technologies, platforms, and work types, the work management system can provide the information which the management process owner requires. The key to having this type information is to capture it at the level of detail that is required to support a manager's responsibilities.

Critical importance of accurate time reporting:

Accurate time reporting is absolutely critical to the success of planning, resource management, cost, and service chargeback management. Associates must reasonably account for their time, and managers must review associate time reporting on a regular basis for any obvious irregularities. IT managers should be provided both online and hard copy reports which allow them to track time reporting integrity. They should periodically review the time reports to validate that associates are reporting reasonable amounts of time to their planned reporting categories. IT associates typically balk at entering time. That's a reasonable reaction. They feel singled out from the rest of the company because few, if any, business units are required to enter time. They are correct in that assumption. IT associates need to understand that time reporting is not a punitive measure, it's just that IT is a very significant company expense, and their time must be carefully managed.

Modify plans grudgingly:

Plans can be modified under proper circumstances, but there must be procedures in place to reasonably track significant changes to a plan. If the current plan is constantly changed to meet current requirements, then the plan is not really a plan, but rather an accounting tool. One way to address plan changes is to have an original plan file and a current year plan file in the planning system. The original plan file is never changed during the course of a yearly planning cycle. The current plan file can be changed during the course of the yearly planning cycle, but changes must be approved, properly identified, and stored in some type of plan change file. Both these plan files can be used in plan status reporting dependent upon the type of status information required.

Central administrative management of the plan:

The IT plan administrator, not individual IT managers or associates, should administer the Work Classification Scheme (WCS). The IT plan administrator works in close cooperation with the IT managers to ensure staff members are using the proper plan work categories for time reporting. If the plan administrator has any doubts about the identity of the work being planned, or if a new plan category is requested, the IT plan administrator must contact the appropriate IT manager to discuss a proper work classification. The process puts the IT manager in the work management loop, and makes the manager more aware of an associate's activity. WCS changes cannot be made indiscriminately, nor be made in response to issues of expediency. Without a disciplined WCS maintenance procedure, the entire work management system can lose its integrity.

Perfection:

Don't initially expect perfection in your planning efforts. It's OK to strive for perfection, but remember an individual can be "perfectly" wrong. Initial planning efforts are a little like playing horseshoes. Close shoes do score points, and can win games. A planner may be surprised how much significant information can be gathered just by some initial planning efforts. Start slowly, expand with experience.

Planning and Resource Management Process

The plan development process requires answers to three simple questions – "Where are we? "Where do we want to be?" "How do we get there?"

The objective of this section of the book is to provide an overall structure of a typical plan development and resource management process. The deliverables of this process are next year's operational, strategic management, and information technology plans. The plan development and resource management processes manage the requirements and issues associated with the development of the plans. The fundamental planning principles and practices remain relatively consistent from company to company, but the appearance and implementation of the plan development process can differ significantly over companies.

The planning process should be taking place at all points and times in the daily work management activities of all managers and associates. It shouldn't be a "one and done" thing. When the company business plan is communicated, and the official plan development process is initiated, many of the planned projects and work initiatives should already be known and discussed so that the planning process is not viewed as some onerous task that "has to be done each year" to satisfy senior management requirements. The planning process is not a serial process. A serial process would deny the business units and IT from shaping the company business plan with suggestions resulting from their own coordinated planning efforts. The process attempts to keep a balance between work requirements and resource capacity. The effectiveness of the planning process is measured when the final plans are distributed and read by the managers and their associates, and few discover any major surprises contained in the plans.

The responsibilities of the business units in the plan development process are often overlooked. IT can do all the right things, but if the business units fail in fulfillment of their responsibilities, the entire process fails. Business units must make their resources available on a timely basis to support the specification of their planned business requirements. There is every reason to expect that the planning process will not be as effective as it could be if IT and the business units use different views of technology, operate from different set of assumptions, have uncoordinated best practices, and work from uncoordinated schedules. A common IT/business unit plan model and plan development process would assist in alleviating many of these plan development obstacles.

Planning Viewed as Answers to a Basic Set of Simple Questions

The process begins by presenting a simple set of three questions, the answers to which basically describe the entire plan development process.

Question one: "Where are we?":

Answering this question forces IT to identify the current status of all work, planned or unplanned. It should include all computer platforms and information technologies.

Question two: "Where do we want to be?":

This question relates to the company's vision, long term objectives, and strategies. The plan should begin with a vision of the future and a set of assumptions concerning what "is" and "what will be". The vision must be a joint effort of business and IT management. No one can predict the future, but a guess of 5% is better than no guess at all. The vision should be "blind" to any existing IT and business support structures or constraints. If a company doesn't know where it wants to be, it just "spins its wheels" and remains where it is today. All resources must be focused towards maximizing progress towards the vision. A vision just can't be a page in a document sitting on a shelf. It needs to be a driver of daily management action.

Question three: "How will we get there?":

The "How" question relates to the strategies that must be developed and the projects that must be launched to achieve the company's vision and objectives. It includes prioritizing and aligning the planned work with the objectives that have been established. All the planning in the world won't get a company "there" unless IT successfully performs the required work.

The three previous questions relate to the more global or structural planning issues, but there are at least five other questions IT must answer that relate to the specific planned work. These questions are less strategic in nature, but important none the less. They are:

- What is the planned work's deliverable?
- What are the costs and expected benefits of implementing the planned work?
- When will the planned work be delivered?

- What existing planned work, if any, may be negatively impacted by implementing the new work?
- Who will pay for the planned work?

Sometimes companies get so involved with these five questions they forget about addressing the three basic questions. This situation is commonly referred to as "not being able to see the forest for the trees". The question concerning the impact of a project on existing work is the question that is sometimes over-looked. Answering this question can result in "opening up a can of worms".

Answering the Question - "Where are we?"

If an individual doesn't know where they are, how can they expect to get where they want to be?

Awareness of the current environment is important because it provides the knowledge base upon which to make intelligent and consistent decisions. A company can't get to where it wants to be if it doesn't know where it is. If you've ever been in a large store or shopping mall with which you weren't familiar and you're trying to find a particular location, you'd probably access a kiosk for directions. The first information item it displays is "You are here". This situation mimics the planning situation where the first question asked is "where are you?" A major objective of this first step is to establish a realistic assessment of current IT resource availability and deployment, and determine how resources are being utilized to satisfy the current business requirements. Are there major gaps or variances between the IT resources currently deployed and the business requirements? If so, where are they? Why? What has changed? What is the status of major initiatives?

Just like an effective plan can't be a document which contains a series of work initiatives unrelated to the attainment of specific visions, objectives, and strategies, neither should a plan be a document that is incidental to a manager's responsibilities. Plans must contain information that is relevant and important to a manager. Plans should be a vehicle around which a manager and subordinate associates can discuss and resolve issues important to each others' job performance. Plans need to be working documents which allow the managers and associates to see the impact of the plans upon IT and company operations.

Planning kickoff meeting starts the plan development process:

IT is a significant partner and sponsor of a company-wide planning kickoff meeting. The meeting is typically scheduled around mid-2nd quarter. It should be a "big deal". All key IT and business management staff should be required to attend. The target date of the meeting assures enough time will be available to complete the plan development requirements for next years' plan. It can take as much as six months of elapsed time to properly complete the plan development process.

A company's Chief Executive Officer (CEO) should establish the tone of the kick-off meeting. The CEO should emphasize the importance of the planning process and the need for everyone's participation. If available, and in a presentable format, the CEO can present highlights of next year's business plan as it is known at the time of the meeting. Those performing the work of the company need to know what the company is attempting to achieve in the next plan year. How else can they perform their job? The senior managers of the strategic business units (SBUs) and IT must incorporate the CEO's vision and objectives within their own strategic unit's plans. The Chief Financial Officer (CFO) is the "dollars person" at the meeting who provides both a "where are we" on the status of the current year's business plan, and a high level view of expense budgeting expectations for next year's plan. Next year's plan expense budgets are often presented as three options.

- Maintain the current level of IT expenditures,
- Decrease the level of IT expenditures ("ouch!"),
- Use the current level of IT expenditure as a baseline budget, but if new projects can be sponsored and cost justified above the baseline budget, then these projects can increase IT budgeted expenditures for next year. Of course, if projects can be eliminated, then baseline expenditures should be correspondingly decreased.

It is very important to note that planning should drive the budget process, not the budget drive the planning process. In some companies the budget is established even before planning starts. This makes the planning process seem almost irrelevant. The first priority in any planning process should be to determine what the company needs to do to achieve its vision, then determine the impact of those needs upon the budget. The result of such an analysis can indicate the needs and wants of the company must be compromised to stay within budget limitations, or the company must find new funding sources to achieve the vision and keep the company competitive.

The Chief Information Officer (CIO) also does a "where are we" at the meeting on the status of IT's current year plan, and presents major IT planning efforts for next year's plan as they are known at the time of the meeting. The CIO should introduce IT's own internal vision and objectives that can become a part of the overall company plan. The IT plan administrator provides primary support to the CIO at the meeting. The IT plan administrator is thoroughly immersed in all the details of the IT plans as they exist, and can respond to specific questions that the CIO might not be able to answer. The IT financial manager is also there to assist the CIO. The company planner, or appropriate designee, coordinates and schedules all company plans, including IT's plans to ensure fit with company planning and budgeting schedules. Other important attendees at the meeting are the company business and IT management staffs and their associates who do the work to make the plan happen.

Major takeaways from the meeting are:

- Importance of planning and resource management to the company's financial well-being
- Overall awareness of the planning process
- The business plan's major objectives and strategies;
- Schedule of plan development events and deliverables
- Identification of key players and their roles in the process

Preliminary planning sessions:

The first order of business after the plan kick-off meeting has been concluded is to schedule and conduct a series of preliminary planning sessions. The preliminary planning sessions can be relatively informal meetings conducted between the business units and their counterpart IT support groups. The meetings are designed to identify, collect, classify, and review work planned for next year. The primary sources of information used at these initial planning sessions are: a *summary business plan,* if available; *the strategic management plan worksheets* which contain the basic IT management process plans and other miscellaneous process plans; and selected reports created from the IT work activity recorded in the work management system during the first 4-5 months of the current year. These documents and reports are packaged into what IT refers to as the *Information Planning Packet.* These packets are distributed to the planning session participants as required. Nothing precludes participants in the planning sessions from suggesting new projects for inclusion in the plans. It is important to identify any current work that may carry-over to the next plan year. The end product of these sessions is the initial development of next year's IT operational plan and the continued development and enrichment of the strategic management plan.

The information gathered at the preliminary planning sessions is periodically sent to the IT plan administrator where it is posted to the appropriate files in the work management system. Reports are rerun and redistributed to the planners for review after the information has been updated. This review/update/redistribute cycle is continued in these sessions until the initial operational plan is completed.

The Information Planning Packet

Summary business plan:

A *summary business plan* provides high level information concerning the company-wide business vision, objectives, critical success factors, cost drivers and SWOT analysis (strengths, weaknesses, opportunities, and threats). If this information is incomplete, or unavailable at this time, IT must "make do" with the information it has at hand. It should be obvious that if the company's plan isn't known, it's very difficult to develop an effective support strategy for it.

Strategic management plan worksheet:

The role of the worksheet was discussed in chapter 2. It provides the initial plans for all the basic IT management processes and thereby "jump starts" the plan development process. It provides an effective vehicle for collecting, organizing, and storing additional plan information. Because the worksheets are stored in a repository, the plan information can be easily shared amongst the planning session participants. Worksheet information is used to update next year's plan file.

Portfolio of current plan status reports:

The portfolio can include reports on a variety of IT areas which collectively represent a broad view of current IT plan status. The reports indicate differences in the way resources were planned as compared to how they are actually being utilized. They provide the manager the opportunity to make mid-plan adjustments. Plan status can be reported on any reporting cycle. A forecasted EOY plan variance is usually a more meaningful number because it considers work scheduling nuances. Plan status can be reported at the production and development work levels only, or a manager can "drill-down" to any required level of detail work. A report or graph which illustrates planned and/or actual work by WCS major work categories as a percent of total planned work and/or total actual work are extremely useful reports. Just a simple graphic depicting total plan requirements, total resource availability, and the gap between the two numbers can be very useful. Reports can be grouped by IT divisions, business units, associates, work categories, or any combination thereof. The status reports mentioned in the book concentrate on reporting status in terms of planned versus actual staff hours, but the reports can just as easily report on budgeted cost versus actual cost. The general types of suggested status reports included in a portfolio of current plan status reports are:

- Current year plan status
- Business unit plan status (discussed as a part of associate status)
- Associate status
- Task or work status
- Project status.
- Management status

No sample reports will be presented in this section. Book 2 presents samples of these reports using data contained in a model company prototype database. Since this book is concerned with principles, only general descriptions of sample reports, including their intended usage in managing IT resources, are presented. What the reader should observe is that if the data is captured at the required level of specificity, generation of queries and reports of all types can be quickly made. The key is knowing what data you need to perform your management responsibilities.

Current Year Plan Status:

These type of reports indicate how well IT is performing against current plan objectives. An example of such a report is a plan variance report indicating YTD status and projected EOY status of planned resources as compared with actual resources utilized. An EOY status would seem to provide more valuable information to the planners than a YTD status.

Associate Status Reports:

IT managers want to know - For which business clients are their associates working? What type of work are they performing? Are they properly accounting for their time? What other IT support units are requesting their services?

One measure of associate status is a report of *associate's percent of effort*. The percent of effort is calculated by dividing the associate's original plan hours, the YTD plan hours, and the forecasted hours respectively by the associate's net available hours. The purpose of this report is to monitor changes in an associate's planned work activities. It allows the IT manager to determine where an associate was originally planned to spend their time; where the associate is currently spending their time; and where the associate is forecasted to spend their time by the end-of-year.

This report provides feedback on the accuracy of the associate's plan. It can serve as a turn-around document to report associate plan changes to the IT plan administrator. Regular review of this information with the associate provides a significant opportunity for the IT manager to gain further knowledge of the associate's work activity. It places the manager in the planning loop, and helps achieve the objective of internalizing planning and resource management in the manager's daily activities.

A report of an associate's *planned utilization of their time* can be used by the IT manager to determine what percent of an associate's net available hours are currently planned. It can be used to identify under-utilized staff, or staff who may need their plan revised to reflect their current planned work.

Accurate entry of time is essential to the success of any work management system. A *time entry efficiency report* can be used by the IT manager to effectively monitor associate time reporting activity status. Time entry efficiency is a percent calculated by dividing the number of hours actually recorded by the associate within a given time period by the total number of hours available for work in the same time period. Time entry efficiency becomes extremely important in cost and service chargeback management. Time entry is the primary means of recovering the cost of staff services. Efficiency percents normally should be in the range of 95% - 105% to satisfy cost and charge back requirements. In a standard costing environment too low an efficiency percent, and IT cannot recover their staff service costs, and too high an efficiency percent, and IT over-charges the business clients. Too high an efficiency percent can create overtime billing issues.

A report of *associate planned and actual time by business unit* enables the IT division manager to review an associate's current work assignments by business unit and IT support units. It helps answer the question - "With which business clients and IT units are my associates spending their time, and what work are they doing for them?" This report can be helpful in discussions conducted among the associate, the IT manager, and the business unit manager. If an IT manager is going to meet with a business unit manager who wants to know which associates are working on their account, and what type of work they are performing, the IT manager may want the report grouped by the IT manager's unit, business unit, work categories, and the associates supporting the business unit. If the CIO, or some member of IT senior staff wants to know how all IT support units are deployed in support of the business units, the report could be grouped by IT department, business unit, IT support unit, and IT associates. This can be a very useful report, one that is valuable in support of the preliminary planning sessions.

A report of *associates with project resource conflicts* enables IT managers to gain control over project leaders, or IT managers, who assign associates to projects without obtaining approval from the associate's manager. Assignment of associates to projects, or non-project work, without first checking with the associate's manager is a significant IT management issue in many companies, and one that planning and resource management can positively impact. These unapproved assignments tend to "remain under the planning radar" until resource conflicts appear in the project schedules. Often project leaders view associates only from their own project perspective, not from the perspective of other IT managers they may be negatively impacting. They fail to recognize, or care, that an associate can be working on other projects, or be carrying a significant production support work requirement. In fairness to project leaders some associates want assignment to a project and they hesitate to bring-up their other commitments to the project leader.

This report is grouped by IT support unit, associate, work priority, and work type (project, non-project). It summarizes all associate non-project work and assigns it a number 1 priority code. All projects currently assigned to the associate are listed in project priority sequence. The non-project and project plan hours are totaled and subtracted from the net hours available for the associate. If this calculation results in a negative amount, the associate is flagged as "Insufficient Resources for Projects" along with the shortage of hours. Use of the priority code makes it easier to determine which project assignments need review. The report doesn't indicate which projects must be adjusted because the report is only measuring the fit of total requirements within a given planning time period. The report can be grouped by project instead of associate in order to list all projects that have significant scheduling conflicts.

A report of other *IT support units requesting resources* addresses the issue of formally requesting associate resources from other IT division managers. Its primary purpose is to keep IT managers informed of which IT divisions are officially requesting their associates' time to work on projects. It provides a simple method and process for IT managers to formally order and report these resource requests. The requestor, and a description of the project/work for which the resources are being requested, are listed in the request description. It is a great communications tool for IT managers. The report accommodates all work categories and all types of resources (e.g. equipment, software, and training) in addition to associate resources that may be required by a project.

Project Status Reports:

"What is the impact of major projects on available IT resources?" Projects, especially enterprise projects, utilize a major portion of IT staff resources. Work on projects can significantly impact production and enhancement work if not properly managed. The percent of resources allocated to project development can approach 50% or more in many companies. This percent can easily increase if resources other than staff resources are considered. Any number of enriched project reports can be produced if a company has a robust project management system.

Task/Work Status Reports:

"What work consumes the most IT resources?" Is the IT plan properly balanced between production and new development work? What systems, or system support functions, require the largest amount of IT staff resources? Reports listing the number of hours IT performs on various work items can be a real "eye-opener" for the business units. IT managers can almost hear the business managers say, as they look at the reports, that they never imagined the size or cost of some of the work initiatives performed on their behalf. Especially enlightening is the amount of work spent on behalf of production support, general systems enhancement, and general management and administration. Information like this helps dispel the perception many business clients have about IT resource availability when they view IT only in terms of headcount.

A *report ranking overall work by actual hours worked* is a report type useful in determining what projects or other work categories are utilizing the resources. An important feature of a report like this is that it combines project work, non-project work, and administrative and management work into a single overall ranking using YTD hours worked. By reporting the various work items on the same report it enables IT and the business community to observe how the various work items compete with each other. The IT manager needs to review situations in which there is a large volume of planned work yet little, or no, actual work recorded. Assuming the work item has been scheduled and initiated, this situation could be indicative of poor planning that can seriously compromise the accomplishment of other work items.

General management and administration is a work item that is usually reported at, or near, the top of the report in resource consumption. The position of this work item is bound to stir some discussion within the business units of any company. It's interesting to observe the relationship of hours worked to the work item's priority on such a report. The expectation would generally be that the higher priority projects would demand a relatively higher share of the resources, but before the IT manager makes that determination they need to consider scheduling and the planned resources required by the work item. A priority work item may just have been initiated, or it may not have been scheduled to begin at the time of reporting. Not all priority work items need involve a significant allocation of resources. A relatively high ranking of general systems/programming enhancements should be expected. This is another work item that often "runs under the radar screen", and doesn't get noticed until it shows-up on a report like this one.

A companion report can easily be written that provides a ranking of work items based upon the amount of planned resources. It provides management a relative sense of the magnitude of the projects being planned. Reports can also be ranked on total cost of the planned work. It seems everyone has a good idea of the value of a dollar.

Management Status Reports:

Reports in this category address the general question—What is the overall health of the IT department? Management issues are divided into two categories based upon organizational scope or impact of a management issue. The first category relates to issues at the IT department, division, group, or associate levels, and it can be addressed by the use of a dashboard type utility. The second category relates to company-wide issues.

A dashboard is designed to provide graphical overviews of key information items that provide the managers with the basic information they need to manage their area of individual responsibility. Liken it to the design and purpose of an automobile's dashboard. On a dashboard the driver may want to see every gauge which enhances successful operation of the vehicle, or the driver may only want to see selective gauges that focus concentration on the most important status indicators of the automobile's performance. It could be that the speedometer is the only gauge required when driving a sports car. The IT manager's first task is to identify the status indicators they want to monitor.

Dashboards can be grouped by IT department, individual IT units, business units, IT associates, work categories, or any combination of these options. The "health" of any IT organizational unit is reflected in the information provided to answer a series of questions about the IT unit. Is the unit within its budget? Who are the unit's business clients? Are the clients getting their expected share of the available resources? What is the unit's on-time, within budget performance record? What type of work does the unit perform? Is the unit fully utilized? Is the unit entering the expected amount of time in the system? Where are the areas within IT that are experiencing the majority of the resource conflicts? What business application systems require the most maintenance and production support? Why do systems require excessive resources? Are there any enterprise projects that are "in trouble"?

Company-wide management issues is the second management status category. Status of these issues are normally found in the statement of company and IT strengths, weaknesses, opportunities, and threats (SWOT). If projects have been aligned properly to address these issues, the status of the projects aligned with the issues can provide a more precise statement of the general health of the company and IT department. There are any number of SWOT alignment reports that can be designed to assist in identifying and addressing these issues. These issues should also have been identified in the IT strategic management plan worksheet.

Answering the Question - "Where do we want to be?"

"An accurate forecast is very difficult to make, especially when it is about the future." Yogi Berra, New York Yankees.

The business managers rely on IT to assist them in imagining the potential, positive impact of the new technologies on company's future operations. Potential negative factors also need to be anticipated. Changes in governmental regulations can adversely affect a company. Business competition can decrease sales. Skilled staff required to operate the manufacturing plants and develop new products might not be available or become unaffordable. Robotics can have a significant impact on jobs. Visioning is truly a cooperative process between IT and the business community.

Creating a vision of a company's future position, and attempting to forecast the plans required to achieve the vision, is a very difficult task, as stated by Yogi Berra. Don't be discouraged by others, especially Yogi, from attempting to develop a long range vision. No one can predict the future with even near 100% accuracy, but if there is a process in place that sets reasonable expectations about the future, and reacts quickly to variances in these expectations as they occur, then major steps towards developing a realistic look into the future can be obtained.

One of the first things that has to be determined is - exactly how far away is the future? Is it 5, 10, 15, 20 years, or more from today. In the not too distant past, and from a visioning perspective, a company may have thought the future was a minimum of 15-20 years away, but with the rapid advances in technology development a company's vision is probably better reset to 5-10 years. A five year IT plan is compatible with a 5-10 year vision. A plan has two major components - a business plan/vision, and a statement of the specific objectives, strategies, and the detail work that must be performed to achieve the business plan/vision. The vision can easily span any number of years because it represents a more generalized statement of what might happen, but a statement of the specific objectives, strategies, and the detail work that is required to achieve the business plan/vision is more difficult to plan at a detail level beyond the initial five year period.

The IT five year plan is a "rolling" type plan that is re-projected by one additional year each new planning cycle. It isn't like a planner has to start the plan from "scratch" each year. This re-projection permits a reassessment and review of the vision and any major changes to the assumptions upon which the vision is based.

Even though the company's business plan acts as a compass that directs IT planning efforts, IT must realize the business plan may not be complete even in the later stages of the plan development process. The company goes through a similar business plan development process as does IT, so it is reasonable to expect some degree of incompleteness in the business plans provided to IT. Considering the fact that any company's strategic business plan is probably structured like IT's "rolling" five year plan, it seems reasonable that IT should not feel like they have to scramble if the current business plan is still in the development stage at this time in the process. It's not like each year the company's business plan radically changes, unless there has been a significant change in top management or company direction. IT must go with what it is given and make revisions when additional information becomes available.

Answering the Question - "How do we get there?"

If you know where you want to be, but you don't have a map to guide you there, then seek the guidance of those who have been there before. Ask them for directions and what resources are needed to support the journey.

A significant amount of planning information is gathered and organized in answering the first two planning questions, but there's one more question to be answered—How do we get there? Without a "how to" response, a plan is just a bunch of words. To provide answers to the "how" question, IT and the company business units must meet again in a series of more focused planning meetings designed to create a final operational plan that represents all company interests. The plans identified in the preliminary planning sessions must be assimilated into a company plan and prioritized across business units, not just within business units. Work must be clearly aligned with business unit objectives, and right-sized to the resources that have been approved. It is inevitable that there will be many more plan requirements than available resources; therefore, objective criteria must be used as a basis of determining which work items will be included in the final operational plan.

Business planning meetings:

The series of semi-formal preliminary planning sessions now gives way to an entirely new series of meetings between IT and the business units. These meetings are referred to as the business planning meetings. They continue until the final operational plan is completed. The meetings are more structured than the preliminary planning sessions. They exercise a greater level of planning precision. The meetings' "flavor" shifts from an emphasis on current year plan activity and status to the finalization of next year's operational plan. Attendees at the meetings can vary in number and content. A company should use whatever structure works best for them considering the company's culture, resources, and organizations, but one thing must be present in the meetings, empowered individuals.

The meetings should be supported by a new series of reports, although nothing precludes supplementing the new reports with reports used in the previous preliminary planning sessions. The new reports can include such reports as: business planning worksheets; prioritization reports; plan alignment reports; and gap analysis reports

The new reports should be created from the perspective of the business units, not necessarily from IT's perspective. IT needs to make sure that the business units understand the services they will be provided in the coming plan year; what IT support units and associates will provide these services; what these services will cost; and what level of resource availability will be assigned to the business units. The business units almost always come to the meetings with a list of requirements that far exceed IT's ability to satisfy them. IT needs to know "when push comes to shove" in the meetings what work needs to be included in next year's plan, and what priority it should be assigned.

Business planning worksheets:

These reports are the primary reports used to support the business planning meetings. They are an excellent "centerpiece" around which to conduct the meetings. They function as the official document used to record decisions made at the meetings. Work that was identified in the preliminary planning sessions are included on the report for review and selection as candidates for final operational plan inclusion. New planned work can be added, or existing work deleted. The expectation is that the business units will review the list of currently planned work and verify two items: Is the work listed on the worksheets the work currently being requested? Are next year's planned amount of resources for the listed work the correct amount? Planned work can be accepted "as is", or the work can be accepted with changes noted on the worksheet. A planned work item that is not to be included in next year's plan is marked for deletion. Work items that are not listed on the worksheet, but should be included, are entered at the end of the worksheet for further evaluation. The worksheet is a working, turn-around type document.

In addition to providing the planning requirements in terms of staff hours, the worksheet includes non-staff budget items such as computer test time, new software acquisitions, or special equipment purchases. At the end of the worksheet all these planned items are costed and compared to the business unit's IT budget, and a budget variance is produced.

Selection of planned work at this stage of plan development doesn't necessarily guarantee the inclusion of the work in the final plan. Projects selected are viewed from a broader, company-wide focus in which the work of each business unit competes for priority and inclusion in the final operational plan with the other business units' work. Priority is determined by the degree to which the work is best aligned with the achievement of business plan and supporting IT objectives. Any agreed-upon actions taken at the meetings is communicated to the IT plan administrator via the marked-up worksheets so that the information can be posted to the appropriate files in the work management system. After the changes are applied, the reports are rerun and redistributed to the meeting participants. The process is repeated until all planned work is resolved.

Plan prioritization reports:

The most difficult part of prioritization occurs when shortages of resources cross major company organizational lines. Establishing cross-organization priorities is the true test of caring about the common good of a company. Conflicts in cross organizational prioritization can result from political motives in which a business unit's needs are put above company needs. Ignorance of each other's needs can also be a source of conflict. Use of the plan model and the plan layers will assist in making sure all plans get a proper audience. A particularly difficult area of cross-prioritization occurs between IT sponsored projects and business sponsored work. Business units are not always happy sharing their scarce resources with the IT department, even though the work IT performs is on behalf of the general business community. Too often business units work within their own management silos. Working within a silo can produce a different view of what is important to the company. A well-created priority scheme can help build a sense of understanding what work is important to each SBU, and why it is so important. Hopefully SBU heads utter statements after reviewing the priority reports that they never knew that such work was so important to another SBU. In many ways it is the business plan, if properly prioritized and communicated, that has the key to opening the doors to the management silos.

A factor compounding the issue of priorities is that a given project or work item can have multiple priorities. In designing the planning functions consider that a project can have a business unit priority, a division priority, a departmental priority, and possibly a company priority, and these priorities can be different across planning periods (i.e. current year and next year).

Some work priorities are a "given". Work that "keeps the lights on" in a company is one of those work categories. Included in this non-discretionary work category are not only computer operations, production support, and break/fix work, but also compliance work, security, and installing required vendor maintenance and required system "patches". Discretionary work, like the name implies, requires the planners to exercise more judgment in setting priorities. All too often major enterprise projects "bump" tactical projects and system enhancement work much to the dismay of the business unit managers whose required work has been "bumped". System enhancements and tactical projects work are considered discretionary to some business managers, but there are other business managers who make a strong case for these tactical resources which they claim enhance their current systems in order to remain competitive with the rest of the industry. The failure to deliver some level of basic system enhancements can cause inefficiencies and workarounds in the business units. There are at least two options available to solve the conflict. The first option is to allocate a certain amount of priority system enhancement resources to each business manager in the plan development process. These resources would be treated as non-discretionary for purposes of planning. The second option is to contract with a staff augmentation firm to employ contractors to address the enhancement requirements.

Another issue surrounding priorities is a little more company-wide in scope. Business managers can sometimes think that the allocation of planned IT work and resources is not fair and equitable. They need to know of the work and resources allocated to them over which they have control, and the work that is "pushed into" their plan. If IT doesn't educate them in the process of work and resource allocations, they can get downright paranoid about the resource allocation process. They begin to think the other business units are getting a larger share of the resources to perform their work. This is a real issue that IT must address by educating the business managers how resources are allocated.

The business managers need to know that resource allocations are driven by the priority of the work assigned to each business area, not by some arbitrary allocation method. They need to understand that there is work performed on their behalf of which they may be unaware (e.g. administration, production support, and required maintenance). Enterprise projects also affect the resources available to the business managers to perform their work. Infrastructure work impacts their resource allocations similarly. Planning reports can assist IT in educating the business mangers about the issues of prioritization and resource allocations.

Plan alignment reports:

As a general planning principle, if someone says they are going to achieve an objective, just ask them "How?" Objectives, plans, visions cannot be achieved without some specific work activity assigned to their accomplishment. Alignment provides the answers to the "How" question. Alignment also assists in establishing work priorities. Work tends to assimilate the priority of the objectives to which it is aligned. Work not aligned to objectives may be more difficult to prioritize. At this stage of plan development process IT needs to assure itself that the work currently identified in the planning process is really the work that best satisfies the company's business plan objectives. Work can align with multiple objectives. Current year, on-going work efforts should be reviewed to determine if they are still properly aligned with planned objectives.

There will be misalignments between objectives and work items, both in the current and forecasted plans. Some amount of planned work without alignment to specific objectives should not be considered a major concern unless the amount of planned work involves significant resources. Determining if this is an issue worthy of addressing is strictly a judgment call on IT management's part. If alignment is made too rigid a process, IT runs the risk of "turning off" the IT and business managers to the planning process. Alignment can become an exercise in minutia. The situation in which major objectives have no corresponding work items aligned to them should generate concern. Sometimes major objectives are just "filler" items designed to enrich plan reports. IT needs to work to eliminate these types of objectives from their plans, but if upon further investigation IT proves these objectives are "for real", then IT better plan the work necessary to accomplish them.

Cost drivers and SWOT analysis items (strengths, weaknesses, opportunities, and threats) represent management objectives/issues. They normally identify very specific objective/issues that if addressed, can produce significant improvements in IT operation. IT needs to get these objectives into the plan as a matter of priority, and identify and align the work targeted to accomplish the objectives.

Gap analysis reports:

The IT management gap analysis objective is to manage the gap between available IT resources and required resources to a reasonable equilibrium and still maximize the achievement of objectives that best advances the company towards its business vision.

A gap analysis report typically is run for the entire IT department or for individual IT divisions. The report begins with a statement of the total net available resource hours for the particular entity being analyzed. Work is then prioritized. Non-discretionary work can be grouped together and given a priority code of 1 (the highest priority) since non-discretionary work should be completed before all other work is started. The remaining work is processed against the net availability of resource hours in priority sequence. Processing consists of subtracting the detail work requirements (projects and non-projects) from the running total of net available resource hours. When a work requirement exceeds the running net availability of resource hours, the work, and all subsequent work for the entity, is flagged as having insufficient resources. A very effective grouping of a gap analysis report is by the IT department, priorty, the work requirements, and the individual IT divisions supporting the work requirements. Running the report in this manner isolates which IT division exhausts its resources first for a work requirement, and thus identifies itself as a resource bottleneck.

There are several options available to address the gap issue. Additional IT resources can be acquired; work can be eliminated; or the work can be reprioritized, or a combination of these options can be selected. Don't ignore significant resource gaps, and don't resolve resource gaps by arbitrarily eliminating projects from the plan. Eliminating requirements is not the only way to reduce gaps. Adding resources to a plan is a reasonable alternative in reducing gaps.

Review, Modify, Select, and Approve the Plan

Matters become even more formal and quite contentious at this stage of the plan development process as business units negotiate to get their work included in the final operational plan. If an IT unit's plan at this planning stage is out-sized to net available resources for the IT unit, then the IT unit and the business managers need to collectively, and reasonably, eliminate this gap before a final plan can be determined.

If senior company management won't increase IT's resources to a level that eliminates a gap, then a formal selection process must be used to right-size the plan by eliminating work from it. In reducing the gap, avoid making arbitrary reductions to individual planned work items just to fit the plan within the net resource availability constraints. All this does is "kick the resource conflicts further down the road". Moving decisions out further sets up IT for the Phase 2 projects and "shoe box" systems as previously discussed.

The obvious solution to the resolution of the gap is to eliminate/re-schedule/postpone some projects to reduce the resource gap. Plans are normally supported by other IT support units; therefore, work cannot be arbitrarily excluded from the plan just because one IT support unit can't satisfy its requirements within its available resources or schedule restrictions.

Changes to one IT support group's plans can have far reaching "rippling effects" on the plans and resources of other IT support units and individual business unit plans.

Modifications of a plan are normally made in a series of plan releases. A revised plan is produced and reviewed each time a release is processed. It is very important to keep a log of the changes made to the plan file. Memories are often short, and when the final operational plan is published, there are usually some upset business managers because all their work was not included in the final plan. The work management system should maintain some type of a plan change file which identifies the modified plan items, the modification date, by whose authority the modification was made, and the reason why the work was excluded from the final plan. It is a good idea to print the plan change file after each plan release update is made. A plan file change report is normally grouped by a release number for control purposes. At the end of each report a release analysis can be printed which lists the remaining gap status of the plan. Work that is removed from the plan is maintained as a transaction in a plan change file. Deleted work should be considered candidates for plan inclusion in subsequent planning years. Maintaining the planned work removed from a plan advances the planning process ever closer to a multi-year planning horizon. It also provides a head-start to next year's plan development process. The process of modifying the plan and re-releasing it for review and approval is repeated until the operational plan is reasonably right-sized. When this occurs, the plan is officially approved and released for publication.

Just a note about retaining deleted plans in a plan change file. If a deleted plan constantly appears in the plan change file, it may be time to permanently delete it from the file. It just becomes clutter. There seems to be a reluctance in some managers to delete the plan record even though it has become obvious that the plan item will never be selected.

Scheduling and Other Considerations

Prioritization, plan alignment, and right-sizing don't solve all the planning issues. For example, IT may have developed a plan that is right-sized to the resources, but the resources are not available at the time when needed. Additionally, the staff may not have the skills needed to perform the work at the required time. To address these additional planning questions, work needs to be formally scheduled and linked to a skills database. Without a project management system (PMS) in the system architecture, scheduling and skills based management functionality is greatly diminished.

Scheduling work is more than just sequencing it in a priority sequence. The work management system discussed in this book only provides the assurance that there are enough resources to complete the work in a given plan year, but it makes no attempt at scheduling the work within the plan year.

What if everyone wants their work completed by the 2nd quarter? Obviously, that's not possible. The scheduling requirement can introduce all types of resource conflict situations in the plan that must be reasonably resolved before the plan is finalized. It may force IT to go back and review some previous steps with new information. Various conflict reports mentioned previously in this chapter can assist in identifying where resource conflicts exist, but they won't help in scheduling the work to eliminate the conflicts, or secure the necessary resources to complete the projects.

Formal work scheduling isn't included in the book because it goes beyond the book's scope, but it must be made a part of the planning process. The situation may not be as difficult to remedy as it first appears. Considering the fact that a significant amount of non-project work is classified as non-discretionary in nature, and projects are generally considered discretionary in nature, one would reasonably think that project work should be scheduled around the non-discretionary work requirements. Under this scenario the onus of scheduling project work around the non-discretionary work requirements would seem to be on the Project Management Office (PMO) and its project management system (PMS). The reasonableness of this scheduling approach is tested when some senior business managers consider all their major project work as non-discretionary.

That issue aside, a work management system will do a good job of managing the non-project work because of the nature of the work. Project work assignments should be worked around non-discretionary work; therefore, it makes sense that the scheduling function be performed in a PMS system.

A PMS project scheduling capability is greatly enhanced by a work management system because a work management system can provide an associate's complete work requirements to a PMS. The scheduling requirement is another very important reason to consider having a PMS as a central component of the IT work management architecture. If you don't have a PMS, you'll have to improvise and manually develop a scheduling technique. Even where automatic scheduling features are available, IT often relies upon manual intervention to make the required scheduling changes.

A skills inventory function which assists in ensuring associates with the proper skills are available to support a project at the time required can also be satisfied with many PMS systems. If a PMS doesn't have a skills management function, then other options must be investigated. Where, and how staff skills are stored, accessed, and utilized is a matter of IT choice. Skills can be maintained as a part of the company's legacy human resources/payroll systems, or as an adjunct file in the work management system. Maintenance and use of a skills inventory system is a significant task, one that is not in the scope of this book.

"How do we know we are there?"

We know we are "there" because:

- A plan which clearly stated our destination was developed
- The work required to get "there" was aligned along the path to the destination
- The plan was linked to a budget so the cost of journey was affordable
- The resources required to support the journey were planned and available
- The plan was communicated to everyone making the journey so that everyone knew where they were going and their role in getting to the destination
- Every member did their assigned job in completing the journey

In some ways these six points summarize the entire planning process. It is not all that difficult. It's mostly common sense.

Publish the Formal Plans

It's the journey that matters, and the formal plan documents are evidence that the journey has taken place.

For completeness sake in writing the book, three IT plans types are identified and presented:

- IT operational plan
- IT strategic management plan
- IT technology plan

Most companies probably publish only one IT plan report - the computer generated operational plan created as part of a work management system. The number and types of plans published is up to the discretion of the company and the IT department. The other two plans represent the visions, objectives, and strategies and major initiatives that are represented in the operational plan, and have determined its content and direction.

IT plans cannot be created independent of the company and individual business unit plans. Without a connection to the business plans, the IT plans would be just that – an "IT plan". IT plans have both an internal and external focus with the business plans. From an internal focus, IT must develop a plan for information technology as it directly impacts its internal operations. Included in the IT internal plan are the IT vision, objectives, strategies, critical success factors, cost drivers, strengths, weaknesses, opportunities and threats, and projects. From an external focus, IT's plans must align with, and support, the company and individual business unit's plans and objectives. The interaction and influence of the operational plan flows in both directions between the business units and IT.

Operational plan:

The IT *operational* plan includes the detail work initiatives required to assist in delivering the IT strategic management plan. It has a short planning horizon, most probably a year; includes production and tactical development initiatives, and is tightly linked to operating budgets. The IT operational plan includes a portfolio of planned projects and non-project work for the coming plan year. It addresses the planning question of—How do we get there? Most IT operational plans are administered by a computer-based plan administration system like a work management system. Some companies choose to concentrate on the detail project/work initiatives of the IT plan, but fail to address the strategic management environment within which these project/work initiatives are developed and implemented. If the strategic management objectives are not explicitly or implicitly included in the plan, then for what purpose is the operational work being planned? Without the strategic management element integrated into the operational plan, the operational plan can become just a report of the projects and the work IT intends to accomplish in the next planning period.

The operational plan will most probably be printed in several different groupings. The options in printing the reports is totally dependent upon the company's plan information requirements, and its willingness to capture the information at the level required to report the information. At what level (i.e. detail, work type, or program) the work should be printed is also a matter of choice. Most companies appear to want enterprise projects reported separately. Other work categories they want printed in summary format.

There are four basic ways the IT Operational Plan can be grouped to satisfy the plan information requirements of the majority of companies.

- By company, Strategic Business Unit, Major and Sub-Major Work Categories
- By company, Major and Sub-Major Work Categories
- By IT department, IT division, Major and Sub-Major Work Categories
- By IT department, Major and Sub-Major Work Categories

The report grouping options listed here have not even addressed possible groupings by technology type (e.g. data, voice, text, and image).

Strategic management plan:

The *IT strategic management plan* is mostly an "IT management affair". It addresses the questions of "Where do we want to be?" and "How do we get there?" It establishes direction and purpose for the entire IT planning process. It functions as the IT operational plan "driver". The plan covers a planning horizon of at least five years, and includes the IT vision, objectives, strategies, global technology matters, cost drivers, SWOT (strengths, weaknesses, opportunities, and threats), critical success factors, and any other major management and organizational issue impacting IT. It can include highlights of major projects that impact the direction and vision of the company, but it doesn't typically include the detail operational work initiatives necessary to deliver the strategic objectives unless the operational issues are significant in their impact on IT operations.

The initial information to develop the strategic management plan is derived from the strategic management plan worksheets created prior to the plan development process. There's really no "cookie cutter" approach to the development of the strategic management plan. The worksheets represent a voluminous amount of information. Even though the information is well structured it still will take a significant amount of effort to produce the plan. The IT plan administrator working with the IT senior management team, the IT senior technical team, the IT senior administrative team, and other IT managers as required will combine and organize the information into a strategic information management plan using whatever plan groupings the IT department determines is most suitable.

Information technology plan:

The IT technology plan is a hybrid plan that combines aspects of the IT strategic management and IT operational plans into a high level, coordinated plan document. The technology plan is the formal document distributed throughout the company. The IT strategic management plan contributes most to the vision, objectives, SWOT analysis, critical success factors, and the cost drivers in the development of a hybrid plan. It also provides the strategic management issues and objectives and the major work initiatives to be accomplished. The IT operational plan contributes most to status of the current work initiatives and the planned initiatives for the next year's plan and beyond.

Putting together a formal information technology plan document is a significant challenge because there is so much information to organize and report. Key to creating the plan document is the ability of the IT administrator to form a broad coalition of key IT and business unit managers to help in assembling all the disparate planning information into some meaningful and readable document which managers and associates want to read. The plan should lead the readers through the process from start to finish. It's easy to get lost in the "trees of the technology planning forest".

Some company plans consist of any number of individually-authored plans each having different formats and addressing different segments of the IT complex. Spreadsheets are commonly used for these planning documents. Any overall plan created in this manner tends to be cumbersome to read because it contains so many diverse plans that are not well integrated. The disparate planning documents normally represent a disparate planning process, which can be indicative of a disparate management structure. Many plans seem to concentrate on hardware, software, and technologies and neglect many of the management functions and practices required of a comprehensive plan. Use of the layered plan model as the basic structure around which to develop the information technology plan document can assist in organizing the plan document.

Remember it's the journey, not the final destination that matters. The final plan's importance is that it is evidence that a planning process has taken place. If conducted properly, information in the plan should not contain many surprises for the reader. Don't be disappointed if many readers just gloss over this document and use it as a reference document because they actively participated in the plan development process.

Figure 20 illustrates a suggested technology plan document structure. The illustration uses a cube to describe the plan document consistent with the idea that both the plan document and plan model represent an information plan. The horizontal layers of the plan structure represent the four major technology types of data, voice, text, and image. The vertical layers of the plan structure represent the major report sections. The report sections are directly linked to the strategic management and operational plans.

The technology plan is classified as a five year plan not because it looked five years into the future, but because it included five distinctive planning periods:

- Summary of the previous year's major activities
- Status of the current year plan
- Next year's strategic management plan
- Detail operational plan for next year
- Lesser detailed operational plan for the following two years

The plan is classified as a "rolling" five year plan in that each year it deletes the oldest year from the plan and adds another year to it. Creation of the first edition of the five year plan is by far the most difficult plan to create, but after that, it's all about updating the previous year's plan, and adding that extra year. Visions, strategies, objectives normally carry-over for several years. If they do change frequently, maybe they aren't strategic. It's the projects and individual work initiatives that change, but they can be readily obtained from the work management system.

The following describes the major report sections of the plan document in more depth.

Title Page	The title page reflects the company's decision to develop a five year information plan.
Plan Structure	The structure of the plan is based upon the model. It is critical that the plan reader understand the basic concepts and assumptions upon which the plan model is developed. This section explains, in summary format, the overall structure of the IT plan model and the supporting plan development process.

Figure 20 Suggested Format for the Technology Plan

PLAN DEVELOPMENT PROCESS

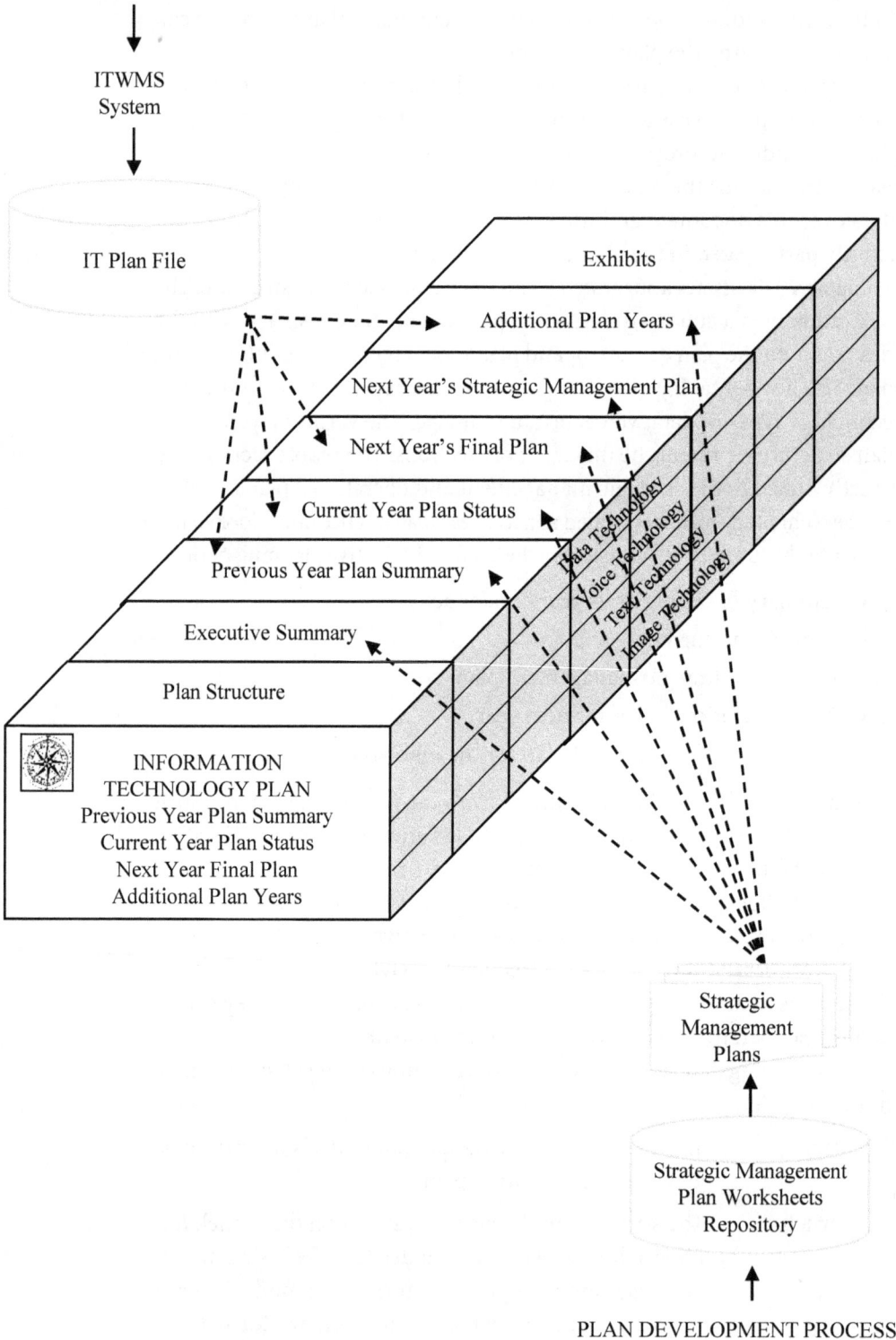

Executive Summary	The executive summary reflects a high level synopsis of all the important planning information. Much of the information reported in this section can be obtained from the IT Strategic Management Plan. Don't be disappointed if many of the readers read only this section of the plan. There are any number of ways to group information in this section. It's a matter of preference. One way of grouping information is by IT, the major strategic business units (SBUs), and the four major technology areas.
Previous Year Plan Summary	This section contains a very brief review and status of last year's major plan accomplishments and management initiatives. Planned initiatives that were not completed should be included. A metric indicating the percent of planned objectives accomplished would be very useful to include in this section. Most of this information can be obtained by reviewing last year's plan.
Current Year Plan Status	This section includes work management system reports which indicate current plan status. Many of the reports are those described in the preliminary planning sessions and business planning meetings. The number and types of reports to include here are up to the planner's imagination.
Next Year's Final Plan	This section contains the final IT operational plan report, and any supporting reports and documents.
Next Year's Strategic Management Plan	This section of the plan is strictly an "IT management affair" as contrasted with the IT operational plan which reports specific work to be performed next year and beyond. It is strategy and objectives focused. The format is narrative in style. It is structured according to the model's management plan layer concept. Accordingly, there are 24 individual plan layer write-ups in this section, each write-up authored by the plan layer owner. Remember too that a plan must be created for each of the four technologies of data, text, voice, and image. A summary of the individual plan layers at the beginning of this section is recommended.
Additional Plan Years	The information in this section represents work that was not selected for next year's plan, but was deemed worthy of consideration in later planning years. It also includes any projects which were specifically targeted for later plan years. Plans in this period of time are typically less structured than those in the immediate plan year.

Consider this report section optional in the early plan development efforts, but at some point it should be seriously considered for inclusion in the plan.

Exhibits   Supporting plan documentation can be included in this section.

Strategic Management Plan Worksheet
Planning and Resource Management Process

Objectives:

Questions asked by many company managers are: Why plan or perform resource management? What is it that IT is attempting to achieve with these functions? Managers don't have the time to do all that formal planning activity. They have work to do. Managers are "doers", not a bunch of "blue sky" planners. Really? Maybe a better question to ask would be - "Why not plan?"

Planning is much more than just writing a nice document containing lots of projects. It's about fundamentally changing the way IT operates. It is about your planning assumptions, the model you use, the IT and company management strategies, structure, organization and best practices that support the plan. It's about architecture. All these things must be addressed to plan effectively.

The following objectives are established for the Planning and Resource Management Process in a "best company" environment. Some of the objectives are repeated over the processes, but a particular process may have unique strategies to achieve them.

- Develop a Better Understanding of IT's Mission within the Company
- Create an IT Business Orientation
- Build Better Business Partnerships
- Enhance IT Management and Associate Effectiveness
- Enhance the Planning Process

Strategies to Achieve Objectives:

The strategies are the action plans concerning how the process will achieve its objectives. Note that strategies can align with multiple objectives.

Develop a Better Understanding of IT's Mission within the Company:

- Develop and communicate a formal mission statement
- Mission - contribute to the company's bottom line
- Mission - operate IT as any other business unit
- Mission - serve and create value-added partnerships
- Mission - deliver information products to its clients

Create an IT Business Orientation:

- Use the business plan to identify business objectives.
- Manage IT as any other business unit
- Implement planning, resource management
- Use common accounting, management best practices, and reporting standards
- Facilitate technical decision making by adding a business dimension to the process
- Obtain better knowledge of company business practices and financial reporting
- Create an atmosphere of metrics and objective measurements
- Report IT activity in financial terms as well as hours, dates, resource units, CPU time, etc.
- Create a view of planning from a business as well as a technical perspective

Build Better Business Partnerships:

- Seek value-added business/technical partnerships
- Develop plan sponsorship and champions to gain visibility and support for IT's planning efforts
- Establish realistic expectations for delivery of IT products and services
- Develop realistic understanding of business resource requirements and IT's capacity to satisfy those requirements by working together in the planning process.
- Promote a service mentality
- Clearly define business clients' responsibilities in the planning process
- Promote the idea that IT associates are businessman who just happen to be professional technologists
- Increase the business unit's awareness that IT needs to be included in upfront project development discussions
- Reinforce the idea that business units sometimes fail to effectively communicate their requirements to IT on a timely basis, or fail to have their resources available to support IT initiatives when required.
- Develop an IT mentality of "projects on time, within budget, and delivered as defined".
- Promote and communicate the importance of teamwork.
- Proactively involve both IT and business managers in the planning process so that they feel they have more control in the process.

Enhance IT Management and Associate Effectiveness:

- Plan the technologies of data, voice, text, and image under the information processing concept
- Promote the idea that a plan is a value-add service to the IT managers, not an encumbrance or restriction of their work.
- Assign management ownership and responsibility for all management functions, facilities, and processes identified in the basic IT management functions plans
- Use the time reporting capability of the planning system to detect areas of operational inefficiency.
- Provide management information not previously available to the IT and business management staffs.
- Promote the management concept that it's not how much information the manager surrounds themselves with, its knowing and using the elements of information that allows the manger to effectively manage their area of responsibility that is important.
- Develop better methods of prioritizing work. Concentrate on assigning priorities for work that cross organizational boundaries.
- Internalize the planning process into daily management practices. Managers need to perform the work that is planned.
- Balance an individual's desire for autonomy with the manager's need to plan and manage overall resources within budget limitations.

Enhance the Planning Process:

- Better synchronize the budget and planning processes
- Create more effective and inclusive plan development process
- Promote creation of a common planning model and process for the business community and IT
- Develop an equitable technology research and development funding process
- Implement a tightly managed plan change process
- Create better coordination of the entire planning process by integrating computer platforms and information technologies.
- Centralize administrative management of the planning process

Strengths, weaknesses, opportunities, and threats (SWOT):

Because the "best company" is the same for each process, the SWOT analysis for this process will not be repeated here. Reference chapter 2, *IT Management Model, Strategic Management Plan Worksheet, Develop and Manage the IT Management Model Process* for the details of the "best company" SWOT analysis.

Cost drivers:

The major cost driver of planning and resource management is the volume and complexity of the work to be planned. Another factor is the completeness and accuracy of the work requirement definitions. On the positive side of matters, IT costs should be reduced because of more effective deployment of IT resources.

Deliverables:

The following lists some of the deliverables (benefits) a company can expect to receive from a successful implementation of the Planning and Resource Management Process.

- Alignment of work with company business plan objectives
- Coordinated IT budget and planning processes
- Expense reductions
- Resources sized to requirements
- Identification of areas of operational inefficiency
- Technical and business based IT/Business Client Partnerships
- Plan management
- Resource management
- Operational, strategic, and information technology plans
- Management and financial reporting
- Work classification scheme

Critical success factors:

What event(s) must occur or strategies be successfully completed in order for the process to achieve its objectives?

- Support of the planning effort by senior business management staff
- Reduce expediency as a factor driving the planning process
- Environment of discipline, responsibility, ownership
- Emphasis on architecture of all types
- Successful implementation of the CPTOIA architecture and its supporting systems and services organization
- Excellent working relationship with the company's accounting and financial divisions
- Timely acquisition of the skills required to build and maintain the new organization and architecture
- Business units actively participating in the planning process and delivering on their responsibilities to IT

Management Function Impact Analysis:

Business plan management:

A process should align with the business objectives listed in the summary business plan example presented in chapter 1. This process aligns with, and is supportive of, the following business objectives listed in the summary business plan example.

- Continuous improvement initiatives
- Effective organizational structures
- Cost awareness
- Plan driven
- Empower staff
- Career development opportunities
- Increase skills and training opportunities
- Customer-focused solutions
- Cost effective products
- Bottom-line oriented
- Financial awareness
- Introduction of new technologies and systems in support of business plan

Process management:

This layer addresses the participants, processes, and procedures required to ensure the proper flow and interchange of information amongst the key managers involved in development and management of the planning and resource management process. The question is how will the process be structured to ensure that the planning and resource management process is properly designed and implemented? The IT plan administrator, as the owner of the process, will define and lead the process. The IT plan administrator will be assisted by members of the IT senior staffs, select members of the senior business management team, and key business managers. Of all the work management processes this is probably the most detailed and complex. The plan development process alone extends for nearly 6 months and involves nearly all the company managers in a series of planning meetings. A major objective of process management is to create a common plan model and plan development process that is shared by IT and the business units.

IT financial management:

The Planning and Resource Management Process shares in the financial management objectives and strategies listed in the Summary Busines Plan. In addition, this process emphasizes the financial management aspects of planning. It facilitates the making of better decisions about the work to be included in the plan because dollars have been added to the decision process. The process addresses the need to better synchronize the company budget and IT planning processes. Plans are more relevant because they are costed and billed. The computer architecture, the systems and services organization, and the consolidation of the four base technologies under the information processing management structure present many opportunities for expense reductions.

IT general management, leadership, organization management:

The objectives and strategies at this management layer include a business plan driven IT department. The plan provides bounds for IT planning activity, and promotes teamwork and value-added partnerships in plan development. The process unifies the management of planning activity for all information technologies and processing platforms. Use of a plan model ensures all IT management functions are planned and assigned ownership and responsibility. The process provides information not previously available to managers and better methods of prioritizing work. An objective of the process is to internalize the planning and resource management process into daily IT management practices. Associate performance reviews are enhanced by the process with the inclusion of planning information in the associate's performance folder.

Cost and service chargeback management:

The process owner has determined that cost management and service charge-back management are major components of the planning process. These management processes are described in detail in chapters 6 and 8. Cost management costs the products and services that deliver the planned work. When the planned work is finalized, cost management re-costs the plan and creates next year's budget. Service chargeback management is initiated after the finalized plan is placed in next year's production cycle. It bills the business client for the utilization of the products and services included in the plan. Service chargeback management requires that all work must be planned. It also needs to know of any new products or services that are included in the plan.

Change management:

Change management is a major part of the annual plan development process. Substantive changes to plans must be logged so plan status reporting can account for changes in projects and work items. An audit log is a common vehicle for logging and reporting such changes. If changes are permitted to be made at will, the planning system ceases to be a planning system and becomes a mere tracking system.

Client relationship (service) management:

The majority of the Planning and Resource Management Process impact on the Client Relationship (Service) Management Function occurs between the IT plan administrator, IT managers, business clients, and the various planning teams that exist around the company. The purpose of the business client relationship is to develop and manage plans to a successful conclusion. The vagaries of planning are replaced with disciplined planning procedures.

Both IT and business associates have clearly defined responsibilities in the planning process. Business clients need to communicate their planning requirements to IT. They need to be available when required to assist in the development and testing of programs and systems. IT needs to be included in upfront project development discussions. It needs to encourage business units to plan the work that is required, not the work the business clients think can be accomplished in the next planning period. It needs to assist the business clients in the development and management of their plans.

Informal type planning activity should occur on a daily basis, but when the annual plan development process begins the planning process between IT and the business clients becomes very structured.

End user computing management:
The Planning and Resource Management Process can have significant impact on this management function. The reason is that the management function is so closely allied with personal computing issues. Company planning initiatives and the concept of personal computing don't necessarily go hand-in-hand. At this management function layer there can be a lot of displeasure displayed toward the company's attempt to introduce a more formal planning structure.

Technology management:
Many times in a company technologies are informally reviewed and analyzed. There's not a lot of structure or process surrounding the management function. The Planning and Resource Management Process with its business plan driven focus on selecting technologies which best enable the company's vision can add needed structure to the entire process of selecting, reviewing, and implementing new technologies in the company. The development of R&D funding strategies will impact the technology management function even more.

Applications management, architecture management, systems software management, database management, hardware (operations) management, and communications and networking management:
Obviously all these management functions are planned and resourced managed. The big change in planning for these areas is the introduction of the computer platform, technology, and organization independent architecture (CPTOIA), along with its support organization. The requirement to support this architecture will be significant at these management function layers. It will require radically different combinations of planning teams because of the integration of computer platforms and technologies. It will also require the infusion of significant new skills and training in a rather short period of time.

Staff education, training, skills management:

Associate training and education should be aligned with the support of the planned work. This practice provides purpose and focus to training and educational efforts. So often an associate takes a training course, but never has the opportunity to apply it to their work. Significant technical training that must occur are:

- Education and training in the CPTOIA architecture and its supporting systems and services organizational structure
- Education and training in the concept of information processing

Training and education not only must address the technical skills and training of associates so that they can perform their technical jobs, but it can be used as a vehicle to promote the concepts and business environment required within IT and the business community for successful implementation of the new technical environment. This type of training can occur in a company seminar type atmosphere in which concepts can be promoted and discussed. Some suggested programs are:

- Program to explain the purpose and concepts of the IT management model
- Program to explain the purpose and concepts of planning and resource management
- Program to obtain a better knowledge of company business practices, especially in the financial area

Potential impact on other management functions:

Use this section to solicit the potential impact of the new process on the process operation of the other management function process owners.

CHAPTER 8
Service Chargeback Management

"One small technical step for IT work management, one giant leap for IT as a business partner"

Paraphrasing Neil Armstrong's famous statement when he first stepped on the moon.

Cost management identifies and costs IT products and services. Planning and resource management plans the work the IT business clients require and identifies the IT products and services required to complete the work. Service chargeback bills the business client for the IT products and services utilized in completing their work, and enters the charges for the work into the company's financial reporting system. This completes the work management "loop", and enables IT to achieve one of its objectives of operating as any other business unit.

Service chargeback is the revenue side of the IT financial management function. It ensures that each management function owner identifies and invoices the business clients for the utilization of their products and services thereby generating the revenue to recover the owner's expenses in providing these products and services. Service chargeback is frequently referred to as IT billing.

Not to trivialize service chargeback, but its implementation from a functional and systems perspective is rather straight-forward. Billing for shared computer equipment and systems utilization is probably the most demanding part of the service chargeback system's functions because of the requirement to gather data used to allocate utilization of shared services to the business clients.

A view of service chargeback from a cultural and management impact perspective is a different story. Service chargeback can be a "lightning-rod" which attracts a lot of strong negative reaction from IT associates and some business clients and managers. Service chargeback must be properly staged and introduced in a company, and especially in IT. No one likes to charge for their services. Few like to record the time they work. Few want to be associated with a service rate that is way beyond their actual rate of pay. These concerns are understandable. IT business clients can be taken aback by the significant price tag for systems and services and decide they can't afford the price tag of IT products and services. A consequence can be that they will not request services they require. This practice is not "good behavior" on the part of the business client. The only way to overcome these negative perceptions is by educating IT and business clients in the service chargeback process, its business objectives, and the manner in which the costs and rates are determined. IT needs to demonstrate that even if the business units don't formally cost and chargeback for their services, they have the same issues except that theirs' are not visible to the rest of the company. Take the advice of Luke Skywalker of Star Wars fame when he said "The force will be with you always". You better use it wisely when it comes to implementing service chargeback. You may need it.

Ownership

It is recommended that the IT financial manager be the owner of this management function. There may, or may not, be an individual service chargeback manager. The IT plan administrator should form a close working relationship with the IT financial manager because service chargeback is so closely linked operationally to planning and resource management functions. The IT financial manager leads the process, but will include the IT senior management teams, select members of the senior business management team, and other key business managers. A key player in service chargeback should be the Chief Financial Officer (CFO). A major company department that must participate in the process is the accounting department.

The management function requires an owner who can develop a *vision* of how service chargeback can change the entire manner in which IT is perceived and operates. Development of *strategies* for successful implementation of the process is an extremely important role played by the service chargeback manager because of the potential explosiveness of the service chargeback function. The ability to *facilitate* the positive interaction and support of both the IT and the business units is another important role that must be played. The *architect* and *chemist* roles are lesser roles because of the cost manager's major role in the areas of product definition and product cost component analysis.

Service Chargeback Architecture, Components and Functions

Service chargeback management is composed of the following major components and/or functions.

Work management system:

Service chargeback is a major sub-system of the work management system. It inter-operates with the sub-systems of planning, resource management, and costing in a common systems architecture. As such it shares in the system functions and features of the other sub-systems, and their connections to other legacy systems, especially the company's financial reporting systems.

Products and services:

IT products and services were defined in cost management (refer to chapter 6, *Cost Management*). They can be maintained in the system file identified as the product file. Service chargeback and cost management can share the same product file. It is important to make the products simple to understand, a concept that IT sometimes has a hard time doing. IT has a responsibility to educate the business clients how product components are combined in various ways to produce higher level type products. The product file operates much like a bill of materials file in the manufacturing industry. Wikipedia. org/wiki/bill of materials defines a bill of materials or product structure as a list of the raw materials, sub-assemblies, intermediate assemblies, sub-components, parts and the quantities of each needed to manufacture an end product. The end products in the case of service chargeback are the IT products and services "sold" to the business client, the other items in the bill of materials are the product cost components.

Business clients:

Who are IT's business clients? They are the business units to whom IT "sells" its products and services. The business clients should already have been identified and maintained in the plan and resource management sub-systems as part of the plan development process. Business units which are not IT business clients can also be stored in this file. These business units are required to support various IT reporting requirements. The development of a business client file should be consistent with the company's chart of accounts in order to maintain reporting data integrity with the company's financial reporting systems; reduce redundant data reconciliation efforts; and ensure the ability of the system to directly export invoice data into the company's financial reporting systems.

Plan file:

Billing information must be imported and stored somewhere in preparation for invoice processing. Where should the billing data be stored? This decision is really up to the discretion of the work management system designer. A good place to consider for storage of this data is the detail plan file (refer to chapter 7, *Planning and Resource Management*) which supports the planning and resource management sub-systems. After all, utilization of the IT products is all being done on behalf of the work planned in the plan file. An alternative storage facility can be a stand-alone billing collection file. This file should have linkage to the detail plan file so that billings can reference the work to which it applies.

Invoice charge types:

Time Reporting:

Associate time reporting can be captured from the planning and resource management time reporting sub-systems. It can also be captured from other legacy systems like help desk and various work request systems.

Recurring billing file:

Certain products or services are regularly billed to the clients each month. These are typically fixed, non-staff charges related to non-shared equipment or other services. It isn't the best utilization of IT resources to reenter these charges each and every month into the system. The recurring billing function automatically creates these charges and posts them to the business clients each month. Recurring expenses are typically identified in the course of the initial examination of the budgets and various company financial reports, but monthly reviews of the company's financial reports should be made to ensure that no new recurring expenses have occurred.

Miscellaneous expenses:

Miscellaneous expenses do not have the recurring nature of the expenses stored in the recurring billing file. As the name implies, these expenses can occur any time during the year, and are often unanticipated; therefore, the company financial reports must be reviewed each month to identify any expenses that have not been billed to the business client. These expenses are not normally included in a product or service rate. They are sometimes referred to as pass-thru expenses. A simplistic input data screen can provide a billing capability to enter these expenses into the system.

Computer Hardware Utilization:

Capture and entry of computer processing and related computer sub-component utilization requires a significant support effort from the IT computer operations and technical services support units. Computer job names, data storage file names, and other computer sub-component names must be changed and/or added to facilitate identification of the work being performed in the data center. Reports and/or files capturing computer processing activity must be provided by the IT operations division to the service chargeback manager on a regular billing cycle so that computer processing charges can be collected and used in the production of invoices.

Shared Software System Utilization:

Certain computer jobs executing on a computer are referred to as online systems. Cost management identified two such systems - Computer Development System and the Online Business Transaction System. These are contrasted with other software systems that are dedicated to a particular business or system function. They are systems within which business or other system applications are developed and executed in order to share common transaction development tools; common access to database management systems; shared business application access; terminal handling; and other facilities.

Billing of shared software systems poses some billing challenges. As a job running on a computer, the cost of the total software system is readily available using the same facilities used to cost any other computer job running on the computer. The challenge is allocating a reasonable charge for each individual's utilization of a shared facility without having to develop some elaborate billing allocation mechanism. Here again the IT computer operations and technical support units can provide some tools to provide the necessary information to make a reasonable allocation of billing charges. The key word is "reasonable". Chapter 6, *Cost Management* discusses two practical allocation methods that can be used.

Invoicing:

Products tend to be more effectively utilized when they have a price tag attached.

Process Overview:

It's the responsibility of the manager of each IT support unit generating charges for IT products and services to export the charges to the service chargeback system where they are formatted and stored in an invoice repository file until ready for release to the invoicing system. Control records should be sent along with batches of invoice data so that the service chargeback manager can verify the correct amount of invoice charges are received. Some of the data exported from the shared computer operations must be allocated before it is stored in the invoice repository file. Allocation methodology is supplied by the cost manager working with the accounting department. The service chargeback manager acts as the consolidator and validator of the invoice data. Once the data has been balanced and formatted, it is released for invoicing to the business client. A direct feed of the invoice information is exported to the company's financial reporting systems for inclusion in normal company financial reporting procedures.

Capture of client product utilization data:

Figure 21 illustrates how invoice data flows into service chargeback for consolidation and assembly for business client invoicing. The service chargeback objective is to use regular work management system activity reporting whenever possible to support the IT billing process. For example, time reporting statistics can be collected as a part of the daily planning and resource management sub-systems. Computer processing charges can be generated directly from statistics generated by the computers themselves. Eventually legacy systems like a company's fixed asset system or accounts payable system can be used as sources of invoice data as the service

Figure 21 Capture of Client Product Utilization Data

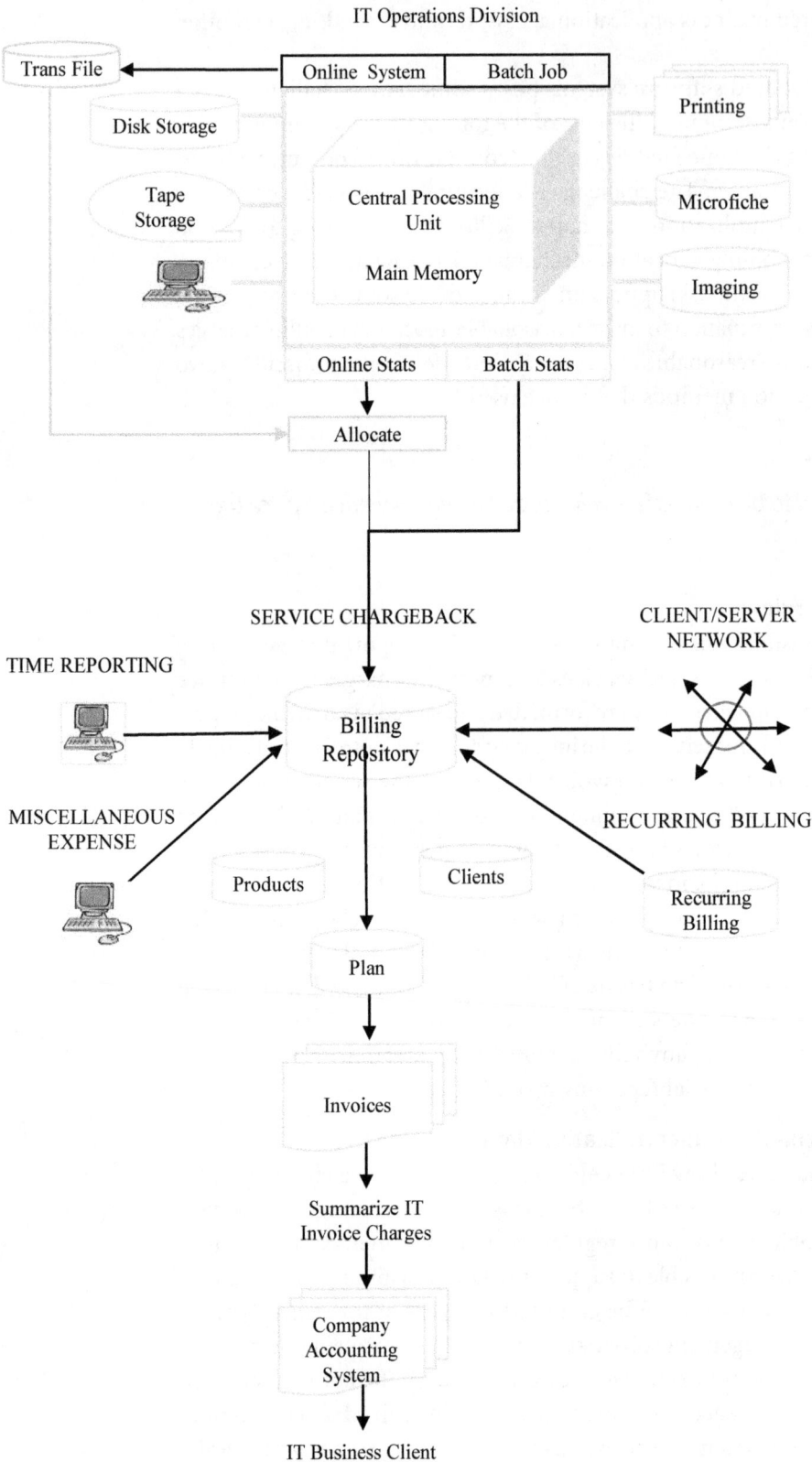

IT Operations Division

Trans File

Online System | Batch Job

Disk Storage

Printing

Tape Storage

Central Processing Unit

Main Memory

Microfiche

Imaging

Online Stats | Batch Stats

Allocate

SERVICE CHARGEBACK

CLIENT/SERVER NETWORK

TIME REPORTING

Billing Repository

MISCELLANEOUS EXPENSE

RECURRING BILLING

Products

Clients

Recurring Billing

Plan

Invoices

Summarize IT Invoice Charges

Company Accounting System

IT Business Client

chargeback system matures. The concept behind service chargeback is to make the billing input process a part of a system's normal processing activities.

Invoice preparation:

Invoices will vary in design and purpose for each company. Invoices can be viewed as just a vehicle to collect revenue from the IT business clients, or they can be viewed as an important management report. Many companies choose to view the invoice as a management report that the IT business clients definitely want to review; one that may trigger the request for additional reports to delve more deeply into the IT charges. It may be the only report that most business clients want to review. For these reasons, some serious thought should go into the design of an invoice.

To satisfy the varying invoice design requirements demanded by companies, a "best company" recommendation is to define a base invoice format for use by each IT support unit that provides a billing for its services. The objective of this basic invoice format is to satisfy the basic business requirements that invoicing is intended to satisfy, which are:

- Who is the IT business client receiving the products or services?
- What IT support unit (i.e. division) provided the products or services?
- When were the products and services provided?
- What technology class are the products and services (i.e. data, voice, text, or image)?
- What major types of service were provided (i.e. Administration, Production, or Development)?
- What specific products or services were utilized (i.e. Staff Services, Software, Development Computer Processing, or Computer Processing)?
- Was a particular business system application or business unit involved in the work (e.g. Accounts Payable System, Accounting Department, etc.)?
- If the work involved a project (e.g. Enterprise or Tactical) what was the project type and name?
- If the work involved staff services, what type of service was provided (e.g. Admin Support, Customer Service, Production Support, Required Maintenance, Design, Program, Enhance, or Demand Reports)?
- How much of the product or service was utilized?
- What is the billing rate for the product or service?
- Most importantly, what did the product or service cost?

The next issue to address is the issue of how the base invoice should be grouped and printed. Selection of an invoice grouping scheme is a company's choice driven by its information requirements.

Figure 22 illustrates an example of a base invoice with suggested groupings. In essence this grouping example provides a base invoice that groups all services by major work type, product or service, and business unit or

Figure 22 Example of Base Invoice Groupings

Information Technology Invoice (Client: Business unit receiving invoice) Technology: (data, voice, text, Image)				Invoice No: X Service Provider: (IT division)
Major Work Type Level	Product or Service Level	Application or Business Unit Level	Project Level	Work Cat Level
Administration	Staff Services	Bus Unit		Admin Support
Production				
	Computer Proc	Bus App or Bus Unit		
	Software	Bus App or Bus Unit		
	Staff Services	Bus App or Bus Unit		Customer Serv
				Prod. Support
				Required. Maint
Development				
	Dev Computer Proc	Bus App or Bus Unit		
	Software	Bus App or Bus Unit		
	Staff Services	Bus App or Bus Unit	Enterprise, Tactical	Design, program
	Staff Services	Bus App or Bus Unit	General Enhance	Programming
				Enhance
				Demand Reports

business application. Development work, except for dev computer proc and software, can be additionally grouped by project. All staff services products or services are grouped by work category. Most every item in the base invoice illustrated above could have been invoiced at the project level, if so desired. The choice of what items, and at what level of granularity they will be reported on an invoice is a matter for each company to decide based upon it's information requirements and the amount of dollars they are willing to pay to gather and report the invoice information.

To further address invoice grouping and granularity requirements the invoice can be included in a billing report packet. The packet can include a series of management reports that can be viewed as subsidiary billing reports. They can roll-up and summarize base invoice activity from the associate level to any and all appropriate upper level business and IT reporting units, in any manner or level of detail the company requires.

Financial systems interface:

IT invoices are summarized at a business client level and exported to the company's financial reporting systems on a regular reporting cycle basis. The charges are posted to the appropriate business client and IT ledger accounts. The invoice charges are considered IT revenue which should offset IT expense. To the IT business clients, the invoice charges represent real expenses which have the same impact as their other business expenses. With the implementation of service chargeback, the business client's accounting ledger reports will contain the business client's budgeted IT expenses, the actual IT expenses, and the variance between the two numbers. If the business client wants the detail of the charges reflected on their ledgers, they can review the IT invoices and a host of other service chargeback system reports that support the charges.

Conversely, IT account ledgers and statements will contain the IT expense budgets, the actual expenses, and the revenue associated with the client's invoices. The variance between the actual expenses and the revenue generated from client invoices provides IT a type of "profit/loss" statement. Importing the IT invoices into the business clients' accounting ledgers brings home the point to the business clients that IT service chargeback is not dealing in "funny money."

Monthly expense and revenue variance analysis:
If IT uses a standard method of costing as described in the book, billing variances will most probably occur throughout the course of a plan year. Both expense and revenue variances must be monitored and corrected by a coordinated expense and revenue analysis effort. A reexamination of cost, billing, and product utilization rates could be in order if any of these variances become significant. It is very important to review the monthly IT billings and the supporting company's financial reports to determine if all expenses are being properly recovered in accordance with the IT standard rates currently in effect. Within a reasonable amount of variance, a monthly billing should recover a month's actual expenses. Each company must decide how much variance can be tolerated before a corrective action must be taken. Variances can originate from errors in expense and/or revenue calculations when establishing the billing rates.

For purposes of this book, and from the perspective of IT, variances are either negative indicating that the revenue generated by IT invoicing was less than IT expense, or variances are positive meaning that IT revenue from invoicing exceeded IT expense. The causes for these variances vary, but one thing that won't vary is that variances will occur when you use standard costing procedures. Variances occurring during the year should be addressed as required, but all variances must be resolved by year-end, and the IT and business client ledger accounts adjusted. Either type of variance can cause IT planning and resource management issues for the business clients. For example, if a business client developed their plan on the basis of rates that were greater than the actual expense of the IT products that supported their plan, the business client may have planned for fewer resources when they could have afforded more resources. The business client in this instance may have eliminated needed work from their plan because of this situation. Significant positive variances can be very upsetting to a business client. Conversely, if a business client developed their plan on the basis of rates that were less than the actual expenses of the IT products, a negative variance would be created. Depending upon the amount of the negative variance, the business client could become quite upset when their ledger account is adjusted to eliminate the variance.

Service chargeback must be closely monitored on a regular basis because it can be the cause of making bad business decisions. IT should have a strategy that engages the business client in the regular analysis of their IT invoices.

Strategic Management Plan Worksheet
Service Chargeback Management Process

Objectives:

What the reader will discover in reading the objectives is that service charge-back management is so much greater in scope that just creating an IT billing system. Of the management functions discussed in the book, service chargeback has a tremendous potential to change the culture and manner in which IT operates within a company. Proper introduction and use of this function is the best guarantee the changes generated by service chargeback will be positive.

Many of the service chargeback objectives are similar to those established for cost management. Both focus on the creation and use of information to isolate areas of IT inefficiencies so that corrective management action can take place. The difference between cost management and service chargeback management is that the information created in costing is more mechanical or technical in nature, and is designed for use by the IT staff, whereas the numbers in service chargeback are ultimately represented in dollars, a language a business manager better understands. In essence, service chargeback not only assists IT, but just as importantly, it creates the opportunity to get the business manager in the business of looking for inefficiencies in their own operation.

For example, a business associate might be running an excessive number of printed reports. Before service chargeback's introduction, the business manager may not have been concerned about this situation either because they chose to ignore it, or because the cost of this excessive reporting was unknown. Even if there were service chargeback, but the system wasn't linked to the company's financial reporting systems, the business manager may still have been unaware of the costs because IT's billings were considered "funny money". When the business manager begins to receive an IT invoice for services provided, and the invoice is posted to the business manager's ledger account, the excessive reporting practice becomes too hard to ignore. Corrective action is taken. This is the type of "good behavior" IT anticipates service chargeback can create in its business client base.

The following objectives are established for the Service Chargeback Management Process in a "best company" environment. Some of the objectives are repeated over the processes, but a particular process may have unique strategies to achieve them.

- Create a positive attitude toward service chargeback
- Engage business clients in addressing areas of inefficient business operation
- Create "good behavior" in use of IT products and services
- Better engage the business client in the management of IT resources
- Move IT closer to operating as any other business unit
- Gain a working knowledge of the company's financial reports and operating procedures
- Create a financial awareness of the costs of technology in both the IT and the business communities

Strategies to Achieve Objectives:

The strategies are the action plans concerning how the process will achieve its objectives. Note that strategies can align with multiple objectives.

Create a positive attitude toward service chargeback:

- Address the "why me" attitude in IT. Even though business and IT associates have common cost components for the delivery of their services, IT is typically the one associate group that gets singled-out for service chargeback. This creates a "why me" refrain in IT associates. The concern and angst is real, and must be addressed by IT management.
- Promote the concept that business and IT associates all have similar cost components in the development of a billing rate for their services. Business associates have salaries, office support, education and training issues, supplies, etc. just like IT associates. Cost and service chargeback issues in the business environment just haven't been made as visible as in IT.
- Demonstrate to IT managers and associates that service chargeback adds value to their jobs by providing another dimension upon which to make technical analyses
- Change the manner in which IT partners with its managers, associates, and business clients by adding a financial as well as a technical "flavor" to the IT/business client relationships.
- Use dollars in describing IT resource utilization to better engage the business client in the IT resource management process
- Use the invoice as a means of engaging business clients in isolating areas of business operation inefficiencies.
- Account for and report IT revenue activity in the company's financial reporting systems
- Internalize IT service chargeback reporting as a regular part of IT management activities

- Create awareness programs to promote positives of service chargeback

Gain a working knowledge of the company's financial reports and financial operating procedures:

- Develop on-going working relationships with the company's accounting department.
- Educate IT managers in the knowledge of company financial procedures and the proper use of company financial reports
- Distribute expense and revenue management oversight responsibilities to IT managers

Create "good behavior" in use of IT products and services:

- Emphasize use of service chargeback information to increase operating efficiencies and decrease IT costs.
- Emphasize the added-value service chargeback information provides to the business decision making process in matters of technology.

Better engage the business client in the management of IT resources:

- Include IT invoicing activity in the company's financial reporting systems to obtain the business client's attention on the utilization of IT products and services
- Provide additional billing-oriented management reports

Move IT closer to operating as any other business unit:

- The introduction of service chargeback with its connection to the company's financial reporting systems completes the work management "loop" and positions IT to be viewed and managed as any other business unit
- Use awareness programs to remove the element of mystique from IT operations

Create a financial awareness of the price of technology in both the IT and the business communities:

- Invoicing for products and services gets IT's and the business clients' attention very quickly because it communicates in the universal language of dollars.
- Include dollars and computer metrics on IT management reports where appropriate

Strengths, weaknesses, opportunities, and threats (SWOT):

Because the "best company" is the same for each process, the SWOT analysis for this process will not be repeated here. Reference chapter 2, *IT Management Model, Strategic Management Plan Worksheet, Develop and Manage the IT Management Model Process* for the details of the "best company" SWOT analysis.

Cost drivers:

The prime drivers of service chargeback costs are:

- Number of IT products and services billed
- Complexity of the products and services billed
- Amount of time and effort to accumulate the billing utilization data
- Detail and complexity of the invoice and supporting reports.

Deliverables:

The following lists some of the deliverables (benefits) a company can expect to receive from a successful implementation of service chargeback management.

- Expense reductions
- Formal product list of IT products and services
- Direct input of invoices into company financial reporting systems
- Enhanced partnerships with business clients
- Better, more informed, business and technical decision making
- More informed business client concerning IT products and services
- Reduction in inefficient computer utilization

Critical success factors:

What event(s) must occur or strategies be successfully completed in order for the process to achieve its objectives? The most critical success factor is the "selling" of service chargeback to the IT staff as a positive move forward towards IT's objective of being managed as any other business unit. This will require an excellent implementation strategy. Secondarily, the business community needs to be "sold" the idea that service chargeback is a value-add function for business users of IT products and services.

Management Function Impact Analysis

Business plan management:

A process should align with the business objectives listed in the summary business plan example presented in chapter 1. This process aligns with, and is supportive of, the following business objectives listed in the summary business plan example.

- Continuous improvement initiatives
- Cost awareness
- Plan driven
- Customer-focused solutions
- Cost effective products
- Bottom-line oriented
- Financial awareness

Process management:

This layer addresses the participants, processes, and procedures required to ensure the proper flow and interchange of information amongst the key managers involved in development and management of the Service Chargeback Management Process. The question is how will the process be structured to ensure that it is properly designed and implemented? The IT financial manager, as the owner of the process, will lead the effort, and will be assisted by members of the IT senior staffs, select members of the senior business management team, and key business managers. The accounting department and the IT managers play particularly important roles in service chargeback implementation. This process will impact all of IT and its community of business clients. The process to develop this management function needs to have a good upfront marketing and "selling" campaign that clearly delineates the process's objectives.

IT financial management:

IT is committed to support the business plan driven objectives of increasing operating efficiencies and adding to company profits. IT is to be managed as any other business unit, and it wants this done in a fiscally responsible manner. In this vane IT will emphasize and exercise expense and revenue management practices. IT's fiscal and accounting practices and policies will be fully integrated with those of the company's accounting and financial reporting departments. The service chargeback system will export IT invoices directly to the company's financial reporting systems to "marry with" expenses that are already there. Charges for IT products and services will hit the "bottom lines" of both IT and business clients. Significant responsibility for managing the expense and revenue associated with an individual IT manager's budget will be distributed to the individual managers. This policy is consistent with the company's and IT's belief in the concept of a distributed management style. IT managers who are assigned budgets must review their budgets on a regular basis to make sure all expenses are being covered by the revenue generated from IT billings. Billing information will be used by the business clients to look for, and address, areas of inefficient

IT product utilization. Excessive billing dollars, not IT units of measure, will be the factor used to detect these potential areas of inefficient utilization.

Plan, resource, and cost management:

The process owner has determined that plan, resource, and cost management functions are major components of this process. These management processes are described in detail in chapters 6 and 7. Service chargeback is initiated after the new plan is placed in next year's production cycle. The Service Chargeback Management Process bills for the utilization of products and services that the Planning and Resource Management Process planned and the Cost Management Process identified and costed.

IT general management, leadership, organization management:

Service chargeback fundamentally changes an IT manager's approach to management practices by adding a new dimension, a financial one, to the way they must manage their resources. They become both a technician and a business person. IT division managers are expected to take an active role in service chargeback. They are expected to manage their "bottom-lines" to ensure the revenue generated from the utilization of their products and services are sufficient to cover their expenses. They must become familiar with the company's financial management procedures and practices. Accurate time reporting must be aggressively managed. Because service chargeback activities will impact IT and business financial performance, its implementation will cause some serious tension in converting to the new ways of IT management. There will be push-back from both IT and the business clients.

Change management:

A change of price must be carefully made for the same reason that a change of cost must be carefully made. Billing-induced variances can be the result of a price change that was not equal to the established standard cost.

Client relationships (service) management:

The key IT/business client relationship in service chargeback is normally between the owner of the product or service and the business client who utilizes the product or service. Questions about an invoice matter can be discussed directly between the product or service user and its owner, or if more detail is required, the service chargeback manager can become involved to assist in resolving an invoice matter. Service chargeback functions as the creator and provider of the invoices.

The Service Chargeback Management Process can create some initial bad behavior in the business clients' reaction to IT invoices. A common refrain heard from the business client is – I can do this work for free! The client is right, but only because they have no chargeback system installed for the services they provide.

Application management:

The most significant impact of the Service Chargeback Management Process is that it provides the business client with the total cost to operate their business application systems. The cost of the business application system is presented in terms of the cost to operate it (i.e. computer processing costs); the cost to support it (i.e. production support and required maintenance); and the cost to enhance it (i.e. enhancements, tactical projects). Service chargeback puts the business client in a position to assist in managing the costs of business application systems because the information is reported in dollars, a language a business client understands.

End user computing (EUC) management:

A major impact of service chargeback on the End User Computing (EUC) Management Process is the manner in which desktop PCs are billed to clients. As mentioned earlier PC users tend to only consider the hardware and software costs. The addition of the other PC burdened costs upsets them. It's more a matter of control than a technical support issue. EUC and service chargeback need to constantly address this issue. EUC also impacts service chargeback in the sheer number of products to be billed. The issue here again is how granular does IT want to be in billing for PC component costs?

Architecture management, technology management, systems software management, database management, hardware (operations) management, and communications and networking management:

Significant changes in these management function areas are caused by the introduction of the CPTOIA architecture, the systems and services organization, and the continued movement towards an information processing concept. The service chargeback process will be impacted in two major ways by the introduction of these new concepts and facilities. First, there will be the need to develop new products and services, and second, there will be the need to capture new product utilization statistics and costs which will be used in billing the business client for use of the products. The cost management process will be similarly impacted.

Staff education, training, skills management:

Service chargeback management should work with the professional IT education and training staff to develop the programs required to educate the company, as well as IT associates, on the why's and how's of service chargeback. The training programs should be directed at addressing attitude adjustment issues related to the "Why me?" attitude of IT, and the education of the business community in the understanding that business associates are not "free" as they sometimes like to think they are when dealing with an IT associate that operates under IT chargeback procedures. A program is also needed to facilitate the development of enriched partnerships be-tween IT and the company's accounting department, and between IT and its business clients.

Potential impact on other management functions:

Use this section to solicit the potential impact of the new process on the process operation of the other management function process owners.

Concluding Comments

A fitting conclusion to this book is contained in the theme statement of chapter 4, the *Information Technology Management Process*. This chapter includes the main topic of the book, yet it consumes only about 5% of the book's printed pages. Possible reasons for this occurrence are: I didn't adequately describe the technology management process, or maybe I chose the wrong topic for the book. I think something else occurred, and it relates to the book's constant reminder that information technology management cannot be developed in a vacuum. The other 95% of the printed pages describe the what, why, and how of this vacuum.

One can't simply implement "information technology management". That's the 5% part of the effort. The other 95% of the effort represents the management and technical infrastructure that information technology management requires for successful implementation. What fills the vacuum are things like the company business plan and supporting IT plans; an IT management model; the management functions IT performs; the IT work that has to be completed; a system to plan, manage, cost, and bill the work; management best practices; and an organization and computer architecture designed to support an information processing complex. Depending upon the status of a company's current information technology management infrastructure, the effort to develop an information technology management process represents a significant IT reengineering initiative. A company needs to be committed to this effort if it wants to be successful.

So why would any company want to undertake such a significant initiative? The answer to that question should be that the company wants to gain significant benefits from the initiative. A multitude of benefits to be obtained were mentioned throughout the book. Information technology management assists in keeping the company competitive with others in the industry. It reduces IT expense by using the management techniques of resource leveraging, plan alignment, gap analysis, and right-sizing. It creates a cost effective IT complex that can produce the new technology products and service options business clients demand. It creates an atmosphere of discipline, ownership, and accountability which challenges and empowers staff. It creates an entirely new view of IT as a business partner which adds a new dimension to information technology management, and demonstrates IT's commitment to contributing to the "bottom-line" of the company.

Like Ted Kennedy said, "Why not?"

About the Author

Dennis McBreen. Master's degree in experimental psychology (Miami University, Oxford, Ohio). Retired, vice president of information technology. Over 46 years of information technology experience working in the insurance, financial services, and manufacturing industries, including 15 years managing his consulting company which provided project consulting and systems development services to a variety of companies including several Fortune 500 companies. Adjunct college instructor teaching multiple information technology topics for 15 years at both the MBA and the under-graduate levels.